THE
THE ANCIENT ROMANS

THE BOOK
OF THE
ANCIENT ROMANS

BY

DOROTHY MILLS

Angelico Press, 2012
First edition, G. P. Putnam's Sons, 1927

For information, address:
Angelico Press, 4619 Slayden Rd., NE
Tacoma, WA 98422
www.angelicopress.com

Library of Congress Cataloging-in-Publication Data

Mills, Dorothy.
The book of the ancient Romans
/ by Dorothy Mills.—Facsimile ed.

p. cm.
Originally published: New York: G. P. Putnam's Sons, 1927.
Includes index.
ISBN 978-1-59731-354-4 (pbk.: alk. paper)
ISBN 978-1-59731-379-7 (hardback: alk. paper)
1. Rome—History. 2. Rome—Civilization. I. Title.
DG210.M6 2008
937—dc22   2008023152

Jacket Design: Michael Schrauzer

PREFACE

THIS book, like its two predecessors, was used in its original manuscript form by one of my history classes. It carries on the story of the way in which man has been learning how to live down to the Fall of Rome in 476 A.D. and so concludes this series on the Ancient World.

The spirit of a nation is expressed and its history is recorded in three ways: in its political history, in its literature and in its art. The aim of this book has been to use such parts of the political history of the Romans, of their literature and of their art as seem to have been the outward and visible signs of the spirit that inspired them.

The writing of this book in this way would not have been possible without the permission of publishers to use certain copyright translations, and I am glad to take this opportunity to express my thanks for such permission, to Messrs. G. Bell and Sons for passages from the translation of *Horace* by Conington; to Messrs. J. M. Dent and Sons for passages from the translation of the *Aeneid* by Fairfax Taylor and from *Livy* by Canon W. M. Roberts; to the Executors of the late Dr. Thomas Hodgkin for his translation from *Claudian* on p. 421; to the Editors of the Loeb Classical Library for passages

iii

from the translations of *Sallust* and *Suetonius* **by**
J. C. Rolfe and of *Appian's Roman History* by Horace White; to Messrs. Macmillan and Company for
passages from the translation of *Marcus Aurelius*
by Gerald H. Rendall and of the *Annals of Tacitus*
by Church and Brodribb; to the Oxford University
Press for passages from the translation of the *Odes
of Horace* and of *Catullus* by Sir William Marris, of
Virgil by James Rhoades, of the *Histories and Germania of Tacitus* by W. Hamilton Fyfe, and of
Epictetus by P. E. Matheson; and to the Walter
Scott Publishing Company for passages from the
translation of *Pliny's Letters* by J. B. Firth.

The three books of this series are intended as an
introduction to the history and civilization of the
ancient world, and they in no way aim at covering
the whole ground.   My aim will have been accomplished if they should create a desire not only to
know something more of this great heritage that has
come down to us from the past, but also something
of its further history and development during the
fourteen hundred years that have gone by since the
Fall of Rome.

DOROTHY MILLS.

NEW YORK.

CONTENTS

THE ROME OF MYTH AND LEGEND

ROME THE CONQUEROR AND LAWGIVER

PART I. ROME THE MISTRESS OF ITALY

CONTENTS

CONTENTS

CHAPTER   PAGE

IV.—ANTONINUS PIUS . . . 396

V.—MARCUS AURELIUS . . . 397

XXI.—RELIGION IN THE ROMAN EMPIRE

I.—DECAY OF THE OLD ROMAN RE-
LIGION 400

II.—STOICS AND EPICUREANS . . 402

III.—THE MYSTERY RELIGIONS . . 406

IV.—THE CHRISTIAN CHURCH IN THE
ROMAN EMPIRE

(a) THE FIRST CENTURIES OF
CHRISTIANITY . . 408

(b) THE EARLY CHURCH . 412

XXII.—THE CIVILIZATION OF THE ROMAN EMPIRE

I.—ROME THE CONQUEROR OF THE
WORLD: THE ROMAN ARMY . 416

II.—ROME THE RULER OF THE WORLD:
ROMAN LAW AND UNITY . 419

III.—ROME THE CIVILIZER OF THE
WORLD:

(a) ROMAN ARCHITECTURE . 421

(b) LANGUAGE AND LITERA-
TURE 423

(c) ROMAN ROADS AND COM-
MERCE . . . 424

ILLUSTRATIONS

The illustrations are grouped at the end of the book, with the exception of the map facing page 1 and the chronological chart facing page 456.

THE BOOK OF THE ANCIENT ROMANS

THE BOOK OF THE ANCIENT ROMANS

Others, no doubt, from breathing bronze shall draw
More softness, and a living face devise
From marble, plead their causes at the law
More deftly, trace the motions of the skies
With learned rod, and tell the stars that rise.
Thou, Roman, rule, and o'er the world proclaim
The ways of peace.   Be these thy victories,
To spare the vanquished and the proud to tame.
These are imperial arts, and worthy of thy name.[1]

IN these words, Virgil, the great Roman poet,
set forth what he believed to be the mission of
Rome.   He lived at a time when Rome had become
a mighty Empire.   Looking back across the centuries, he could see how she had grown from being
only a small settlement to be the ruler of the world.
She had conquered the world, and not only the
Mediterranean world with its great civilizations, but
lands far beyond the shores of that ancient sea,
lands inhabited by men of strange speech and
uncouth ways.   In the thought of the poet, that
had been the first step in her mission, to conquer;
then, having conquered, she was to rule and crown

[1] Aeneid, VI.

the peace she had established in her empire with law and order. This mission she worthily fulfilled. We, looking back to the days of Virgil, can see that she accomplished yet a third great task, for having conquered and then wisely ruled it, she civilized the world.

The spirit of a nation expresses itself and its history is recorded in various ways: in the social relations of the people both with each other and with other nations, and this is called its political history; in its language, which expresses itself in its literature; and in its building, which is its architecture.[1]

It is in the political history, the literature and the architecture of Rome that we find the story of how she made her own that which came to her out of the East, and of how greatly she fulfilled her mission not only of conquering, but also of ruling and of civilizing the world.

[1] *The Book of the Ancient Greeks.*

THE ROME OF MYTH AND LEGEND

CHAPTER 1

The Land of Italy

The peninsula of Italy divides the Mediterranean world into two parts, the Eastern and the Western. Italy turns her face to the West, for the Apennines are very steep and rugged on their eastern side, but slope more gently down to the plains in the West. There are more good harbours on the western coast than on the eastern, which brought the earliest inhabitants of Italy into communication with countries to the South and West of them rather than with those in the East. This was often a source of danger, for the neighbouring peoples in the Western Mediterranean were not always friendly, and the southern and western coasts of Italy were open to attack both from Europe and the north coast of Africa.

Greece turned her face to the East and looked out upon lands that had a more ancient civilization than her own; the face of Italy was turned to the West, and when her history began she looked out upon lands that were almost unknown, inhabited by peoples who knew very little of what is called civilization, who could not write, who had no lit erature, who knew almost nothing of the art of building, and whose pottery and weaving were of the crudest and most elementary type. Italy lay between the ancient East and the unknown West, between lands which had marked characteristics of their own and behind which lay long centuries of history, and lands which as yet had no fixed character and whose history lay in the future.

As the Apennines turn Italy towards the West, so do the Alps, her northern boundary, turn her to the South. The Alps were a barrier between Italy and the rest of Europe, but they did not make a very secure wall of defence, for though they are difficult of ascent from the South, they are not very hard to cross from the North. In early times many tribes migrated into Italy, where the inhabitants were not very well able to defend themselves against these enemies who came down upon them so easily from the mountains, which they themselves found so hard to climb.

This danger of attack from enemies had a marked influence on the character of the people who lived in Italy, especially on the early Romans who were destined to become the rulers of the land. Constantly exposed to danger, from the earliest days they experienced the sternness and seriousness of life; self-defence forced them to unite, and often their very existence depended on a life of the strictest self-discipline and control. All this made them stern, practical and capable. From the very beginning they had a sense of the tremendous possibilities there were in life both for achievement and also

for failure, and this developed in them to a marked
extent that quality that is best expressed by the
word *character*.

The land of Italy is a sunny land and a beautiful
one, with its mountains and rivers and rich fertile
plains. From early times there were fields of grain,
vineyards which produced wine, olives which gave
oil, and good pasture land for the cattle and flocks
of sheep which supplied not only food, but good
wool for clothing. The Romans were not the keen
lovers of beauty that the Greeks were, but they
were proud of their land and of all that their race had
done to make it great. "Here," said Virgil,

Blooms perpetual spring and summer here
In months that are not summer's; twice teem the flocks:
Twice doth the tree yield service of her fruit.

. . . .

Mark too her cities, so many and so proud,
Of mighty toil the achievement, town on town
Up rugged precipices heaved and reared,
And rivers undergliding ancient walls.

. . . .

A land no less that in her veins displays
Rivers of silver, mines of copper ore,
Ay, and with gold hath flowed abundantly.
A land that reared a valiant breed of men.

. . . .

Hail! land of Saturn, mighty mother thou
Of fruits and heroes.[1]

[1] Georgic, II.

CHAPTER II

THE EARLY PEOPLES OF ITALY

IN very ancient times Italy was inhabited by a number of different peoples, about whom very little is known. It is thought that in those far-away, misty days when the peoples of the world were wandering in search of homes, certain tribes crossed the Alps and came down into Italy. They must have found some of the prehistoric inhabitants in possession of the land, and they probably fought them and overcame them, slaying many and then mingling with the rest and occupying the land. These first settlers are now looked upon as the original inhabitants of Italy. Some of these tribes settled north of the Tiber and then spread over Central Italy, the Umbrians in the districts near the Adriatic and the Sabines in the mountains of the interior. All the hill-tribes in Central Italy were considered as descended from the Sabines who sent out numbers of colonists to neighbouring districts. At one time, when the Sabines had been engaged in a long war with the Umbrians, they made a vow that they would consecrate to the gods all the products of that spring, called by them the Sacred Spring. All the children born during that season were consecrated to Mars, and when they had grown to manhood they were sent forth, with a bull as their leader, to seek new homes wherever the gods willed. The bull lay down to rest in a certain village, whereupon the Sabine youths drove out the inhabitants and, after sacrificing the bull to Mars, established themselves in that place. These colonists became known as Samnites.

To the banks of the Tiber came another tribe, the Latins, who gave to the region where they settled the name of Latium. This was a fertile land, and the Latins soon grew more prosperous than the tribes in the more hilly interior. At first, like all early peoples, they consisted of a number of separate tribes, but Latium was a district much exposed to attack from hostile neighbours, and the Latins soon found that for mutual protection and defence it was necessary to form some kind of organization. So it came about that thirty communities joined together and formed the Latin League. As some centre was necessary for such a league, a place where a common assembly could be held, where justice could be dispensed and where there might be a common sanctuary, Alba Longa was made the chief town and head of the League. Very little is known about the early history of the Latin League, but it is important because the joining together of a number of communities with one common centre which belonged to them all, was the beginning of that sense of national unity which was to become a characteristic of the Roman people.

These were the early Italian peoples who lived in

Italy, but as early, probably, as from the eleventh
century B.C. onwards, other peoples appeared, two
of which left an abiding mark on the early civilization of Italy.   These were the Etruscans and the
Greeks.

The Etruscans settled in the coast region north
of Rome and there they developed a civilization of
their own.   The Romans seem always to have
regarded them as intruders and as strangers in the
land, though their settlements were made in very
early times, some of them at least as early as 1000
B.C., but it was towards the end of the seventh century B.C. that they were at the height of their power.
Very much still remains to be learnt about the
Etruscans, when they came into Italy and whence
they came, for their writing has not yet been fully
deciphered, but Roman writers have left some
account of what they knew about them.   They were
ruled by a king who wore a crown and a purple robe
and who sat on an ivory throne, and they had a
code of laws which gave them rules for the conduct
of daily life in the community and for different ways
of interpreting the will of the gods.   They were
specially skilled in the art of augury, the art which
interpreted signs in nature as outward expressions
of the will of the gods, and they believed that special meanings were attached to such phenomena as
thunder and lightning and the flight of birds.

The Latins were much influenced by the Etruscans and learnt many things from them.   The Etrus-
sans may themselves have been influenced by the
early Greeks, especially in their architecture, paint-

ing and sculpture. They were richer, more prosperous and more skilful than their neighbours and were a people of great importance in early Italy. They were a commercial people, but they do not seem to have had an adventurous spirit like that of the Phoenicians or the Greek colonists, and they waited for trade to come to them rather than sail out on to uncharted seas in search of it. Etruscan influence can be seen in the early art and architecture of the Latins, in some of their amusements, such as gladiatorial shows, and in their religious beliefs. A great many Etruscan tombs have been found, and from the care with which the dead were buried and the articles which were buried with them, the Etruscans evidently believed in a future life.

Greater than the Etruscan influence on the early peoples of Italy was that of the Greeks. Colonists from Greece had settled in the South of Italy and as far North as the Bay of Naples, and they gave the name of Magna Graecia to this whole region. The Greek cities were active in trade, powerful, wealthy and luxurious. One of the most important was Tarentum, a city which had an excellent harbour, and which was one of the most prosperous trading ports in the South of Italy. Tarentum was noted for its fine wool and purple dye, which were as famous as those of Tyre.

There were also Greek colonies in Sicily, an island noted then, as now, for the loveliness of its situation and its beauty in the springtime of the year. The Sicilians themselves held to the tradition that the island had been given by Jupiter as his gift to Proserpine on her marriage with Pluto, and there were many other legends of gods and goddesses who were said to have dwelt in the island. The chief cities were along the coast, and Pindar called them "a gorgeous crown of citadels."

These were the peoples who in historic times first inhabited Italy. In time one city, very small and unimportant at the beginning of her history, was to rise from their midst, destined to conquer them all, to unite them and to rule them. Where Greece had failed, Rome was to succeed, for having first united the peoples not only of Italy but of the then known world, she was to give them a real sense of national unity.

CHAPTER III

THE FOUNDING OF ROME

IT is very difficult to know the truth about the early history of Rome, because there are so few historical records of that far-off period. In 390 B.C. when Rome was burnt by the Gauls, all the public records were destroyed, and it was not until long after that date, that out of the traditions and legends which had been handed down, a history was made. But if reliable historical records are scanty, legend and tradition are full of tales which tell us what the Romans themselves believed as to their own origin. Though these tales must not be looked upon as real history, they have, nevertheless, a distinct importance of their own. For the character of a nation is influenced by what that nation believes about its origin and by the traditions on which it brings up its youth. It is from such traditions that we can learn what a people admired and what it despised, what kind of heroes were held up as examples to be followed, what was considered noble and honourable, and what was held to be petty and mean.

According to the most ancient tradition, **Aeneas,** after the fall of Troy, fled from the burning cit

accompanied by his father and his little son, Ascanius, together with a few faithful followers. After
many adventures he reached the coast of Italy,
where, so good omens assured him, should be his
home and the land over which his descendants
should rule. The King of Latium came out to
drive back the strangers, but he was defeated by
Aeneas, who then made peace with him and after a
time wedded his daughter, Lavinia. After the
death of the King, Aeneas ruled in his place, until
he was slain in battle fighting against the Etruscans. Ascanius then became King, and finding the
city in which his father had lived too small for the
increasing population, he founded Alba Longa and
made it his chief city.

The descendants of Aeneas ruled in Alba Longa
for three hundred years. At the end of this time the
rightful King was Numitor, but he was dethroned
by his brother Amulius, who, fearing lest Rhea
Silvia, the daughter of Numitor, should have sons
who might grow up and claim the kingdom, caused
her to be made a priestess of the goddess Vesta.
Amulius thought that all was well and that his
brother would never be strong enough to regain his
kingdom, when news was brought to him that Rhea
Silvia had twin sons of great beauty, whose father
was none other than the god Mars. "But neither
gods nor men sheltered her or her babes from the
King's cruelty; the priestess was thrown into prison,
and the boys were ordered to be thrown into the
river."[1]

[1] Livy, I, 4.

Now it happened that just at this time, the Tiber had overflowed its banks and the servant who had been charged to drown the infants, left them in the shallow water on the bank, thinking that it would be deep enough to drown them.   But the river went down and the infants were left on dry ground at the foot of a fig-tree.   Here, tradition tells us,

a thirsty she-wolf from the surrounding hills, attracted by the crying of the children, came to them, and nursed them, and was so gentle towards them that the king's flock-master found her licking the boys with her tongue.   According to the story this man's name was Faustulus.   He took the children to his hut and gave them to his wife to bring up.[1]

Faustulus knew who these boys were, and he brought them up well, and, it is said, actually

with the knowledge and secret assistance of Numitor. They went to school and were well instructed in letters and other accomplishments befitting their birth.   And they were called Romulus and Remus.   As they grew up they proved brave and manly and of undaunted courage.   But Romulus seemed rather to act by counsel, and to show the sagacity of a statesman, and in all his dealings with their neighbours, whether relating to feeding of flocks or to hunting, gave the idea of being born rather to rule than to obey.[2]

Both boys were noted amongst the shepherds for their skill in protecting the flocks and driving off

[1] Livy, I. 4.   [2] Plutarch: *Life of Romulus.*

robbers and in delivering from injury all who were oppressed.

When Romulus and Remus had reached manhood, they learned who they were, and how Amulius had taken the throne which belonged of right to their grandfather. A plot was formed, Amulius was slain, and Numitor replaced on the throne. But Romulus and Remus had been so long accustomed to take the lead amongst their companions, that they were not content

to dwell in Alba without governing there, nor would they take the government into their own hands during the life of their grandfather. Having therefore delivered the dominion up into his hands and paid their mother befitting honour, they resolved to live by themselves, and build a city in the same place where they were in their infancy brought up.[1]

They began to build, but the brothers could not agree as to which should be the founder of the city, or who was to give his name to it and rule it. So they decided to consult the guardian gods of the place by means of augury, and in this way to settle the dispute. Romulus went up on to the Palatine Hill and Remus to the Aventine in order to make their observations. Remus is said to have seen six vultures and Romulus double that number; though some declared that Remus did truly see his number and that Romulus only pretended to see his. Others declared that Romulus had seen the

[1] Plutarch: *Life of Romulus.*

twelve vultures, though they had appeared after
the six seen by Remus, but that the gods undoubtedly
favoured him because to him had appeared double
the number seen by his brother. Angry words
passed between the two brothers, and then Remus

contemptuously jumping over the newly raised walls
was forthwith killed by the enraged Romulus, who exclaimed: "So shall it be henceforth with everyone who
leaps over my walls." Romulus thus became sole ruler,
and the city was called after him, its founder.[1]

Thus, according to tradition, was Rome founded,
on the twenty-first day of April in the year 753 B.C,
and that day of their country's birthday was kept
by ancient Rome and is still kept in Rome today as
a national holiday.

According to the earliest foundations of the city
laid bare by modern excavations, there had been in
Rome a very much older settlement than that of
Romulus. It is believed that whoever these earliest Romans were, they were in some way connected
with their Latin neighbours, for from the beginning
of their history the Romans spoke Latin, they worshipped Latin gods, and the official titles given to
their magistrates and assemblies were all Latin.

The site of Rome possessed great natural advan-
tages. The city was surrounded by a fertile plain
with distant hills on one side of it and the sea on
the other. The first settlement was on the Palatine,
the hill in the centre of the seven hills on the Tiber,

[1] Livy, I, 6.

all of which were to become part of the city.   The
Palatine was a secure stronghold in itself and it was
protected by the ring of hills which surrounded it.
But these hills did not cut off the early settlement
from the river.   The Palatine controlled the earliest
and best known ford across the Tiber and so not
only was access to the sea secured, but communication with the interior of Italy was open to those who
settled on this hill.   Livy, the Roman historian,
said of the site of Rome:

Not without good reason did gods and men choose
this spot as the site of a City, with its bracing hills,
its commodious river, by means of which the produce
of inland countries may be brought down and inland
supplies obtained; a sea near enough for all useful purposes, but not so near as to be exposed to danger from
foreign fleets; a district in the very centre of Italy,
in a word, a position singularly adapted by nature for
the growth of a city.[1]

[1] Livy, V, 54.

CHAPTER IV

THE SEVEN KINGS OF ROME

753–509 B.C.

I. ROMULUS

ACCORDING to the old Roman traditions, Rome was ruled by kings for nearly two hundred and fifty years. The first of these kings was Romulus, the founder of the city. In order to secure a large enough population for the new city, Romulus encouraged all manner of men to settle there, and he made the city

a sanctuary of refuge for all fugitives, where they received and protected all, delivering none back, neither the servant to his master, the debtor to his creditor, nor the murderer into the hands of the magistrate, saying it was a privileged place, and they could so maintain it by an order of the holy oracle; insomuch that the city grew presently very populous.[1]

Romulus then set to work to build his city, and he did it in what is known to have been the ancient method of founding a settlement.

[1] Plutarch: *Life of Romulus.*

He sent for men out of Tuscany, who directed him by sacred usages and written rules in all the ceremonies to be observed as in a religious rite. First they dug a round trench about that which became the Comitium, or Court of Assembly, and into it solemnly threw the first-fruits of all things either good by custom or necessary by nature; lastly, every man taking a small piece of earth of the country from which he came, they all threw it in together. Making this trench the centre, they built the city round it. Then the founder fitted to a plough a brazen ploughshare, and, yoking together a bull and a cow, drove himself a deep line or furrow round the bounds; while the business of those that followed after was to see that whatever earth was thrown up should be turned all inwards towards the city. This line was to be the wall, and where they designed to make a gate, there they took out the share, carried the plough over, and left a space; for which reason they consider the whole wall as holy, except where the gates are.[1]

The gates were not considered holy, because things that religion held to be unclean had sometimes to be carried out through them.

Romulus had founded his city and peopled it with men who were brave warriors and loyal followers of the King, but a state in which there were no women could not last, for there would be no children to grow up and take the place of the founders of the city. The states in the neighbourhood of Rome belonged to the Latin League, and their laws forbade intermarriage with other states, unless

[1] Plutarch: *Life of Romulus.*

special treaties had been made to allow it.   Romulus, therefore,

sent envoys amongst the surrounding nations to ask for alliance and the right of intermarriage on behalf of his new community.   It was represented that cities, like everything else, sprang from the humblest beginnings, and those who were helped on by their own courage and the favour of heaven won for themselves great power and great renown.   As to the origin of Rome, it was well known that whilst it had received divine assistance, courage and self-reliance were not wanting.   There should, therefore, be no reluctance for men to mingle their blood with their fellow-men.

Nowhere did the envoys meet with a favourable reception.   There was a general feeling of alarm at the power so rapidly growing in their midst,[1]

and insulting messages were sent back to Romulus, telling him that if he wanted wives for his men, he had better offer his city as a refuge for women thieves and outcasts, for only such women were fit to wed with his men.   When these messages were delivered, the Roman youths were very angry, and they determined to avenge these insults and to secure their wives by force.

To secure a favourable place and time for such an attempt, Romulus, disguising his resentment, made elaborate preparations for the celebration of games in honour of Neptune.   He ordered public notice of the spectacle to be given amongst the adjoining cities, and

[1] Livy, I, 9.

his people supported him in making the celebration as magnificent as their knowledge and resources allowed, so that expectations were raised to the highest pitch.

There was a great gathering; people were eager to see the new city, all their nearest neighbours were there, and the whole Sabine population came, with their wives and families. They were invited to accept hospitality at the different houses, and after examining the situation of the city, its walls and the large number of dwelling-houses it included, they were astonished at the rapidity with which the Roman state had grown.

When the hour for the games had come, and their eyes and minds were alike riveted on the spectacle before them, the preconcerted signal was given. Romulus rose from his seat, gathered up his robe and threw it over his body, and the Roman youth dashed in all directions to carry off the maidens who were present. Alarm and consternation broke up the games, and the parents of the maidens fled, distracted with grief, uttering bitter reproaches on the violators of the laws of hospitality and appealing to the god to whose solemn games they had come, only to be the victims of impious perfidy.

The maidens were just as despondent and indignant, but Romulus went round to them all in person, and pointed out to them that it was all owing to the pride of their parents in denying right of intermarriage with their neighbours. They would live as honoured wives, sharing in the property and civil rights of their husbands, and would be the mothers of freemen. He begged them to lay aside their feelings of resentment and give their affections to those whom fortune had made masters of their persons. They would find their husbands all the more affectionate, because each would do his utmost, so far as in him lay, to make up for the loss of parents and country.[1]

The Romans were successful in soothing the feelings of the Sabine maidens, who soon settled down and grew to love those whom they had begun by hating and fearing.

The Latin tribes in the neighbourhood of the Roman settlement on the Palatine did not allow it to grow larger and stronger without opposition. The Roman territory was invaded and there was constant war, but the Romans proved the stronger and during the reign of Romulus the Capitoline and Quirinal hills became part of Rome, various tribes became subject to her, their land was added to the Roman territory and their inhabitants became Roman citizens. This was the beginning of the policy which made Rome great, for "there was nothing that did more advance the greatness of Rome, than that she did always unite and incorporate those whom she conquered into herself."[2]

The greatest of these wars was waged against the Sabines. These sent ambassadors to Rome asking for their daughters back, but Romulus refused to return the maidens and proposed instead an alliance between the Sabines and Rome. The warlike Sabines, who were jealous of the success of Romulus, refused to enter any alliance with him, and war resulted. Some of the Sabine tribes were defeated and made part of Rome, but others under their King attacked the Roman citadel which had been

[1] Livy, I, 9.   [2] Plutarch: *Life of Romulus*.

built on the Capitoline Hill and which was called the
Capitol.   This hill was almost inaccessible and it
was strongly guarded.   But Tarpeia, the daughter
of the Roman captain who was in command of the
Capitol, having gone outside the fortifications to
fetch some water, was seized by the King of the
Sabines, and when she saw the rich gold bracelets
the Sabines wore, she offered, "in return for what
they had on their left arms," to betray the citadel
into their hands.   The promise was made, and that
night she opened one of the gates and admitted the
enemy.   The Sabines kept their part of the promise.   In their left hands they always bore their
shields, and when they had taken possession of the
Capitol, they crushed Tarpeia to death under the
weight of these heavy shields, "that her example
might be left as a warning that no faith should be
kept with traitors."[1]   Later generations did not
forget her base deed, for they used to cast down
malefactors from that part of the Capitol which she
had betrayed, and they called the spot the Tarpeian
Rock.
   The Sabines were now in possession of the citadel.

   The next day the Roman army was drawn up in
battle array over the whole of the ground between the
Palatine and the Capitoline Hill (where later the Forum
was built), and angry over the loss of the citadel, they
determined to recover it and advanced to the attack.[2]

But the Sabines met them and advanced with so
fierce an onslaught that the Roman line broke and

[1] Livy, I, 11.   [2] Livy, I, 12.

the Romans fled to what was then the gate of the Palatine. Even Romulus was being swept away by the crowd of fugitives, and lifting up his hands to heaven he exclaimed:

Jupiter, it was thy omen that I obeyed when I laid here on the Palatine the earliest foundations of the City. Now the Sabines hold its citadel, having bought it by a bribe, and coming thence have seized the valley and are pressing hitherwards in battle. Do thou, Father of gods and men, drive hence our foes, banish terror from Roman hearts, and stay our shameful flight! Here do I vow a temple to thee, Jupiter Stator, as a memorial for the generations to come that it is through thy present help that the City has been saved.

Then, as though he had become aware that his prayer had been heard, he cried: "Back, Romans! Jupiter bids you stand and renew the battle."[1] The prayer so heartened the Romans that they regained courage and their fears changed into confidence.

Both sides were about to begin fighting again, when they were prevented by what must have been the strangest sight they had ever seen.

For the Sabine women, whose wrongs had led to the war, throwing off all womanish fears, in their distress went boldly into the midst of the battle, with dishevelled hair and rent garments. Running across the space between the two armies, they tried to stop any further fighting and calm the excited passions, by appealing to their fathers in the one army and their husbands in the other not to bring upon themselves a curse by stain-

[1] Livy, I, 12.

ing their hands with the blood of a father-in-law or a
son-in-law. "If," they cried, "you are weary of these
ties of kindred, these marriage-bonds, then turn your
anger upon us; it is we who are the cause of the war,
it is we who have wounded and slain our husbands and
fathers. Better for us to perish than live without one
or the other of you, as widows or as orphans." The
armies and their leaders were alike moved by this appeal, and there was a sudden hush and silence in both
the hosts.[1]

The appeal of the women was heard, and a truce
was made whilst the leaders discussed the terms of a
treaty.

The women, in the meantime, brought and presented
their husbands and children to their fathers and brothers;
gave those that wanted meat and drink, and carried the
wounded home to be cured, and showed also how much
they governed within doors and how indulgent their
husbands were to them.[2]

Conditions of peace were soon agreed upon. The
women were to be free to stay where they were if
they chose, but they were to be exempt from all
drudgery and labour, except that of spinning wool;
the two nations were to be united in one state; the
royal power was to be shared between Romulus
and Tatius, King of the Sabines; and the seat of
government for both nations was to be Rome.

For five years Romulus and Tatius ruled together,
then, Tatius having been slain by an enemy, Rom-

[1] Livy, I, 13.   [2] Plutarch: *Life of Romulus.*

ulus ruled alone.   Both in his wars and in his wise
rule in time of peace, Romulus so strengthened the
power of Rome, that the city was able "to enjoy an
assured peace for forty years after his departure."[1]
Romulus was regarded by all who came after him as
"a god, the son of a god, the King and Father of
the City of Rome," and it was believed that he had
never tasted death like an ordinary mortal, but had
been taken by the gods while still alive to dwell with
them.   For on a day when he was speaking to the
people without the city

on a sudden, strange and unaccountable disorders and
alterations took place in the air; the face of the sun was
darkened, and the day turned into night, and a great
tempest arose, during which the people dispersed and
fled, but the Senators kept close together.   The tempest
being over, and the light breaking out, when the people
gathered together again, they missed and enquired for
their King; the Senators suffered them not to search or
busy themselves about the matter, but commanded them
to honour and worship Romulus as one taken up to the
gods.[2]

Some of the people believed this, but others accused
the Senators of having taken the life of the King.
These suspicions were, however, laid to rest by one
of the elders, whose word had great weight in all
matters.   He came before the people a few days
later and said to them:

At the break of dawn today, the Father of this City
suddenly descended from heaven and appeared to me.

[1] Livy, I, 16.   [2] Plutarch: *Life of Romulus.*

Whilst, thrilled with awe, I stood rapt before him in deepest reverence, praying that I might be pardoned for gazing upon him, "Go," said he, "tell the Romans that it is the will of heaven that my Rome should be the head of all the world. Let them henceforth cultivate the arts of war, and let them know assuredly, and hand down the knowledge to posterity, that no human might can withstand the arms of Rome."[1]

Great credence was given to this man's story, and the grief of the people was soothed by this belief in the divinity and immortality of Romulus. "It was in the fifty-fourth year of his age and the thirty-eighth of his reign that Romulus, they tell us, left the world."[2]

II. NUMA POMPILIUS

After the death of Romulus, a year went by before a successor to him was elected. Rome was still a young state, and there was no family sufficiently important to take the lead, but the two nations, the Romans and the Sabines, united by Romulus, were jealous of each other, and at first it seemed as if neither would be willing to be ruled by a King from the other. At last the Senators, the elders who advised the King,

began to grow apprehensive of some aggressive act on the part of the surrounding states, now that the City was without a central authority and the army without a general. They decided that there must be some head

[1] Livy, I, 16.   [2] Plutarch: *Life of Romulus.*

of the state, but no one could make up his mind to con-
cede the dignity to anyone else.[1]

So they arranged for what was called an *interregnum*,
during which time the Senators ruled in turn. But
the Roman people did not like this, and they complained that instead of one master they had a hundred. The Senators realized that there was a growing determination amongst the people to elect their
own King, and so they decided to give to the people
freely what otherwise would be taken by force if
they delayed, but they did it

in such a way that they did not give away more privilege
than they retained. For they passed a decree that
when the people had chosen a King his election would
only be valid after the Senate had ratified it by their
authority. The Assembly of the people was called together and one of the Senators addressed it as follows:
"Elect your King, and may heaven's blessing rest on
your labours! If you elect one who shall be worthy
to follow Romulus, the Senate will ratify your choice."
    There was living, in those days, in one of the Sabine
cities, a man of renowned justice and piety, Numa
Pompilius, a man whose temperament and training had
been moulded by the rigorous and austere discipline
of the ancient Sabines, which was the purest type of
any that existed in the old days.[2]

It was determined by both Romans and Sabines that
this was the man best fitted to rule, and ambassadors from Rome went to him and asked him to be

[1] Livy, I, 17.   [2] Livy, I, 17–18.

King. To their surprise, he not only did not accept at once, but he required a great deal of persuasion, as he was unwilling to leave his quiet and peaceful life for an office for which he did not consider himself fitted.

At length his father and one of his kinsmen, taking him aside, persuaded him to accept a gift so noble in itself, and tendered to him rather from heaven than from men. "Though," they said, "you neither desire riches, being content with what you have, nor count the fame of authority as having the already more valuable fame of virtue, yet you will consider that government itself is a service of God, who now calls out into action your qualities of justice and wisdom, which were not meant to be left useless and unemployed. Cease, therefore, to avoid and turn your back upon an office which, to a wise man, is a field for great and honourable actions, for the magnificent worship of the gods, and for the introduction of habits of piety, which authority alone can effect amongst a people."[1]

Numa heeded this appeal to the duty of his accepting such a trust as was placed before him, and after offering sacrifices to the gods he returned with the ambassadors to Rome. Headed by the Senate, the people came out to meet him and he was received with great joy. But he refused to wear the robes of office until it should be made clear that it was the will of the gods that he should be King. He was led up to the Capitol, where the chief of the augurs laid his hand upon his head and offered this prayer:

[1] Plutarch: *Life of Numa Pompilius.*

"Father Jupiter, if it be heaven's will that this Numa Pompilius, whose head I hold, should be King of Rome, do thou signify it to us by sure signs."[1] In silence and devotion the assembled people stood below in the Forum. Then, even as the prayer went up to Jupiter, they saw the auspicious birds flying across the sky, whereupon "Numa, taking upon him the royal robes, descended from the hill to the people, by whom he was recognized and congratulated with shouts and acclamations of welcome, as a holy King, and beloved of all the gods."[2]

Having in this way been made King, Numa set to work to show the Romans that peace was better than war. The first inhabitants of the city had been men of a daring and warlike spirit, who had seen the state grow stronger and larger by warfare. Numa determined to show them that peace tended equally to prosperity. He built a temple to Janus, a legendary hero, half-god and half-king, who was said to have spent his life in raising mankind from brutal and savage customs to a more civilized manner of life, for which reason he is depicted "with two faces, to represent the two states and conditions out of the one of which he brought mankind, to lead them into the other."[3] When the gates of the temple of Janus were closed, it signified that Rome and all the surrounding nations were at peace; when they were open, it meant that the state was at war.

[1] Livy, I, 18.
[2] Plutarch: *Life of Numa Pompilius.*
[3] Ibid.

During the reign of Numa, those gates were never seen open a single day, but continued constantly shut for a space of forty-three years together; such an entire and universal cessation of war existed.[1]

But only twice again in the later history of Rome were the gates of this temple closed, so seldom was the state at peace.

Numa loved peace, but he knew that occasions would arise when there would be disputes that must in some way or other be settled. In order to make it possible to settle such disputes without going to war, Numa instituted an order of

guardians of the peace, whose duty it was to put a stop to disputes by conference and speech; for it was not allowed to take up arms until they had declared all hopes of accommodation to be at an end.[2]

Numa has been called the founder of Roman religion. He desired that the people

should apply their minds to religion as to a most serious business, and that they should make their prayers to the gods, not by the way and as it were in a hurry, or when they had other things to do, but with time and leisure to attend to it.[3]

Numa made laws concerning the appointment of the priests, and all the regulations bearing on religious matters were written down and placed in the hands of the chief priest, the Pontifex Maximus.

[1] Plutarch: *Life of Numa Pompilius.*   [2] Ibid.   [3] Ibid.

Numa also instituted the order of the Vestal Virgins, the priestesses of the goddess Vesta, whose duty it was to see that the sacred fire was always kept burning.[1]

Another of the reforms of Numa was the making of a new calendar, not, we are told, "with absolute exactness, yet not without some scientific knowledge,"[2] and he divided the year into twelve lunar months, some of which to this day bear the names given them by this ancient Roman King.

In order to encourage the people as much as possible in the arts of peace, Numa divided the land that had been conquered by Romulus amongst all the poorer people, and encouraged them to cultivate it well, for he believed that nothing would give such a keen wish for peace as agriculture and a country life. He valued such a life far more for its influence on the character of men than for any wealth or profit it might bring.

After the union of the Sabines with Rome, the people, whilst all being part of Rome, had, nevertheless, thought of themselves as either Romans or Sabines and there had been a good deal of rivalry and jealousy between the two. To do away with this, Numa divided the people by their trades into companies or guilds. He formed the companies of musicians, goldsmiths, carpenters, dyers, shoemakers, skinners, braziers and potters; and all the other trades he united in one guild. Each guild had its own place of meeting and worshipped its own gods. In this way the old distinctions fell out of

[1] See p. 128.   [2] Plutarch: *Life of Numa Pompilius*.

use, and through the guilds much greater harmony amongst the people prevailed.

It was not only the Romans who were influenced by the mild and peace-loving Numa.

but even the neighbouring cities, as if some healthful and gentle air had blown from Rome upon them, began to experience a change of feeling, and partook of the general longing for the delights of peace and order, and for life employed in the quiet tillage of soil, bringing up of children and worship of the gods.   Festival days and sports, and the secure and peaceful interchange of friendly visits and hospitality prevailed all through Italy.   The love of virtue and justice flowed from Numa's wisdom as from a fountain, and the serenity of his spirit diffused itself, like a calm, on all sides.[1]

Numa lived to be more than eighty years old, and we are told that he died gently and peacefully of old age.   All the neighbouring states did him honour at his funeral, showing by the presence of their ambassadors that they were living in peace and friendship with Rome.

These first two kings of Rome had each in a different way advanced the greatness of the state. Both by the lessons of war and by the arts of peace Rome had become strong and disciplined.

III. TULLUS HOSTILIUS

Numa Pompilius was a Sabine, the first King had been a Roman.   Tullus Hostilius, the grandson of a

[1] Plutarch: *Life of Numa Pompilius.*

Roman who had fought with great valour in the war against the Sabines in the reign of Romulus, was now

chosen King by the people and their choice was confirmed by the Senate.   He was not only unlike the last King, but he was a man of more warlike spirit even than Romulus, and his ambition was kindled by his own youthful energy and by the great achievements of his grandfather.   Convinced that the vigour of the state was becoming enfeebled through inaction, he looked all round for a pretext for getting up a war.[1]

Such a pretext was not very difficult to find.   It was a warlike period, in spite of the long years of peace during the reign of the gentle Numa, and a quarrel was easily made with Alba Longa.   It happened that Roman peasants at that time were in the habit of carrying off plunder from the Alban territory, and the Albans from Roman territory. Both sides sent envoys at almost the same time to demand redress, but Tullus was determined on action, and he brought it about that his demands were refused, upon which he declared that he had just cause for war.

Both sides prepared for what was almost like a civil war, for the Romans and Albans were of kin, and both could claim Aeneas as a common ancestor.   Now there happened to be in each of the armies three brothers, fairly matched in years and strength, and the Kings suggested to them that they should each fight on behalf of their country, the

[1] Livy, I, 22.

three Horatii for Rome, and the three Curiatii for the Albans, and that the country of whichever side prevailed should receive the submission of the other. They consented; time and place were fixed, and the six combatants armed themselves. They were greeted with shouts of encouragement from their comrades, who reminded them that their fathers' gods, their fatherland, their fathers, every fellow-citizen, every fellow-soldier, were now watching their fight. The signal was given, and with uplifted swords the six youths charged at each other. Not one of them thought of his own danger, their sole thought was for their country, their one anxiety that they were deciding its future fortunes. At first neither side seemed to be gaining any advantage, but the fight was so fierce, that soon two of the Romans fell dead, and all three Albans were wounded. Horatius was now left alone, one man against three. He was not wounded, and though he knew he was not a match against the three together, he felt sure of victory, could he but fight each separately. So he feigned flight and ran some distance from the spot where they had been fighting. The Albans pursued him, but they were wounded, and could only come up with him one after the other. Horatius fought with each in turn and slew all three. Great then was the triumph of the Romans, for instead of Rome submitting to her neighbour, Alba Longa would now fall under Roman rule.

The Roman army now marched back to Rome, with Horatius at its head, bearing the spoils, the weapons and cloaks of the enemy. Horatia, the sister of Horatius, had been betrothed to one of the Curiatii. With other Roman women she came out of the gates of the city to greet her brother on his victorious return, but when she saw him wearing on his shoulders the cloak of her betrothed which she had made with her own hands, she burst into tears and tore her hair, calling on her dead lover by name. The triumphant soldier was so enraged by his sister's outburst of grief in the midst of his own triumph and public rejoicing, that he drew his sword and ran it through her body, saying as he did so: "So perish every Roman woman who mourns an enemy!"

The people were horrified at this deed and Horatius was brought before the King for trial. The custom required that he should be put to death for the murder of the maiden, but the father of Horatius interfered to save his life. He declared that his daughter had been justly slain, that if it had not been so, using the authority given to him as a father, he would himself have punished his son.[1] Then he implored the judges not to bereave him of all his children, and pointing to the spoils of the Curiatii, he said to the people, "Can you bear to see bound and scourged and tortured beneath the gallows the man whom you saw, lately, coming in triumph adorned with his foemen's spoils?" The young soldier bore himself with great courage and was ready to meet whatever it was decreed should befall him. His bravery and his father's tears were too much for

[1] See p. 57.

the people, and they acquitted him. But it was because they admired his bravery rather than because they considered his cause a just one. To make atonement for the deed of his son, the father offered many sacrifices to the gods.[1]

The Albans were now subject to Rome, but they did not keep the peace, and at last Tullus decided that Alba Longa should be destroyed and its inhabitants removed to Rome. He announced his intention in these words:

I shall take a course which will bring good fortune and happiness to the Roman people and myself, and to you, Albans; it is my intention to transfer the entire Alban population to Rome, to give the rights of citizenship to the plebeians, and enroll the nobles in the Senate, and to make one City, one State. As formerly the Alban state was broken up into two nations, so now let it once more become one.

In grief and sorrow the Albans left their city, seizing hastily what they could carry and leaving behind their hearths and household gods and the homes in which they had been born and brought up.

When the Albans had left their city, the Romans levelled to the ground all the public and private buildings in every direction, and a single hour gave over to destruction and ruin the work of those four centuries during which Alba had stood. The temples of the gods, however, were spared in accordance with the King's proclamation.

[1] From Livy, I, 24–26.

The fall of Alba led to the growth of Rome. The number of citizens was doubled, the Caelian Hill was included in the city, and that it might become more populated, Tullus chose it for the site of his palace, and for the future lived there.[1]

Alba Longa had been the chief city in the Latin League. After the Roman conquest of the city, Rome began to gain supremacy in the League, by which her power was greatly increased.

Tradition tells that after other wars, Tullus attempted to appease the anger of Jupiter, which he had incurred by his neglect of all sacred things, by certain sacrificial rites. But the King had so long neglected all religious observances, that he

marred these rites by omissions and mistakes. Not only was no sign from heaven vouchsafed to him, but the anger of Jupiter was roused by the false worship rendered to him, and he burnt up the King and his house by a stroke of lightning.

Tullus had achieved great renown in war and had reigned for two and thirty years.[2]

IV. ANCUS MARTIUS

On the death of Tullus, the people chose Ancus Martius, the grandson of Numa, to be King, and the Senate approved the choice. Ancus knew that great as had been some of the achievements of Tullus, he had neglected the religion of his country, and so he determined that Rome should once more carry out

[1] Livy, I, 29–30.   [2] Ibid., 31.

all the religious observances as had been done in
the days of Numa. The Latin states, with whom
Tullus had made a treaty, thought that Ancus was
so much occupied with these matters that he would
not fight, and so they planned to attack Rome.
Now Ancus believed that peace had been the great
need for Rome in the days of Numa, but he saw
that it would not be possible to preserve that peace
unbroken in his own time. He set out with an army
and defeated his enemies and took their city. Following the custom of the earlier kings who had enlarged the state by receiving its enemies into Roman
citizenship, he transferred the whole of the population to Rome. The Palatine had been settled
by the earliest Romans, the Sabines had occupied
the Capitoline Hill with the citadel on one side of
the Palatine, and the Albans the Caelian Hill on the
other; the Aventine was now assigned to the new-
comers. With all this increase of population in
Rome, there was also an increase of wrong-doing and
many secret crimes were committed. To overcome
this growing lawlessness, a prison was built in the
heart of the city overlooking the Forum.

Ancus Martius also brought the Janiculum into
the city boundaries, not because the space was
wanted, but to prevent such a strong position from
being occupied by an enemy. This hill was connected with the city by a bridge for the convenience
of traffic. This was the first bridge built over the
Tiber and was known as the *Pons Sublicius*, the
Bridge of the Wooden Piles. Strict laws were
passed concerning the building of this bridge; no

:ron of any kind was to be used in its construction
or in its repair, and the beams were to be so placed
as to be easily and quickly removed in the event of
the approach of an enemy.

The additions made by Ancus Martius were not
confined to the city. He extended the Roman
dominion to the sea, and built the port of Ostia at
the mouth of the Tiber.

The reign of Ancus lasted for twenty-four years
and his deeds, we are told, both in the field and at
home, were equal to any of those of the Kings who
had reigned before him.[1]

V. LUCIUS TARQUINIUS PRISCUS

During the reign of Ancus, there came to Rome
from Etruria, Lucius Tarquinius Priscus, a wealthy
and ambitious man. He was not himself an Etruscan by birth, but he had married Tanaquil who
belonged to one of the foremost families in Etruria.
Rome was still a young state where nobility was
won by personal merit, and both Tarquin and Tanaquil felt that there would be more room in Rome
for a man of courage and energy than in the older
state of Etruria. They said to each other that
even the Kings of Rome had not always been Romans. Numa had been a Sabine, and Ancus Martius was only Roman on his father's side. If Sabines
could rule in Rome, why not perhaps some day an
Etruscan? So they packed up their belongings and
removed to Rome.

[1] Livy, I, 33.

They had got as far as the Janiculum, when a hovering eagle swooped gently down and took off the cap of Tarquin as he was sitting by his wife's side in the carriage, then circling round the vehicle with loud cries, as though commissioned by heaven for this service, replaced it carefully upon his head and soared away. It is said that Tanaquil, who, like most Etruscans, was expert at interpreting heavenly omens, was delighted and bade her husband look for a high and great destiny, for such was the meaning of the eagle's appearance.

Full of hopes they entered the city. The fact that Tarquin was a stranger and a wealthy one, brought him into notice, and by his courteous demeanour, his lavish hospitality, and many acts of kindness he won all whom it was in his power to win, until his reputation reached even the palace. Once introduced to the King's notice, he soon succeeded in getting on to such familiar terms that he was consulted in matters of state, as much as in private matters. At last, after passing every test of character and ability, he was actually appointed by the King's will guardian to his children.[1]

When Ancus died, his sons had almost reached manhood. This made Tarquin all the more anxious that the election of the new King should be held as soon as possible, and when the day had been fixed, he arranged that the two sons of Ancus should be out of the way on a long hunting expedition. Tarquin is said to have been the first who actually canvassed for the crown, and he delivered a long speech to secure the interest of the people. He pointed out to them that it was not a new thing for a foreigner

[1] Livy, I, 34.

to become King. The Sabine Tatius had not only
not been a Roman, but he had once been even the
enemy of Rome, and Numa was an entire stranger to
the city when he was called to the throne. He then
went on to say that he had chosen Rome as his
home, and that he had lived there as a grown man
for a longer period than he had lived in his own country, that he knew the laws of Rome and all her civil
and religious ceremonies. He so roused the enthusiasm of the Roman people that they unanimously
elected him King.

Tarquin continued the warlike policy of the
Kings before him and gained great victories over
both the Latins and the Sabines. After one of his
campaigns a quantity of rich plunder was brought
to Rome, and to celebrate his victory Tarquin
determined to hold more splendid Games and on a
much larger scale than any that had taken place
in Rome before. Then for the first time a space was
marked for what was known afterwards as the *Circus
Maximus*. Spots were allotted to the patricians
where they could build for themselves stands from
which to view the Games. The contests were
horse-racing and boxing, the horses and boxers
having mostly come from Etruria.[1] Games were
at first only held on special occasions, but they soon
became an annual event and were called sometimes
the *Roman*, and sometimes the *Great Games*.

When Tarquin had brought his wars to an end,
he began to improve the city, and we are told that
he kept the people so busy with his new buildings

[1] Livy, I, 35.

that they had no more quiet at home than they had in the field. He drained the Forum and the low-lying parts of the city near it, and built a great sewer called the *Cloaca Maxima* to carry off the water into the Tiber. He divided the ground round the Forum into building sites, and arcades and shops were built, but above all, he began a great Temple to Jupiter on the Capitoline Hill.

Now about this time a strange incident took place.

It is said that whilst Servius Tullius, a slave boy living in the palace, lay asleep, his head was suddenly seen by some who were standing by, to be surrounded by flames. The cry which broke out at such a sight aroused the royal family, and when one of the servants was bringing water to quench the flames, the Queen stopped him, and after calming the excitement forbade the boy to be disturbed until he woke of his own accord. Presently he did so, and the flames disappeared. Then Tanaquil took her husband aside and said to him, "Do you see this boy, whom we are bringing up in such a humble style? You may be certain that he will one day be a light to us in trouble and perplexity and a protection to our house. Let us henceforth bring him up with all care and indulgence, one who will be the source of glory to the state and ourselves." From this time the boy began to be treated as their child and trained in all those arts by which a man's character is formed for high office. The youth turned out to be of a truly kingly disposition and when search was made for a son-in-law to Tarquin, none of the Roman youths could be compared with him in any respect, so the King betrothed his daughter to him.

When Tarquin had been about thirty-eight years on the throne, Servius Tullius was held in by far the highest esteem of anyone, not only with the King but also with the patricians and the commons. Now the two sons of Ancus had always felt it most keenly that they had lost the throne through the treachery of their guardian. They were not only angry that Rome should be governed by one who was as great a foreigner as Tarquin, but still more so that after his death the crown would descend to a slave—that crown which Romulus, the offspring of a god, and himself a god, had worn whilst he was on earth, was now to be the possession of a slave, born a hundred years later! They felt that such a thing would be a disgrace to the whole Roman nation, and they determined, therefore, to repel that insult by the sword. But it was on Tarquin rather than on Servius that they sought to avenge their wrongs, for they knew that if Servius were killed, the King would still make anyone he chose heir to the crown.[1]

The sons of Ancus formed their plot and hired two shepherds to assassinate the King. But the blow did not kill the King on the spot, though he was mortally wounded. As he lay dying, Tanaquil, the Queen, sent for Servius, and taking him by the hand, she showed him the dying King and said to him:

The throne is yours, Servius, if you are a man; it does not belong to those who have, through the hands of others, wrought this worst of crimes. Follow the guidance of the gods, who by the sacred fire foretold your greatness. Rouse yourself, and follow my counsels.

[1] Livy, I, 39–40.

Tanaquil then caused the doors of the palace to be closed, after which she appeared to the people at a window. She bade them not despair, the King was not dead, only stunned; he had already recovered some consciousness and it was his will that Servius Tullius should rule in his place until he were able to do it himself once more. So for several days Servius ruled, sitting in the royal chair and administering justice.

At length sounds of mourning arose in the palace, and it could no longer be hidden from the people that the King was dead. Servius, protected by a strong bodyguard, now publicly took possession of the throne. No one opposed him, the sons of Ancus withdrew into exile, and Servius Tullius became King. He was the first to ascend the throne without being elected by the people, but the Senate made no opposition and he was recognized by everyone as King.

VI. SERVIUS TULLIUS

Servius Tullius began his reign by a work of the greatest importance. Just as Numa had been the author of religious laws and institutions, so Servius is remembered as having divided the inhabitants of the state into divisions according to the wealth each man possessed. In ancient times every able-bodied man was expected to serve in the army, but as the soldier had to provide all his own armour and weapons, Servius divided the state into five classes according to the kind of armour and weapons that each could be expected to provide. The army thus formed was divided into groups of a hundred men, called *Centuries*, and gradually these Centuries acquired the powers of the old assembly called the *Comitia Curiata*[1] and became a voting body called the *Comitia Centuriata*. Summoned by the sound of a trumpet, the Centuries used to meet in this assembly outside the walls of the city in the *Campus Martius*, or Field of Mars. In order to find out exactly who were the inhabitants of the city, Servius instituted the census, which was taken every five years, and from the census the classes and the centuries were formed.

Servius Tullius then enlarged the city. He added the two other of the hills which encircled the Palatine, the Viminal and the Esquiline, and he enclosed the whole city, which had now become the City of the Seven Hills, by a wall, parts of which are still standing.

Servius next entered into friendly relations with his neighbours, especially with the Latin nations. He made a treaty of peace with them and built a temple to Diana on the Aventine in honour of the treaty, and the Latins now definitely acknowledged that Rome was the head of Latium.

After a long and honourable reign Servius had gained a firm hold on the kingdom and was much beloved by the people. He had two daughters who had married two young Tarquins, the sons of Tarquinius Priscus, and it came to the ears of Servius that one of these Tarquins, Lucius, was saying that

[1] See p. 57.

he was reigning without the consent of the people. In order to be sure of their good-will, Servius gave to each man amongst the people a piece of land that had come to Rome by conquest, and then he put to them the question whether it was their will that he should reign. The result of his enquiry was that he was recognized by a more unanimous vote than had been given before to any other King. But this did not satisfy the ambition of Lucius Tarquin, who aimed at nothing less than being King himself. In this he was aided by his wife, Tullia the daughter of Servius, a very wicked woman. He and Tullia plotted wickedly together and one day, accompanied by armed men, Tarquin entered the Forum and before anyone could stop him, seated himself in the royal chair in the Senate House, and ordered the Senators to be summoned "into the presence of King Tarquin." Servius, who had been hastily sent for, arrived on the scene while Tarquin was speaking, and when he saw him in the royal seat and heard his insolent words, he exclaimed in loud tones: "What is the meaning of this? How dare you with such insolence summon the Senate or sit in that chair whilst I am alive?" Tarquin replied in insulting words that he was occupying his father's seat, and that as a King's son he had more right to it than one who was a slave. A great tumult arose upon this, everyone present taking the side of either Tarquin or the King. In the midst of the confusion Tarquin seized Servius in his arms, and being a younger and a stronger man, carried him out of the Senate House and flung him down the steps into the

Forum below. The friends of the King fled, and Servius, already half dead from terror and violence, was put to death by men whom Tarquin sent after him.

It was believed that all this was done at the suggestion of Tullia, and these were deeds quite in keeping with her general wickedness. It is known that just as her father had been so cruelly murdered, she drove down to the Forum in a two-wheeled chariot, and was the first to greet her husband as King as he came out of the Senate House. He told her to leave such a scene of tumult and violence, and she was departing, when she saw the body of her father lying before her in the road. In rage and anger she filled up the measure of her wickedness by ordering her charioteer to drive the chariot right over her father's body.

Servius Tullius had reigned for forty-four years, and even a wise and good successor would have found it difficult to fill the throne as he had done. His rule had been moderate and gentle and the glory of his reign was all the greater, because with him perished all just and lawful kingship in Rome. [1]

VII. TARQUINIUS SUPERBUS

Lucius Tarquin, called Tarquin the Proud, now began to reign.

He had done nothing whatever to make good his claim to the crown except actual violence; he was reign-

[1] Livy, I, 46–48.

ing without either being elected by the people, or confirmed by the Senate. He was the first of the Kings
to break through the traditional custom of consulting
the Senate on all questions, the first to conduct the
government on the advice of his palace favourites.
War, peace, treaties, alliances, were made or broken
by him, just as he thought good, without any authority
from either people or Senate.[1]

Tarquin the Proud was cruel and oppressive, and he
ruled as a tyrant, but he was successful in war and
made the power of Rome greatly respected.

One day, when Tarquin was at the height of his
power, a strange old woman, unknown to any of
those who surrounded the King, came before him,
and offered to sell him nine books, which she said
were sacred because certain oracles concerning
Rome were written in them. She asked so large
a sum of money for them, that the King asked her
if she were mad. For answer, she burnt three of
the books in the King's presence, and then offered
him the remaining six for the same price. Again
the King ridiculed her offer and refused to buy the
books. Whereupon the old woman placed three
more upon the fire, and then offered the King the
last three, still at the same price. Impressed by
her strange deeds, the King bought the three remaining books, and the old woman departed with the
money and was seen no more. It was found that
these books did indeed contain certain oracles concerning Rome, and that the old woman was the
Wise Woman, or Sibyl, of Cumae. The books were

[1] Livy, I, 40.

called the Sibylline books and were counted as some of Rome's greatest treasures.

Tarquin the Proud became more and more tyrannical and was hated and feared by everyone. He was so wicked that the thought of the gods and of how they might perhaps punish him often filled even him with anxiety. One day a strange sign appeared in the palace, for a snake glided out of a wooden column. Tarquin was so frightened that he decided to send two of his sons to Delphi to ask the oracle for the meaning of this sign. Their kinsman, Lucius Junius Brutus, went with them. The young men had not only their father's business to attend to, but also an enquiry of their own that they wished to make. They asked Apollo which of them should reign in Rome after the death of Tarquin. The answer came at once: "Whichever of you young men shall be the first to kiss his mother, he shall hold supreme sway in Rome." The two brothers then drew lots as to which should be the first to kiss their mother on their return to Rome. But Brutus saw another meaning in the words, and pretending to stumble, he bent and kissed the ground, for, he said, the earth is the mother of us all.

Soon after the return of the two brothers from Delphi they were with Sextus, the third son of Tarquin, who had not gone with them to the oracle, and their cousin Collatinus in camp. At a wine-party given in their leisure hours, the conversation turning upon their wives, each began to praise his own and to say how much better a wife she was than the others.

As the dispute became warm, Collatinus said that there was no need of words, for it could in a few hours be ascertained how far his Lucretia was superior to all the rest. "Why do we not," he exclaimed, "mount our horses and pay our wives a visit and find out their characters on the spot? What we see of the behaviour of each on the unexpected arrival of her husband, let that be the surest test." They all shouted, "Good! Come on!" Setting spur to their horses they galloped off to Rome where they arrived as darkness was beginning to close in. They found the King's daughters-in-law passing their time in feasting and luxury with their acquaintances, but they found Lucretia very differently employed. She was sitting at her wool-work in the hall, late at night, with her maids busy round her. So the palm in this competition was awarded to Lucretia.[1]

Sextus was as wicked as his father, and not long after he so gravely insulted Lucretia that she called upon her father and her husband to avenge her, and then in grief and shame she plunged a knife into her heart. Hearing of this, Brutus stepped out before those who were present when the dreadful story was told and said:

I swear, and you, O gods, I call to witness, that I will drive hence Lucius Tarquinius Superbus, together with his wicked wife and his whole family, with fire and sword and every means in my power, and I will not suffer them or anyone else to reign in Rome.

He then went down into the Forum where a crowd collected round him. Everyone had his own com-

[1] Livy, I, 57.

plaint to make of the wickedness of the royal house, and Brutus soon found himself at the head of an armed band.   They closed the gates of the city and a decree of banishment was passed against Tarquin, his children and all his race.   Tarquin went into exile amongst the Etruscans and his sons followed him.

In this way the Tarquins were expelled, and monarchy in Rome came to an end.

Lucius Tarquinius Superbus had reigned for twenty-five years.   The whole duration of the kingly government from the foundation of the City to the expulsion of the last Kings was two hundred and forty-four years. Rome now became a Republic, and two Consuls were elected in the Comitia Centuriata.   These Consuls were Lucius Junius Brutus and Lucius Tarquinius Collatinus.[1]

[1] Livy, I, 60.

CHAPTER V

'ROMAN SOCIETY IN THE DAYS OF THE KINGS

IT is not until the establishment of the early Roman Republic in 509 B.C., about two hundred and fifty years after the traditional founding of Rome, that we know very much of which we can be historically certain about Roman society and government. The chief authority for this period is Livy, who lived in the latter part of the last century B.C. long after the events he narrates had taken place. He himself says of this period of the Kings:

> The facts were obscure, dim as events seen from afar. This was the result of their antiquity. But also in those times written records were extremely rare, and they alone can be trusted to preserve faithfully the memory of events.

But it was during this period of the Kingdom that the customs and usages which prevailed later were developed, and though we do not know very much, a few things stand out of which we may be certain.

To the early Roman the most sacred and the most important of all human institutions was the Family. The Father was the head of the Family, and his word was law over all the members of his household. He could exercise the power of life and death over his sons, and if he chose, he might even sell them into slavery. A group of Families, each of which was descended from a common ancestor, was called a *Gens*, and several of these groups bound together by common interests, common festivals, a common hearth and the worship of the same god formed a *Curia*. Ten Curiae made a Tribe, and three Tribes formed the early Roman state. But the Tribe did not last very long as a political division of the people, and it was the Curia that became of much greater importance, for the thirty Curiae included all the freemen of the early state. These freemen were supposed to be descended from the leading families in the small communities which had existed before Rome became a single state. As time went on and the state grew larger, these men claimed privileges for themselves because of their birth and position, and they were given the name of *patricians*, the *patres* or Fathers of the state. They sat in an assembly called the *Comitia Curiata*. It was they who elected the King, who on his part chose a Senate of three hundred men to advise him, and whose business it would be to ratify the elections made by the Comitia Curiata.

The King was the chief priest, the chief ruler, and the chief general of the Roman people. As chief priest it was his duty to preserve peace and harmony between the city and the gods who watched over it. It was believed that Jupiter revealed his will by the sending of certain omens, by thunder and lightning

and in the flight of birds. These omens were called
the *auspices* and those who interpreted them the
augurs. The college of augurs was held in such
honour that nothing was undertaken in peace or war
without its sanction; the Comitia Curiata, all matters of the highest importance were suspended or
broken up if the omen of the birds was unfavourable.
The college of the augurs was responsible for the
interpretation of the auspices, and the college of
the priests or pontiffs for settling which days were
to be held sacred and to decide any difficult religious
question that arose.   In Egypt, where they had very
similar duties to perform, the priests sometimes became more important than the King, but in Rome,
the chief of the college of priests, the *Pontifex
Maximus*, was often the King himself, and it was
the King who was usually the Chief Augur.
The King was also the chief ruler, and though in
theory the Senate was there to advise and the
Comitia Curiata to ratify or reject his decisions, in
practice he had almost unlimited power.   This royal
power was called the *imperium*, a word which in
various forms still survives today.   To the Roman,
this word *imperium* meant discipline and order in the
state; it stood for the firm Roman conviction that
when lawful authority had been entrusted to an individual by the members of a state, that authority
must be absolutely obeyed.   The early Roman
method of electing a King ensured that every care
would be taken to elect the right man, but when
once elected and acknowledged as King by the
people, his power was absolute.   The outward sym-

bols of this *imperium* were the rods borne before the King whenever he appeared in public by twelve attendants called lictors. Each lictor carried a bundle of rods called the *fasces* in the centre of which was an axe, the symbol of the royal power over the life and death of his subjects. The lictors with their rods were introduced by the Etruscan Kings, who had also brought with them to Rome the other insignia of the kingly power: the gold crown, the ivory sceptre, the ivory throne called the curule chair, and the white robe with purple border.

The patricians were the most important people in the early Roman kingdom, but they were not the only inhabitants of Rome. The patricians were those who belonged to the ancient noble families, but there were also large numbers of people of lower rank. These were the descendants of those who had settled in Rome later than the patrician families, and they were called *plebeians* from the Latin word *plebs* meaning the *multitude*. They were freemen, but they could neither hold office nor sit in the Senate, these were privileges for the patricians only.

As far as we can disentangle it from legend and tradition, this was the early society and the early government of Rome during the period when she was ruled by Kings. Certain facts in this early history stand out clearly to us. From very small beginnings and from being less powerful than her neighbours, Rome had gained for herself order and freedom within the city, independence and supremacy amongst her nearer neighbours. At the opening of the period of the Republic, we see Rome determined to make her supremacy over the surrounding states secure and lasting; she was beginning to realize that there were possibilities for communication with the world that lay even beyond the shores of Italy, and to feel that she had within her the strength to expand far beyond the bounds of the seven hills that encircled the city and that had once been the limit of her rule.   The first step in this expansion, that was to be greater than she dreamed of when she found herself free from the rule of the later Kings who had oppressed her, was the conquest of Italy, of which before three centuries had passed she was to be the Mistress.

ROME

THE CONQUEROR AND LAWGIVER

PART I

ROME THE MISTRESS OF ITALY

CHAPTER VI

How Rome Conquered Italy

THE Roman people expelled the Tarquins in the year 509 B.C. and the chief government then passed from the hands of the Kings into those of two magistrates called Consuls, who were elected every year by the Comitia Centuriata. Within the city the power of the Consuls was limited, but in war-time when they took the field as generals of the army, their authority was supreme. The elders of the city still sat in the Senate, and as all those who had been Consuls generally became members of the Senate, it grew to be a body of men of practical experience as well as of ripe wisdom. When the state was threatened by any great peril, the Consuls, acting with the approval of the Senate, could appoint one man to be sole ruler with unlimited powers for a definitely fixed time. This ruler was called a Dictator.

When the Republic was established, Rome was still a very small nation, ruling little more than the land immediately outside the city and the seven hills, and she was surrounded on all sides by enemies. For the space of two centuries and a half Rome struggled against her neighbours, until she finally overcame them and in 264 B.C. was the acknowledged mistress of Italy.   During this same period she was also struggling with herself, learning how to govern herself, learning the meaning of justice and teaching her sons that those who would rule must first learn how to obey.   Rome learned these lessons in a stern school.   She understood, as no other nation of the ancient world understood, that true greatness in a nation or an individual is always bought at a price, and that price is sacrifice.   The history of these two hundred and fifty years is the history of a nation that counted discipline and duty amongst the greatest of the virtues, and those whom the Romans of a later day looked upon as their heroes, whose examples were to be followed, were men who by steady training in discipline and self-control were unfaltering in treading the path of sacrifice in obedience to what they believed to be their duty.

Before Rome became the mistress of Italy she had to subdue powerful rivals.   The most important of these rivals were the Etruscans, some of the peoples in the plains and hills surrounding Latium, and the Greeks; and in addition to these enemies she had to face a terrifying invasion of Gauls from the North.

I. WARS AGAINST THE TARQUINS

The Tarquins did not submit tamely to their exile.   Everyone in Rome expected that as soon

as they could gather an army they would declare
war on the newly-formed Republic, but no one
thought that the first attempt to restore them
would be by the treachery of Romans.   But it was
discovered that a conspiracy had been formed with
the intention of admitting the Tarquins secretly
one night into the city.   This plot had been made
by some of the young Roman nobles who had been
the companions of the young Tarquins.   During the
reign of the last King they had done very much as
they pleased, and they missed the licence and the
King who had given them all they wanted, whether
it was lawful or not.   When the plot was discovered, it was found that the two sons of Brutus, the
Consul, were among the conspirators.   The traitors
were all sentenced and condemned to be executed.

Their punishment created a great sensation owing to
the fact that in this case the office of Consul imposed
upon a father the duty of inflicting punishment on his
own children; he who ought not to have witnessed it,
was destined to be the one to see it duly carried out.
Youths belonging to the noblest families were standing
tied to the post, but all eyes were turned to the Consul's
children, the others were unnoticed.   The Consuls took
their seats, the lictors were told off to inflict the penalty;
they scourged their bare backs with rods and then beheaded them,[1]

and Brutus, the Consul, yet also the heartbroken
father, sat in his seat of office, never flinching from
the stern duty required of him.

[1] Livy, II, 5.

When Tarquin heard of the failure of his plans, he was very angry, and he persuaded two of the cities of Etruria to support him, and to help him recover his throne and punish the Romans.

So two armies from these cities followed Tarquin to recover his crown and chastise the Romans. When they had entered the Roman territory, the Consuls advanced against them. As Tarquin drew near he recognized Brutus and in great rage he exclaimed: "That is the man who drove us from our country; see him proudly advancing, adorned with our insignia! Ye gods, avengers of kings, aid me!" With these words, he dug his spurs into his horse and rode straight at the Consul.[1]

Brutus was slain, but the victory was with the Romans.

The Tarquins now

took refuge with Lars Porsena the King of Clusium, whom they sought to influence by entreaty mixed with warnings. At one time they entreated him not to allow men of Etruscan race, of the same blood as himself, to wander as penniless exiles; at another they would warn him not to let the new fashion of expelling kings go unpunished. Porsena considered that the presence of an Etruscan upon the Roman throne would be an honour to his nation; accordingly he marched with an army against Rome.[2]

The Romans were in a state of great alarm, for the power of Porsena was believed to be very great,

[1] Livy, II, 6.   [2] Livy, II, 9.

and the Senate feared that the people, if they became panic-stricken, might admit the Tarquins into the city, even though they knew what kind of rule they would re-establish. Added to this fear, there was the danger of famine owing to a shortage of food.

Porsena advanced with his army upon Rome.

On the appearance of the enemy the country people fled into the city as best they could. The weak places in the defences were occupied by military posts; elsewhere the walls and the Tiber were deemed sufficient protection. The enemy would have forced their way over the Sublician Bridge, had it not been for one man, Horatius Cocles. The good fortune of Rome provided him as her bulwark on that memorable day. He happened to be on guard at the bridge when he saw the Janiculum taken by a sudden assault, and the enemy rushing down from it to the river, whilst his own men, a panic-struck mob, were deserting their own posts and throwing away their arms. He reproached them one after another for their cowardice, tried to stop them, appealed to them in heaven's name to stand, declared that it was in vain for them to seek safety in flight whilst leaving the bridge open behind them, there would very soon be more of the enemy on the Palatine or the Capitol than there were on the Janiculum. So he shouted to them to break down the bridge by sword or fire, or by whatever means they could, he would meet the enemies' attack so far as one man could keep them at bay. He advanced to the head of the bridge, a conspicuous figure, as he stood there alone. The enemy were astounded at his courage. Two men were kept by a sense of shame from deserting him—Lartius and Herminius—both of them men of high birth and renowned courage. For a brief interval the three men repulsed the wild, confused onset of the enemy. Then, whilst only a small portion of the bridge remained and those who were cutting it down called upon them to retire, he insisted that his companions should retreat. Looking round with eyes dark with menace upon the Etruscan chiefs, he challenged them to single combat. For some time they hesitated, each looking round upon the others to begin. At length shame roused them to action, and raising a shout they hurled their javelins from all sides on their solitary foe. He caught them on his outstretched shield, and with unshaken resolution kept his place on the bridge. They were just attempting to dislodge him by a charge when the crash of the broken bridge and the shout which the Romans raised at seeing the work completed stayed the attack by filling them with sudden panic.   Then Horatius said: "Tiber, holy Father, I pray thee to receive into thy holy stream these arms and this thy warrior." So, fully armed, he leaped into the Tiber, and though many missiles fell over him he swam across in safety to his friends. The State showed its gratitude for such courage; his statue was set up in the Forum, and as much land given to him as he could drive the plough round in one day. Besides this public honour, the citizens individually showed their feeling; for, in spite of the great scarcity, each, in proportion to his means, sacrificed what he could from his own store as a gift to Horatius.[1]

Lars Porsena was repulsed, but not defeated, and he now changed his plan from assault to blockade. This caused food in the city to become more and more scarce and corn was sold at famine prices.

[1] Livy, II, 10.

There was a young noble, Caius Mucius, who regarded it as a disgrace that whilst Rome in the days of her servitude under the kings had never been blockaded in any war or by any foe, she should now in the day of her freedom be besieged by those very Etruscans whose armies she had often routed.

He determined to avenge this disgrace by making his way alone into the enemy's camp.

So he went to the Senate. "I wish," he said, "Fathers, to swim the Tiber, and if I can, enter the enemy's camp, not to plunder or to avenge the pillaging of our land. But I purpose, with heaven's help, a greater deed." The Senate gave their approval, and concealing a sword in his robe, he started. When he reached the camp he took his stand in the densest part of the crowd near the royal throne. It happened to be the soldiers' pay-day, and a secretary, sitting by the King and dressed almost exactly like him, was busily engaged as the soldiers kept coming up to him. Afraid to ask which of the two was the King, lest his ignorance should betray him, Mucius struck out, but he killed the secretary instead of the King. He tried to force his way back through the dismayed crowd, but he was seized and dragged by the King's bodyguard to the royal throne. Here, alone and helpless, and in the utmost peril, he was yet able to inspire more fear than he felt. "I am a citizen of Rome," he said, "men call me Caius Mucius. As an enemy I wished to kill an enemy, and I have as much courage to meet death as I had to inflict it. It is the Roman nature to act bravely and to suffer bravely. I am not alone in having made this resolve against you, behind me is a long list of men who aspire to the same distinction. You will have every hour to fight for your life, and find an armed foe on the threshold of your royal tent. This is the war which we, the youth of Rome, declare against you. The matter will be settled between you alone and each one of us singly."

The King, furious with anger, and at the same time terrified at the unknown danger, threatened that if he did not at once reveal the nature of the plot he was darkly hinting at, he should be burnt alive. "Look," Mucius cried, "and learn how lightly these regard their bodies who have some great glory in view." So saying he plunged his right hand into a fire burning on the altar. Whilst he kept it burning there as if he did not feel it, the King, astounded at such conduct, sprang from his seat and ordered the youth to be removed from the altar. "Go," he said, "you have been a worse enemy to yourself than to me. I would invoke blessings on your courage if it were displayed on behalf of my country; as it is, I send you away exempt from all the rights of war, unhurt and safe." Then Mucius, in return for this generous treatment, said, "Since you honour courage, know that what you could not gain by threats you have obtained by kindness. Three hundred of us, the foremost amongst the Roman youth, have sworn to attack you in this way. The lot fell to me first, the rest, in order of the lot, will come each in his turn, till fortune shall give us a favourable chance against you."[1]

Mucius returned to Rome and he was afterwards given the name of Scaevola, which means Left-handed, because he had lost his right hand. Lars Porsena was so unnerved by this first attempt on his life and the knowledge that there would be many

[1] Livy, II, 12.

others that he made proposals of peace to Rome. On surrender of certain hostages, the Etruscans withdrew from the Janiculum and left the Roman territory. As a recognition of his services the Senate gave Caius Mucius a piece of land.

The honour thus paid to courage incited even women to do glorious things for the state. The Etruscan camp was situated not far from the river, and the maiden Cloelia, one of the hostages, escaped, unobserved, through the guards and at the head of her sister hostages swam across the Tiber amidst a shower of javelins and restored them all safe to their relatives. When the King heard of this he was at first very angry and sent to demand the surrender of Cloelia, the others he did not care about. But afterwards his feelings changed to admiration; he said that the exploit surpassed those of Horatius and Mucius, and announced that whilst on the one hand he should consider the treaty broken if she were not surrendered, he would on the other hand, if she were given back, send her home to her people unhurt. Both sides behaved honourably; the Romans surrendered her as a pledge of loyalty to the terms of the treaty; the Etruscan King showed that with him courage was not only safe but honoured, and after praising her, sent her home with half the remaining hostages as a gift.

After peace was thus re-established, the Romans rewarded the extraordinary courage shown by a woman, by an extraordinary honour, namely an equestrian statue. On the highest part of the Sacred Way a statue was erected representing the maiden sitting on horseback.[1]

[1] Livy, II, 13.

Lars Porsena made several other attempts to procure the return to Rome of the Tarquins, but they were all fruitless, and at last, seeing that the determination of the Romans not to have a King was unalterable, he made a lasting peace with them.

"Since," he said, "this is your fixed and unalterable determination, I will not harass you by fruitless proposals, nor will I deceive the Tarquins by holding out hopes of an assistance which I am powerless to render. Whether they insist on war or are prepared to live quietly, in either case they must seek another place of exile than this, to prevent any interruption of the peace between you and me." He followed up his words by still stronger practical proofs of friendship, for he returned the remainder of the hostages and restored the territory which he had formerly taken. So the peace between Rome and Lars Porsena remained unbroken.[1]

One more attempt at return was made by the Tarquins. They joined the army of the Latins who were threatening war on Rome, and when the Romans heard that they had done so, they were so enraged that they determined to engage in battle at once. Then was fought the battle of Lake Regillus, one of the fiercest battles the Romans had ever yet fought. Legend says that the twin gods Castor and Pollux fought on the side of the Romans and gave them victory. A little after the battle it is said that two tall and comely men were seen in Rome. They were cooling their horses, which were foaming from the haste of their ride, near a

[1] Livy, II, 15.

fountain in the Forum, and to the first man that
spoke to them they gave the news of the victory.
Then they vanished, and the Romans, believing that
the strangers were the Twin Gods themselves,
built in their honour a temple in the Forum.

A few years later Tarquin the Proud died, and
Rome was troubled by him no more.

II. ROME AND THE VOLSCIANS AND AEQUIANS

c. 486–405 B.C.

It was just after the final defeat of the Tarquins
that Rome made a treaty of alliance with the Latins.
Under the later Kings the Latins had already
acknowledged the leadership of Rome, but they
had revolted, and now in 493 B.C. they made a
lasting peace.

Let there be peace between the Romans and all the
Latin cities as long as heaven and earth shall remain
in their present position.

Let them neither make war upon one another themselves, nor bring in foreign armies, nor grant a safe
passage to those who shall make war upon either.

Let them with all their forces assist one another when
attacked by enemies, and let both have equal shares
of the spoils and booty taken in their common wars.

Let nothing be added to, or taken from these treaties
except by the joint consent of the Romans and all the
Latins.

It was well that Rome should be at peace with
the Latins, for she soon had other wars on her

hands. The first was against the Volscians who
lived in the southern plains of Latium near the
coast. The chief Volscian city was Corioli, and this
city was besieged by the Romans. Amongst the
most distinguished of the young soldiers in the
Roman camp was a patrician, Caius Marcius, and
he happened to be on guard one day when the
Volscians suddenly opened the gates and made a
sally into the Roman camp. Owing to the brilliant
leadership of Marcius, the Romans entered the
town and took it, and as a reward for this deed,
Marcius, the hero of Corioli, was given the name
of Coriolanus.

Not long afterwards there was a famine in Rome,
and the price of corn was so high that the poorer
people were unable to buy any. But just when
the people were suffering most, a large quantity of
corn from Sicily arrived. Some of this had been
bought, but an equal quantity had been sent as a
present from the Tyrant of Syracuse. Everyone
hoped that now that food was plentiful again, the
corn would be sold at the old reasonable price, and
that the corn which had been sent as a gift would be
distributed freely amongst the poorer people. But
Coriolanus, who was an arrogant, insolent young
patrician, opposed these measures vehemently.
This so much angered the people that he was tried
by the Senate as an enemy to the state and condemned to perpetual banishment. Then he did,
what did not often happen in the history of Rome:
he fled to the enemy, to those very Volscians whose
city he had taken and in fighting against whom he

had gained such great renown. Not only did he flee to their land, but he offered them his services as general to march against Rome, promising to tell them everything he knew which would be an advantage to them.

The Volscians accepted the offer of Coriolanus who immediately went out at the head of a Volscian army and captured several Roman towns, until at last he was only a few miles from Rome itself. The Romans were greatly alarmed, and the Senate sent ambassadors to ask him to return to Rome where his sentence of exile should be recalled, and imploring him to deliver his country from the misery and terror of war.   But Coriolanus returned them a sharp answer, full of bitterness and resentment, and refused to listen to them unless they would promise to restore to the Volscians all the land and cities they had taken from them. The ambassadors returned to Rome, but when they went back a second time to Coriolanus, he refused even to see them.

After that a body of priests, wearing their sacred robes, went to him, but their mission, too, was fruitless. Then it was that Valeria, a noble Roman lady, went to Volumnia, the mother of Coriolanus, and begged her to bring Virgilia, his wife, and his children, and join her and other Roman women in going to the Volscian camp and entreating Coriolanus to spare the city. Volumnia consented, and the women set out.

On their arrival at the camp a message was sent to Coriolanus that a large body of women were present.

He had remained unmoved by the majesty of the state in the persons of its ambassadors, and by the appeal of the priests; he was still more obstinate when he saw the tears of the women. Then one of his friends, who had recognized Volumnia, standing between her daughter-in-law and her grandsons, and conspicuous amongst them all in the greatness of her grief, said to him, "Unless my eyes deceive me, your mother and wife and children are here." Coriolanus sprang from his seat to embrace his mother. But she, changing her tone from entreaty to anger, said, "Before I admit your embrace, suffer me to know whether it is to an enemy or a son I have come, whether it is as your prisoner or as your mother that I am in your camp. Has a long life and an unhappy old age brought me to this, that I have to see you an exile and from that an enemy? Had you the heart to ravage this land, which has borne and nourished you? However hostile and menacing the spirit in which you came, did not your anger subside as you entered its borders? Did you not say to yourself when your eyes rested on Rome, "Within those walls are my home, my household gods, my mother, my wife, my children?""[1]

When she had finished speaking, she

threw herself down at his feet, as did also his wife and children, upon which Coriolanus cried out, "O Mother! what is it you have done to me!" and raised her from the ground. "You have gained a victory," said he, "fortunate enough for the Romans, but destructive to your son, whom you, though no one else have defeated."[2]

[1] Livy, II, 40.
[2] Plutarch: *Life of Coriolanus.*

He then embraced his family and sent them back
to Rome, after which he moved his camp away from
Roman territory.   It is not known for certain what
was the end of Coriolanus.   One tradition says that
the Volscians, in their anger at not being led on to
Rome, killed him, but it was also said that he dwelt
amongst the Volscians until he was very old, when he
was quoted as having said that "it is not until a
man is old that he feels the full misery of exile."

When Volumnia and the Roman women returned
to the city, great honours were paid them for what
they had done, and a temple was built to serve as a
memorial of their deed.

The next war in which the Romans were engaged
was against the Aequians, who lived to the north-
east of Rome on the slopes of the Apennines.   The
Aequians used to come down from the mountains
and plunder and destroy the Roman territory.   On
one occasion they actually surrounded the camp of
one of the Consuls and besieged it as if it had been
a city.   The other Consul was not equal to the
emergency, and the Senate decided to appoint a
Dictator.   They chose a man named Cincinnatus
and sent messengers to tell him of his appointment.   Cincinnatus had a small farm on the other
side of the Tiber, to which he often went in order
that he might enjoy the pleasures which cultivat-
ing his own land gave him.   It was here that he
was found

either digging a ditch or ploughing or as all are agreed
in saying, doing some kind of farm work.   After a

friendly greeting, he was requested to put on his toga
that he might hear the commands of the Senate, and
the messengers expressed the hope that it might turn
out well for him and for the state. He asked them in
surprise, if all was well, and bade his wife bring him his
toga quickly from the cottage. Wiping off the dust
and sweat he put it on and came forward, on which the
messengers greeted him as Dictator, and congratulated
him and asked him to come immediately to the city.[1]

Cincinnatus obeyed the Senate and put himself
at once at the head of the army. In a very short
time he had relieved the besieged camp and forced
the Aequians to surrender to him completely. He
told the leaders who were brought to him in chains
that

he did not require their blood, they were at liberty to
depart; but, as an open admission of the defeat and
subjugation of their nation, they would have to pass
under the yoke. This was made of three spears, two
fixed upright in the ground, and the third tied to them
across the top. Under this yoke the Dictator sent the
Aequians.[2]

This victory was considered so great, that it was
decreed in Rome that

Cincinnatus with the army he was bringing home, should
enter the city in triumphal procession. The commanding officers of the enemy were led in front, then the
military standards were borne before the general's
chariot, and the army followed laden with spoil, and

[1] Livy, III, 26.   [2] Livy, III, 28.

songs of triumph were sung as the procession moved along.[1]

Such an entry of a victorious Roman general into the city was called a Triumph, and it was only accorded to those who had signally distinguished themselves in a war. A crown of gold of a pound in weight was voted to Cincinnatus as a reward, but he cared nothing for high honours or for wealth, and glad only that he had been able to serve his country, as soon as he was able to do so, he laid down his office and returned to the quiet of his farm in the country.

III. ROME AND THE ETRUSCANS

405-396 B.C.

Rome had fought against the Etruscans when these had helped the Tarquins in their attempts to regain the throne. One of the last great struggles of these two nations took place at Veii, one of the wealthiest and most luxurious cities of Etruria. The Romans besieged this city, but at this time they had not had much experience in sieges, and year after year went by, and still Veii withstood them.

In the midst of the war a strange sight which caused much anxiety was observed in the Alban Lake. It was the beginning of autumn, a long dry summer had just come to an end, and in many places the lakes, brooks and springs were very dry. But to the amazement and fear of everyone, the

[1] Livy, III, 29.

Alban Lake began to rise until it overflowed its banks and flooded the surrounding country. An aged man of Veii declared that an ancient prophecy had foretold that the Romans would never get possession of the city until the water had been drawn off in a certain way from the Alban Lake. No one believed him, but the prophecy was talked about. At length a young Roman seized the old man and carried him before the commander-in-chief, who questioned him and then sent him to the Senate in Rome. There he repeated again that

it stood recorded in the Books of Fate, that whenever the water of the Alban Lake overflowed and the Romans drew it off in the appointed way, the victory over Veii would be granted them; until that time, the gods would not desert the walls of Veii.[1]

But the Senate wanted more advice as to what they should do under these strange circumstances, so they sent messengers to Delphi to consult the oracle. When they returned, the answer agreed with the words spoken by the Etruscan soothsayer. The answer ran:

See to it, Roman, that the rising flood
At Alba flow not o'er its banks and shape
Its channel seawards.   Harmless through thy fields
Shalt thou disperse it, scattered into rills.
Then fiercely press upon thy foemen's walls,
For now the Fates have given thee victory.

[1] Livy, V, 15.

That city which long years thou hast besieged
Shall now be thine. And when the war hath end,
Do thou, the victor, bear an ample gift
Into my temple, and the ancestral rites
Now in disuse, see thou celebrate
Anew with all their wonted pomp.[1]

As soon as the people had heard the word of the
oracle, they set to work and did as they had been
commanded. The festival of the Latin League,
which had not been celebrated for some time, was
held once more and a sacrifice offered on the Alban
Mount. Then, following the instructions of the
Etruscan soothsayer, the overflowing water of the
Alban Lake was properly drained off. The siege,
however, still went on, until in the tenth year, Camillus, who was 'a good general, was made Dictator,
and under his leadership the city was at last taken by
storm (in 396 B.C.) and an enormous amount of
plunder carried off. It was then proposed that the
territory of Veii should be distributed amongst the
Roman citizens, and that half the population of
Rome should be removed to Veii. This proposal
was popular amongst the poorer people in Rome, for
they thought it would make them prosperous, but
Camillus, paying no heed to the unpopularity it
would bring him, opposed the measure, because he
did not think it a good one. It was rejected, and
Camillus was looked upon with suspicion as a "hater
of the people and one that grudged all advantage to
the poor."[2] This suspicion and dislike soon took

[1] Livy, V, 16.   [2] Plutarch: *Life of Camillus.*

an active form and Camillus was accused of having kept "certain brass gates, part of the Tuscan spoils, in his own possession."[1] The people were excited and ready to believe anything against him. His friends were not powerful enough to protect him, but they promised him that should he be condemned to pay a fine, they would contribute towards the paying of it. But Camillus,

not able to endure so great an indignity, resolved, in his anger, to leave the city, and go into exile; and so, having taken leave of his wife and son, he went silently to the gate of the city, and there stopping and turning round, stretched out his hands to the Capitol, and prayed to the gods, that if, without any fault of his own, but merely through the malice and violence of the people, he was driven out into banishment, the Romans might quickly repent of it; and that all mankind might witness their need for the assistance, and desire for the return of Camillus.[2]

IV. THE INVASION OF THE GAULS

390 B.C.

There is not a Roman but believes that immediately upon the prayers of Camillus, a sudden judgment followed, and that he received a revenge for the injustice done unto him; for almost immediately after his departure such a punishment visited the city of Rome, and an era of such loss and danger and disgrace so quickly succeeded.[3]

[1] Plutarch: *Life of Camillus.*   [2] Ibid.   [3] Ibid.

The disaster which fell upon Rome was the invasion of her land by the Gauls.   These were fierce
Celtic tribes from the North who had crossed the
Alps and were invading Etruria.   The Gauls were
tall fair-haired warriors, with flashing eyes and
insolent manners.   They were brave, impetuous and
intelligent, but proud and quarrelsome.   They were
good fighters but merciless, and they disliked discipline and order and lacked the perseverance to finish what they began.   They wore heavily embroidered robes, which they threw off when they went
into battle, and a broad gold ring as a collar round
the neck.   Their voices were fierce and threatening, and they were much given to feasting and
wine-drinking after their battles.   Such were the
men who had now come into Etruria and were only
a few miles from Rome.

The Romans, alarmed for the safety of the city,
marched out with their whole army to meet the barbarian invaders.   They encamped by the river Allia,
a small tributary of the Tiber, and here the Gauls
came upon them.   A terrific battle followed, in
which the Romans were utterly defeated.   Their
Latin neighbours, who should have been their
allies, failed them in this hour of great peril, and the
greater part of the Roman army was destroyed.   Of
the survivors, some fled to Veii and took refuge there,
whilst others made for Rome with the tale of the
disaster.

Had the Gauls immediately marched on to Rome,
nothing could have saved the city; the whole of it
would have been ruined and no one left alive to

tell the dreadful tale. But the Gauls did not realize what a victory they had won, and they spent some time in feasting and dividing the spoil before deciding on their next move. This was wholly characteristic of the Gauls. They had no idea of settling down and they made no effort to take possession of the land they conquered. They fought fiercely as long as they were victorious, but when they were defeated they vanished as speedily as they came, leaving behind them wasted lands, burning cities and memories of terror.

The delay of the Gauls in marching on Rome gave those who were left in the city time to prepare for their coming. Some of the Romans decided to escape from the inevitable fate they saw coming upon the city, others resolved to stay. These,

realizing the hopelessness of attempting any defence of the City with the small numbers that were left, decided that the men of military age and the able-bodied amongst the Senators should, with their wives and children, withdraw into the Citadel and Capitol, and after getting in stores of arms and provisions, should from that fortified position defend their gods, themselves and the great name of Rome. If only the Citadel and the Capitol, the abode of gods; if only the senate, the guiding mind of the national policy; if only the men of military age survived the impending ruin of the City, then the loss of the old men in the City could be easily borne.[1]

These old men, some of whom had been Consuls, all of them men of experience and men who in the days

[1] Livy, V, 39.

of their strength had served the state, went to their homes in the city to await the coming of the enemy. Those who had been Consuls

resolved to meet their fate wearing the insignia of their former rank and distinctions. They put on the splendid dress they wore when conducting the chariots of the gods or riding in triumph through the City, and thus arrayed, they seated themselves in their ivory chairs in front of their houses.[1]

The Gauls came, and finding the gates of the city undefended, they entered and following their leader they pressed into the city. Here they found the aged Romans seated in the porches of their houses, and they were

struck with amazement at the sight of so many men sitting in that order and silence, observing that they neither rose, nor so much as changed colour or countenance, but remained without fear or concern leaning upon their staves, and sitting quietly looking before them. The Gauls, for a great while, stood wondering at the strangeness of the sight, not daring to approach or touch them, taking them for an assembly of superior beings. But when one, bolder than the rest, drew near to one elderly Senator, and, putting forth his hand, gently touched his chin and stroked his long beard, the Senator with his staff struck him a severe blow on the head; upon which the barbarian drew his sword and slew him. This was the introduction to the slaughter; for the rest, following his example, set upon them and killed them all and all others that came in their way;

[1] Livy, V, 41.

and so they went on to the sacking and pillaging of the houses. Afterwards they burnt them to the ground and demolished them, being furiously angry with those who kept the Capitol, because they would not yield to a summons; but, on the contrary, when assailed, had repelled them, with some loss, from their defences. This provoked them to ruin the whole city, and to put to the sword all that came to their hands, young and old, men, women and children.[1]

Rome lay in ashes at the feet of a barbarian invader, but the Capitol still held out, and the Gauls began to find it difficult to procure enough food for their army. So they decided to divide their forces; one part was to continue the siege of the Capitol, and the other was to forage amongst the neighbouring states in order to bring back food to the besiegers. Now Camillus was living as an exile not far from Rome.

He was grieving far more over the misfortunes of his country than over his own, and he was eating his heart out in reproaches to gods and men, asking in indignant wonder where were the men who had fought with him and taken Veii, men whose valour in all their wars was greater even than their success.[2]

When Camillus heard that the Gauls were in the neighbourhood of the city in which he was dwelling, he went to the magistrates and persuaded them to raise an army and go out against this savage enemy. Realizing that Camillus was a great general, they

---

[1] Plutarch: *Life of Camillus.*   [2] Livy, V, 43.

listened to his advice, and all in the city who could bear arms were mustered together and placed under his command. They marched out in the dead of night and found the camp of the Gauls unprotected and the barbarians sleeping. They raised a tremendous shout and rushed upon the Gauls, who woke, but so heavy were they with sleep and wine that they offered but little resistance, and the greater number were slaughtered as they lay in their own camp.

The fame of what Camillus had done spread to the neighbouring cities, and the young men of various places came to him and enthusiastically offered to follow him, if he would be their leader. Especially anxious to do so were the Romans who had fled to Veii after the battle of the Allia, and they sent to Camillus and asked him to take the command. But he refused to do so, unless the Romans who were in the Capitol should appoint him, for as long as any Romans held the Citadel, he considered that his country, and he refused to interfere unless they gave their consent. One of the young men offered to go to the Capitol to beg the Romans there to recall Camillus. It was a perilous undertaking, for the hill was closely watched by the Gauls, but the youth was ambitious and anxious to obtain honour, and he set out, reaching the city when it was dark. He went to the side on which the hill of the Capitol was steepest, and, though with great difficulty, he managed to get up and presented himself to the guards, saluting them and telling them his name. He was at once taken before those who

were in command, and he told them what Camillus had done and urged them to make him general.
They consulted for a while, and then decided that
Camillus should be made Dictator. The messenger then returned the same way he had come and
delivered the answer to Camillus, who set forth at
once with the army which was eagerly waiting to
follow him and prepared to fall upon the Gauls.

In the meantime, however, when the dawn came,
some of the Gauls

passing by chance near the place at which the messenger
by night had got into the Capitol, spied in several
places marks of feet and hands, where he had laid hold
and clambered, and places where the plants that grew
to the rock had been rubbed off, and the earth had
slipped, and went accordingly and reported it to the
King, who coming in person, and viewing it, for the
present said nothing, but in the evening, picking out
such of the Gauls as were nimblest of body, and by
living in the mountains were accustomed to climb, he
said to them, "The enemy themselves have shewn us a
way how to come at them, which we knew not of before,
and have taught us that it is not so difficult and impossible but that men have overcome it. Where it was
easy for one man to get up, it will not be hard for many,
one after another. Rewards and honours shall be bestowed on every man as he shall acquit himself."

When the King had thus spoken, the Gauls cheer-
fully undertook the task, and in the dead of night a
good party of them together, with great silence, began
to climb the rock. This proved less difficult than they
had expected, so that the foremost of them having gained
the top, they all but surprised the outworks, and mas-

tered the watch, who were fast asleep; for neither man
nor dog perceived their coming. But there were sacred
geese kept near the temple of Juno, which at other times
were plentifully fed, but now, by reason that corn and
other provisions were grown scarce for all, were but in
a poor condition. The creature is by nature of quick
sense, and apprehensive of the least noise, so that, being
watchful through hunger and restless, they immediately
discovered the coming of the Gauls, and running up
and down with their noise and cackling, they raised
the whole camp, while the barbarians on the other side,
perceiving themselves discovered, no longer endeavoured
to conceal their attempt, but with shouting and violence
advanced to the assault. The Romans, every one in
haste snatching up the next weapon that came to hand,
did what they could on the sudden occasion. Marcus
Manlius, a man of consular dignity, of strong body and
great spirit, was the first that made head against them,
and engaging with two of the enemy at once, with his
sword cut off the right arm of one just as he was lifting
up his blade to strike, and running his shield full in
the face of the other, tumbled him headlong down the
steep rock; then mounting the rampart, and there standing with others that came to his assistance he drove
down the rest of them. The Romans having thus escaped danger, took the captain of the watch and flung
him down the rock on the heads of their enemies, and
to Manlius for his victory they voted a reward.[1]

The Gauls had failed to take the Capitol and the
siege continued, but they were in a very bad plight.
They had little food, for fear of Camillus prevented
them from going very far to get any, and worse

[1] Plutarch: *Life of Camillus*.

even than the lack of food was the sickness which was amongst them. They were accustomed to a country where in the summer they could obtain shelter from the heat and could easily reach the coolness of the hills when the plains became intolerable. But encamped round the Capitol they had no shelter, the low-lying land was very unhealthy, and they were stricken with fever. So many of them died, that the living, themselves sick almost to death, were unable to bury them, and conditions grew steadily worse and worse.

The Gauls had besieged the Capitol for seven months and the case, had they but known it, was not much better with the besieged than it was with the besiegers. At last the leaders on both sides let it be known that they were willing to make terms,

and an agreement was arrived at by which a thousand pounds of gold was fixed as the ransom of a people destined ere long to rule the world. The humiliation was great enough as it was, but it was aggravated by the meanness of the Gauls who used unjust weights, and when the Romans protested, Brennus, the insolent leader of the Gauls, threw his sword into the scale, with an exclamation intolerable to Roman ears, "Vae victis! Woe to the vanquished!"[1]

But help was near. Whilst this was going on, Camillus arrived at the gates of Rome.

He commanded the main body of his forces to follow slowly after him in good order, and he himself with the

[1] Livy, V, 48.

choicest of his men hastening on, went at once to the Romans; where all giving way to him, and receiving him as their sole magistrate, with profound silence and order, he took the gold out of the scales and delivered it to his officers, and commanded the Gauls to take their weights and scales and depart; saying it was customary with the Romans to deliver their country with iron, not with gold.[1]

The Gauls were very angry, but for the time they withdrew, for night was coming on. At daybreak Camillus appeared before the camp of the enemy, and a sharp battle took place in which the Gauls were routed, and they fled. Thus did Camillus triumph as he deserved, for he had saved his country, and Rome was once more free. The city was soon rebuilt, but one great loss could never be repaired. When the Gauls burned the city, all the public records were destroyed. For this reason the early history of Rome has had to be pieced together from legends and traditions. All the stories cannot be literally true, but they show, perhaps better even than more authentic historical records might have done, what was the rugged, stern and disciplined character of the men who founded the Roman Republic.

V. THE LATIN WAR

340–338 B.C.

For about fifty years after the departure of the Gauls, Rome was occupied in rebuilding the city,

[1] Plutarch: *Life of Camillus.*

in strengthening her position, in subduing her enemies and in winning more territory for herself.
As the population of Rome increased, the question of
the food supply became more and more pressing
and was in many cases the cause of an aggressive
policy of Rome towards her neighbours.

For over a hundred years the Latins had been
the allies of Rome, bound to her by the treaty of
alliance made soon after the final defeat of the
Tarquins. These Latins fully realized the advan-
tages to them of being allied to Rome, but they
resented not having equal rights with the Romans.
Disputes arose between the two nations, and then
the Latins sent ambassadors to the Roman Senate offering terms on which they would live at peace
with Rome.

Recognizing [they said] that we are kindred nations, we
offer peace upon the conditions of equal rights for both,
since it has pleased the gods to give equal strength to
both; though we are quite able to assert the independence
of Latium by force of arms.   One consul must be elected
from Rome, the other from Latium; the Senate must
contain an equal number of members from both nations;
there must be one nation, one Republic.   And in order
that there may be one seat of government and one name
for all, since one side or the other must make some con-
cession, let us, if this City really takes precedence, be
all alike Romans.[1]

A storm of protest arose in the Senate when these
terms were announced.   Titus Manlius, the Consul,
declared that

[1] Livy, VIII, 5.

if the Senate were visited by such madness as to accept these conditions, he would come with his sword drawn into the Senate and kill every Latin he found there. "Hear, O Jupiter!" he cried, "art thou, as though thou hadst been conquered and made captive, to see in thy temple foreign consuls and a foreign Senate!"[1]

The Senate and the people were alike of the opinion that this question could only be decided by war, and war was accordingly declared. The Consuls, Titus Manlius and Decius Mus, went into camp, and it is said that on that first night when all was still and quiet around them, a strange and awful form appeared to each, and announced that victory would be given to that people whose general should sacrifice his life for his country. In the morning the Consuls consulted the augurs as to the meaning of this vision, and were told that from other signs it was clear that the gods required such a sacrifice, if victory were to be gained. The Consuls then arranged with each other that he whose men should first give way before the enemy should be the one to make the sacrifice.

The leaders of the Romans were more than usually anxious that strict discipline should be observed in the army, for they realized that a war against the Latins was not like a war against a foreign foe. The Latins were

a people resembling them in language, manners, arms and especially in their military organization. They had been colleagues and comrades as soldiers, centurions and

[1] Livy, VIII, 5.

tribunes, often stationed together in the same posts and side by side in the same ranks.[1]

In order that no confusion might arise from mistakes, strict orders were given that without permission, no soldier might leave his post to engage in a single encounter with the enemy.

It happened that one of the troop commanders who had been sent out to reconnoitre, was the young Titus Manlius, the son of the Consul. As he came with his men quite near to the camp of the enemy, a Latin commander, a man well-known and of great reputation, not only amongst his own people but also amongst the Romans, came out to meet him. He asked the young Roman in mocking terms if his troop were all the army Rome had, and then challenged him to a single fight that he might show him how much a Latin horseman was superior to a Roman. Either angry, or else too ashamed to decline the challenge, "the high-spirited youth forgot the Consul's edict and the obedience due to a father and rushed headlong into a contest in which victory or defeat were alike fatal."[2] Victory fell to Titus Manlius. He killed his adversary, and taking, as was the custom, the armour and weapons of his fallen foe, he rode back to the Roman camp and went straight into the presence of his father, not in the least realizing either the nature of his deed or its consequences. Throwing the spoils at his father's feet, he said, "That all may say that I am worthy to be of your blood, I bring to you these spoils

[1] Livy, VIII, 6.   [2] Livy, VIII, 7.

taken from a dead enemy who challenged me to single combat." But the Consul made no answer to his son. He turned away from him and ordered a trumpet to sound the Assembly.

The soldiers mustered in large numbers and the Consul began: "Since you, Titus Manlius, have shown no regard for either the authority of a Consul or the obedience due to a father, and in defiance of our edict have left your post to fight against the enemy, and have done your best to destroy the military discipline through which the Roman state has stood till now unshaken, and have forced upon me the necessity of forgetting either my duty to the republic or my duty to myself and my children, it is better that we should suffer the consequences of our offence ourselves, than that the state should expiate our crime by inflicting great injury upon itself. We shall be a melancholy example, but one that will be profitable to the young men of the future. My natural love of my children and that proof of courage which from a false sense of honour you have given, move me to take your part, but since either the Consul's authority must be vindicated by your death or for ever abrogated by letting you go unpunished, I would believe that even you yourself, if there is a drop of my blood in your veins, will not shrink from restoring by your punishment the military discipline which has been weakened by your misconduct. Go, lictor, bind him to the stake."

All were paralyzed by such a ruthless order; they felt as if the axe was directed against each of them; fear rather than discipline kept them motionless. For some moments they stood transfixed in silence, then suddenly, when they saw that his head had fallen, their voices rose in unrestrained and angry complaint; they spared neither laments nor curses. The body of the youth covered with his spoils was burnt on a pyre erected outside the rampart, with all the funeral honours that the soldiers' devotion could pay. "Manlian Orders" were not only regarded with horror for the time, but were looked upon as setting a frightful precedent for the future.

The terrible severity of the punishment, however, made the soldiers more obedient to their general, and not only did it lead to greater attention being paid to the pickets and sentry duties and the ordering of the outposts, but when they went into battle for the final contest, this severity proved to be of the greatest service.[1]

The battle took place near the foot of Mount Vesuvius. At first both armies fought with equal strength and equal determination, but after a time it seemed as if the Romans were giving way before the Latins. Then it was that Decius Mus, remembering the sacrifice that would give his side the victory, in full armour leapt upon his horse and dashed into the midst of the enemy. He fell, pierced with many darts, but his unexpected deed had thrown the Latins into confusion, for wherever his horse carried him, the enemy fled in terror from what they thought was no human form, and when at last he fell, they fled, leaving his body lying alone in a clear space. The Romans, on the other hand, rushed forward, and the more the Latins yielded, the harder they pressed them.

[1] Livy, VIII. 7–8.

The Latins were utterly defeated and were forced
to accept the terms imposed upon them by Rome.
The Latin League was brought to an end; the Latins
became Roman citizens, but their privileges were
limited. With a few exceptions they could enjoy
all the rights of citizenship, of voting and of holding office in their own cities, but not in Rome;
Romans, on the other hand, enjoyed the privileges
of full citizenship in any city ruled by Rome. It
was hard that the Latins, men of the same race and
speech as the Romans, should be denied full citizenship, but it may fairly be said that they had not
done much to deserve it. When Rome had almost
been utterly destroyed off the earth by the Gauls, the
Latins had not come to her aid, even though an alliance bound them together as friends and allies.
They were not looked upon by the Romans as their
equals; they had failed her in the hour of need, and
now they were called upon to pay the price.

VI. THE SAMNITE WARS

343–290 B.C.

During the years when Rome was fighting the
Latins, she was also occupied with other wars on
her frontiers. At one time during this period all
Rome was startled and alarmed by an event which
seemed to be of evil omen.

Owing either to an earthquake or the action of some
other force, the middle of the Forum fell in to an immense depth, presenting the appearance of an enormous

cavern. Though all worked their hardest at throwing earth in, they were unable to fill up the gulf, until at the bidding of the gods, inquiry was made as to what that was in which the strength of Rome lay. For this, the seers declared, must be sacrificed on that spot if men wished the Roman republic to be eternal. The story goes on that M. Curtius, a youth distinguished in war, indignantly asked those who were in doubt what answer to give, whether anything that Rome possessed was more precious than the arms and valour of her sons. As those around stood silent, he looked up to the Capitol and to the temples of the immortal gods which looked down on the Forum, and stretching out his hands first towards heaven and then to the yawning chasm beneath, devoted himself to the gods below. Then mounting his horse, which had been caparisoned as magnificently as possible, he leaped in full armour into the cavern. Gifts and offerings of fruits of the earth were flung in after him by crowds of men and women, and immediately after his disappearance the gulf filled up.[1]

From this incident the spot was known as the "Curtian Gulf."

After the Latin war Rome was mistress of the two plains of western Italy, but the Samnites were still very powerful, and though for a long time the two nations had been at peace with each other, conflicting interests had already begun to make trouble between them, and these troubles now threatened to become serious.

The Samnites were a hardy, brave and high-spirited nation. They fought in glittering armour and of

[1] Livy, VII, 5.

the flower of their army some, we are told, wore
striped tunics and carried golden shields, whilst
others wore white tunics and carried silver shields.
They now began to look jealously at the increasing
power of Rome and would gladly have conquered
for themselves some of the rich western plains that
were gradually being absorbed by Rome.

The first quarrel with Rome came over the possession of Capua, a rich city in Campania.   The
Samnites tried to take it, but Capua appealed to
Rome against the enemy.   The Romans attacked
the Samnites and defeated them, and Capua was
then added to the Roman territory, which gave to
Rome the control of nearly all Campania.   This
first Samnite war came suddenly to an end, for
Rome was willing to make peace on account of the
revolt of the Latins, but soon after the Latin war
was over, a second war broke out against the Samnites, who had again attacked a city that was
friendly to Rome.

At the beginning of this war the Romans met with
a great disaster.   The Consuls and forty thousand
men were entrapped in a narrow valley called the
Caudine Forks, and were taken prisoners.   The
Samnite general was undecided what to do with
these Romans.   His father, an old man and very
feeble, but full of ripe wisdom, advised him either
to let the Romans go free, or to put every man of
them to death.   He believed that by letting the
Romans depart uninjured, the Samnites would
establish a lasting peace and friendship with a very
powerful people; if, on the other hand, the Romans

were put to death, they would at least postpone
further war for some time, as it would take Rome a
long time to recover from the loss of her armies.
His son and the other Samnite chiefs asked if there
were no middle course to follow:

No [said the aged Samnite], once let men whom you
have exasperated by ignominious treatment live and you
will find out your mistake. The Romans are a nation
who know not how to remain quiet under defeat. Whatever disgrace you now inflict will burn into their souls
and rankle there for ever, and will allow them no rest
till they have made you pay for it many times over.[1]

But the Samnite general did not heed his father's
advice. The Roman Consuls were made to agree to a
humiliating peace, and the whole army was condemned to pass under the yoke. When the Consuls returned to the camp with the terms of surrender, there was bitter grief and distress in the army.

So bitter was the feeling that the men had difficulty
in keeping their hands off those through whose rashness,
they said, they had been brought into that place and
through whose cowardice they would have to leave it
in a more shameful plight than they had come. They
had had no guides who knew the neighbourhood, no
scouts had been sent out, they had fallen blindly like
blind animals into a trap. There they were, looking
at each other, gazing sadly at the armour and weapons
which were soon to be given up, their right hands which
were to be defenceless, their bodies which were to be
at the mercy of their enemies. They pictured to them-

[1] Livy, IX, 3.

selves the hostile yoke, the taunts and insulting looks of the victors, their marching disarmed between the armed ranks, and then afterwards the miserable progress of an army in disgrace through the cities of their allies, their return to their country and their parents, whither their ancestors had so often returned in triumphal procession.

While they were uttering these indignant protests, the hour of their humiliation arrived which was to make everything more bitter for them by actual experience than they had anticipated or imagined. First of all they were ordered to lay down their arms and go outside the rampart with only one garment each,[1]

and then, in order of rank, the whole army passed under the yoke.

When the news of this disgrace reached Rome, the whole city put on mourning. The booths in the Forum were shut up, all public business ceased, the Senators laid aside their purple tunics and gold rings, and the gloom amongst the citizens was almost as great as that of the army. When the men returned, they crept into the city late in the evening and went to their homes, and for some days not one of them would show himself in public or in the Forum.

In the meantime the Senators were discussing what had better be done to avenge this humiliation. They declared that they were not bound by what the Consuls had promised, because no Consul had the right to accept such terms. Finally it was decided to reject the terms and to send

[1] Livy, IX, 5.

back to Samnium the Consuls as prisoners. But the army was not surrendered, though the Senate and the people knew quite well that it should have been sent back too, and that it was a breach of faith not to do so.

The Romans recovered from this disaster, and the war began again and dragged on for some time. At last the Samnites agreed to make peace. They gave up what they had conquered and made an alliance with Rome. But it was not a lasting peace and soon after a third Samnite war broke out. This time the Samnites were joined by a number of old enemies of Rome, the Etruscans, some Italian tribes, and Celtic invaders from the North. In a long and bitter fight Rome-broke the power of these enemies, they were all forced to sue for peace, and Rome made them acknowledge her supremacy. Rome now ruled the whole of Central Italy, and her only rivals in the peninsula were the Greeks who occupied the South.

VII. THE WAR WITH PYRRHUS

281–272 B.C.

The wealthiest Greek city in the South of Italy was Tarentum. This was a rich, commercial city, and fearing that Rome might attempt to capture her trade, she had made a treaty with her, by which the Romans promised that Roman ships should not sail past a certain point of the coast in the direction of Tarentum. But the Romans broke this treaty, and their ships sailed into the forbidden waters, where the men of Tarentum promptly sank four of them and took a good many prisoners. The Romans sent ambassadors to Tarentum to demand redress, but they were in the wrong and were insulted, whereupon war soon followed. The Tarentines were not strong enough to fight the Romans alone, so they called to their aid Pyrrhus, the King of Epirus.

This young King was of Greek descent; he had already carried on several victorious campaigns and he was renowned as one of the great generals of the time. Pyrrhus was called by his subjects the "Eagle." He was very ambitious and his imagination had been stirred by the story of the deeds of Alexander the Great. Like Alexander, his ambition was limited neither by seas, nor mountains, nor unpeopled deserts, and one of his dreams was to cross to Italy and free the Greeks settled there from the Romans who threatened to overwhelm them. As Alexander had won for himself an Empire in the East, so would he win an Empire in the West. He would unite the Greeks in Italy and Sicily and then he would overthrow the states, of the strength of which he knew little or nothing, but of which the names appealed to his imagination, Carthage and Rome. So when the Tarentines invited him to come and lead them in the war against Rome, he accepted their offer.

The arrival of Pyrrhus in Italy is one of those events in history which seize upon the imagination. For the first time the Roman was to meet the Greek in battle. It was on Italian soil, but it was the first time that Rome had faced an enemy from beyond the sea, and the enemy was this young, brilliant, chivalrous Greek general who aimed at conquests as far-reaching as those of Alexander. But Pyrrhus was to learn that the new foe against whom he was now to fight was made of sterner stuff than any against whom he had hitherto fought. He brought with him to Italy twenty elephants—animals which the Romans had never before seen, and they called the strange unwieldy beasts the "grey oxen,"— three thousand horse soldiers, twenty thousand foot, two thousand archers and five hundred slingers. At first the Tarentines thought that they could stay at home and amuse themselves while Pyrrhus fought their battles for them, but they soon found out that this was a mistake and that he expected them to take their fair share in the war.

The first great battle between the Romans and Pyrrhus was fought in 280 B.C. at Heraclea. It was in this battle that the Romans saw the elephants for the first time. They were defeated, and Pyrrhus advanced to within forty miles of Rome, but he had suffered such losses in the battle that he sent an ambassador to Rome to discuss a treaty of peace. The Senators were almost ready to yield, when the aged Appius Claudius, a Roman of distinction who had formerly been Consul, but who now by reason of his great age and blindness had withdrawn from public affairs, hearing the report of what the Senate was about to do, ordered his servants to carry him in his chair through the Forum to the Senate House. When he entered, his sons met him and led him to a seat, and so great was the respect in which he was held that the whole assembly was silent. Then the aged Roman entreated the Senate to tell Pyrrhus that if he desired an alliance with them, he must first withdraw his army from Italy, and that then Rome would treat with him. "Tell him," said the proud old man, "that Rome never treats with an enemy while he is on Roman soil."

The ambassador, greatly impressed by the dignity of the Romans, returned to Pyrrhus. He told him that he had failed to make peace, and that the Roman Senate was an assembly of kings. War began again, and Pyrrhus won another great battle, but his losses were so appalling that he could not follow up his victory, and to one who was congratulating him on having won, he said that another such victory would utterly ruin him. From the time of Pyrrhus onwards, a victory won at a price which almost ruins the conqueror has been called a *Pyrrhic Victory*.

Pyrrhus left Italy after this battle and went to help the Greeks in Sicily who were fighting against the Carthaginians. He was successful at first, but when he found it impossible to take the Carthaginian strongholds he returned to Italy, and once more met the Romans in battle. It was at Beneventum, in the year 275 B.C. This time the tide of fortune changed, and the Romans completely overwhelmed Pyrrhus, who was so badly defeated that he was forced to withdraw altogether from Italy. He disappeared as suddenly as he had come, leaving behind him the memory of a great soldier, who was brave, high-minded, courteous, and of a courage that in the midst of his misfortunes had remained unconquerable.

Soon after the departure of Pyrrhus, Tarentum surrendered to Rome, who thereby became mistress of the whole peninsula of Italy.

For more than two centuries Rome had been struggling for the control of Italy, and now she had won it. Fair lands had been wasted, fields had been laid bare, countless lives had been lost, but civilization was on the side of Rome and Rome had triumphed. She had shown herself possessed of vigour and energy; she had created a united Italy; she had laid firm and sure foundations; how was she going to build upon them? Success is, if not a greater, at least as great a test of character as failure. So far Rome had been successful; how would her character stand this test?

CHAPTER VII

How Rome Ruled Italy

I. HOW ROME RULED HERSELF

IN the two centuries and more that went by from the founding of the Roman Republic to the time when Rome found herself the mistress of Italy, the Romans had been doing other things besides fighting. They had been learning how to govern themselves. It has been seen that when the last kings were expelled, the power that had formerly been in the hands of one man, the King, was entrusted to two men, who were given the title of Consuls, and that the Senate, that assembly of the older men, the Fathers of the City as they were sometimes called, men whose knowledge and experience of life had made them wise as well as practical, supported and advised them, as in the days of the kingdom they had supported and advised the King.

To the Consuls was given most of the authority and some of the outward state that had formerly belonged to the King. They wore a white robe edged with purple and sat in the curule chair, and in public they were preceded by the twelve lictors. The *imperium* which had once been the symbol of the royal power was now entrusted to the Consuls, but instead of holding it for life, they held it only for one year, after which they laid down their office. The chief authority was wielded by the two Consuls in turn, and in order to prevent any Consul from attempting to become sole ruler, one of them always had the power to veto the action of the other. And to make any kind of return to a monarchy still more impossible, a law was passed making a Consul ineligible for re-election for ten years after he had held office.

The Consuls had charge of the state treasury, they were judges in all law cases, and in war-time they were the commanders-in-chief of the army. But during the early years of the Republic, Rome was so often at war, that the Consuls were obliged to be away from the city for long periods at a time. In order to ensure that their duties as magistrates would not be neglected during these absences from the city, other officials were appointed to help them. *Quaestors* were appointed to attend to the affairs of the treasury, *praetors* to act as judges, and *aediles* to attend to the general welfare of the city, such as the maintenance of the public buildings and the supervision of the public games.

The Roman Senate was originally made up of patricians only. When new senators had to be chosen, preference was given to men who had been Consuls, for as the Consuls were also generals in the field, such men in the Senate would generally ensure a wise handling of military affairs in time of war. The early Roman Senate was a patriotic body of men

and a very great council. It was greater than any
other ruling body of the ancient world, and for dignity and patriotism, wisdom and practical experience it has seldom, if ever, been surpassed at any
time by any ruling body.

The Senate, however, was not the only assembly
in Rome. In the early days of the city there had
been the Comitia Curiata. Under Servius Tullius
the Comitia Centuriata gradually took its place
and at a later date there was an assembly of the
tribes called the Comitia Tributa. But though these
assemblies of the people existed, and though in theory the power of any magistrate was supposed to
spring from the will of the people, in practice, Rome
was ruled by the patricians, for all the important
offices, those of the greatest honour and trust,
whether political, military or religious, were in the
hands of the patricians, and no plebeian could expect
to fill them. The story of how Rome, during the
period when she was making herself mistress of
Italy, was also learning how to govern herself, is
the story of a long struggle between the patricians
and the plebeians, at the end of which the plebeians
had won the right to share in the government and
to be recognized as the political equal of the patrician.

In the early days of Roman history, the patrician
was probably more fitted than the plebeian to govern, for the art of government requires training like
any other art, and tradition had given all the training and experience to the patrician only. But government by one class is always apt to become a
tyranny, and when the patricians forgot that birth,

wealth and education were not privileges that made them better than anyone else, but a trust which had been given them to use for the welfare of the whole state, their rule became arrogant and insolent, and murmurs of dissatisfaction and discontent amongst the plebeians began to make themselves heard.

The story of how the plebeians won their rights is a long and a complicated one, but it is one of the outward signs of the spirit that helped to make Rome great. From the very beginning of her history as a Republic, not only was there war without the borders, but conflicts within the state and constant struggles between patricians and plebeians. Twice the people threatened actions which endangered the very existence of the state, yet in spite of strife and struggle at home and war abroad, Rome preserved a spirit of practical reasonableness which saved her. She knew that advance could only be made if both sides were willing to give up something, and so she laid strong foundations, that proved equal to the strain of supporting the mighty fabric that was to rise upon them. The Roman had not the imagination of the Greek. He did not spend much time in discussing the philosophy of government or what an ideal state should be. He found himself living in a difficult world, with a great many practical questions pressing on him for an answer, and he solved each problem as it came to him in as practical and as reasonable a way as he could find.

The first great law which recognized that the plebeians had rights as citizens was passed, probably in the very year of the establishment of the Republic, 509 B.C., by Valerius, one of the Consuls. Valerius was a patrician, but he was known to sympathize with the plebeians and he was called Poplicola, the People's Friend. By this Valerian Law two important steps were taken: anyone who tried to make himself King or to assume the chief power in the state without the people's consent, was to be tried as a traitor, and to every citizen who had been condemned for a crime, whether plebeian or patrician, was given the right of appeal to the people.

The Valerian Law recognized that the people had rights, but it did not remove their grievances and some of these were very real. The Republic was engaged in constant war and the people were required to serve in the army, which resulted in the neglect of their farms and other business and reduced them to great poverty. This often brought them into debt, and the laws concerning debtors were harsh and cruel. The debtor was frequently thrown into prison, and his creditor had also the right to seize him and hold him as a slave or even to sell him into foreign slavery, if he could not pay.

Another plebeian grievance concerned the land. It was the custom after a victorious war to distribute part of the conquered land amongst the citizens, but though the plebeians helped to win this land, none of it was given to them, it was to the patricians only that it was granted. The quarrel between the patricians and the plebeians about the public land was known as the *agrarian* trouble, and it lasted for a long time.

At this time there was no written law in Rome, nothing but a great body of tradition which was known only to the patricians and handed down by them from generation to generation. This knowledge of the law was jealously guarded by the patricians, and they were very careful to keep this knowledge to themselves. The people were, therefore, entirely at the mercy of the patricians when the law had to be administered, and these grew more and more harsh in their interpretation of it. The absence of any written law to which appeal could be made, rendered the plebeians helpless and unable to obtain any real redress for injustice.

All these grievances made the plebeians very discontented, and at last they determined to take an action that would show the patricians that they would no longer submit to the injustice of their position. In 494 B.C. at a time when the state was expecting war, the plebeians in a body deserted their commanders and marched out of the city to a place known later as the Mons Sacer or Sacred Mount, where they announced their intention of founding a new city for themselves which should be entirely free from patrician control.

The plebeians remained quite quietly at the Mons Sacer, but

a great panic seized the city. Those plebeians who had been left by their comrades in the City feared violence from the patricians, and the patricians feared the plebeians. "How long," it was asked, "would the multitude who had seceded remain quiet? What would happen if a foreign war broke out?'' They all felt that their hopes rested on concord amongst the citizens, and that this must be restored at any cost.

The Senate decided, therefore, to send as their spokesman, Menenius Agrippa, an eloquent man and acceptable to the people as being of plebeian origin. He was admitted to their camp, and it is reported that he simply told them the following fable in primitive and crude fashion. "In the days when all the parts of the human body were not as now agreeing together, but each member took its own course and spoke its own speech, the other members, indignant at seeing that everything acquired by their care and labour and ministry went to the belly, whilst it, undisturbed in the middle of them all, did nothing but enjoy the pleasures provided for it, entered into a conspiracy; the hands were not to carry food to the mouth, the mouth was not to accept it when offered, the teeth were not to masticate it. Whilst, in their resentment, they were anxious to coerce the belly by starving it, the members themselves wasted away, and the whole body was reduced to the last stage of exhaustion. Then it became evident that the belly rendered no idle service, and the nourishment it received was no greater than that which is bestowed by returning to all parts of the body the blood by which we live and are strong."[1]

This fable made the plebeians think, and they began to realize that without the patricians, who alone understood not only the laws which made for order between man and man, but also all those forms and ceremonies by which peace was kept between the gods and men, they would be helpless.

[1] Livy, II, 32.

The patricians, on their side, also realized how
helplessly the state would lie at the mercy of any
foreign invader, if the plebeians were not there to
take their share in the defence of the city, and so
they were willing to come to some terms with the
plebeians. These returned to the city, and the
patricians agreed to cancel the debts of those who
were unable to pay and to set free those who were
in prison for debt, but the most important conces-
sion made was the institution of two plebeian officials called Tribunes, who were to be elected by the
people and whose duty it was to protect the plebeians from any patrician harshness or unjust severity. The person of a Tribune was to be sacred, and
any man who should injure him or attempt to prevent him from doing his duty was to be laid under a
curse and put to death. During his term of office
the Tribune could not be away from the city for a
night, and he was required always to have his door
open, so that when they had wrongs to be redressed,
the oppressed or injured might always be able to
find him. At first there were only two Tribunes,
later there were five, and then ten.

The plebeians had gained something, but they
still had no means of knowing what was the law.
So the Tribunes, as representing the people, began
to urge the Senate to have the laws written down and
placed where all could see them. For a long time the
Senate refused, but at length it consented, and a
body of ten men, called the Decemvirate, was
appointed to draw up the laws of the state. These
became known as the Laws of the Twelve Tables.

They were not new laws, but they were now placed
in the Forum, in a public place where all could see
them, so that justice could no longer be administered in an arbitrary way.   They were set up in 450
B.C. and from that time onwards the plebeians, as
well as the patricians, could know what were their
rights. So important did the Romans consider
this knowledge of the law, that schoolboys were
required to learn the Laws of the Twelve Tables by
heart.

Soon after the publication of the Twelve Tables
another step was taken by the plebeians in the winning of their rights.   The Consuls, Valerius and
Horatius, men who were friendly to the people, had
a law passed in 448 B.C. known as the Valerio-
Horatian Law, by which, with the consent of the
Senate, the Assembly of the people could make laws
which would be binding on all, and which made the
Assembly of the people of much greater importance
than it had been before.   The importance of this
law was not so much in the actual power given to the
Assembly, as in the recognition of its place as part
of the government of the state.   Further power
was given at this time to the Tribunes, who were
allowed to sit at the door of the Senate House where
they could hear everything that went on within.
They could take no part in the discussions, but if
they had any objection to an act about to be passed
by the Senate, they had the right to cry out, *Veto*, I
forbid. This did not always prevent the Senate
from passing the act, but as time went on, the Tribunes became more and more powerful, until at last

their veto effectively prevented the passing of any law to which they objected.

In 443 B.C. a new office was created in Rome, that of the Censor. There were two Censors at a time, always patricians, and they were elected at intervals, usually about once every five years, when they remained in office for a little over a year. The Censors were generally chosen from the older men of high reputation who were greatly respected both on account of their age and of their standing in the state. Their power was great, but each Censor could, if he wished, veto any decision made by the other. The duties of the Censors were to see that all who claimed the rights and privileges of citizens were really citizens, that every man served in the army when required, and that he paid his taxes justly. The Censors had extraordinary power given to them. They could enquire into the private life of any citizen, find out how he performed his family duties, how he treated his slaves, and whether he indulged in useless luxury. They could inspect any land they chose and find out whether it was being rightly cultivated. To us, the office of Censor may seem to interfere with the private rights of the individual, but the Romans of the early Republic believed that in some way the work of the Censors was for the good of the state, and they looked upon it as a kind of purifying rite that the state needed at intervals.

The office of the Censor was one that was honourable and greatly respected, and the Romans were able to have perfect confidence in the justice and wisdom of the Censors. The Roman love of order and discipline was so great that it submitted willingly to whatever was held to be for the welfare of the state.

The plebeians had now gained many rights and privileges, but one office, the highest of all, was still closed to them: no plebeian could be Consul. For more than eighty years after the passing of the Valerio-Horatian Law the struggle had continued. Laws were passed, concessions were made and much was gained, but it was not until 367 B.C. that the Licinian Laws, called after the Tribune who succeeded in getting them passed, gave the plebeians equal political rights with the patricians, for these laws decreed that of the two Consuls, one must be a plebeian.

The struggle between the patricians and the plebeians had been a long one. Many laws had been passed, many compromises between the two classes had been arrived at, all the questions were not yet solved, particularly those connected with the agrarian troubles, but by the three great laws, the Valerian, the Valerio-Horatian and the Licinian, Rome was learning how to rule herself, and was showing at home that sense of discipline and order and that respect for authority which trained her to rule the world, for only when a nation can rule itself, is it fit to rule others.

II.   HOW ROME RULED ITALY

The Greek with his jealousy of all city-states outside his own had failed to create an empire of which all Greeks would be proud to call themselves citizens, and in defence of which they would lay down their lives. A Greek conqueror always considered himself and his state superior to those he conquered, and conqueror and conquered never met on equal terms. Alexander the Great was far-seeing beyond his age and understood that to knit a world empire together all parts of it must be treated alike, but his vision cost him the friendship of most of his Greek friends, who believed that nothing could ever bridge the gulf that divided them from those whom they called barbarians. Where the Greek failed, the Roman was to succeed, for those whom Rome conquered were treated not so much as conquered subjects, as allies and friends of the Roman people.

The Italians whom the Romans conquered were not a united people, but a number of tribes all speaking different dialects, with no common traditions and no common history. The first step taken by Rome in uniting these peoples was to bind each of them directly to herself, by making separate treaties with each city and nation. Not only did she not try to bind them together, but she did not as a rule allow any such union, partly, probably, because she did not want to run any risk of a combination of these states against her. But there was also a much more far-seeing policy which made her do this. The Samnite could not be made an Etruscan, nor an Etruscan a Latin, but all could be made to feel that they were Roman, and the fact that they all owed allegiance to the same state bound them together as no other policy could have done. It took time, for the conquered could not be expected to feel a sense of patriotism towards their conqueror at once, but Rome could wait. True patriotism is a thing of the spirit and cannot be forced, neither can it be directly taught. It must grow and be nourished by the soil and the sun and the air, by common traditions and common standards of honour and truth and justice. In the beginning, the conquered people of Italy had none of these, but Rome understood how to frame her policy towards them in such a way, that in time they not only called themselves, but were in very truth Roman citizens.

Rome governed Italy in three ways. To some cities she granted all the privileges of full Roman citizenship, that is to say they had the same rights in their own city and in Rome, though the Roman rights could only be exercised in Rome itself. To other cities, and these were chiefly in Latium, she gave what was called the Latin right. The inhabitants of such cities had all the civil rights of Roman citizens, they could trade and intermarry with Romans, but they had no political rights in Rome, they could neither vote nor hold office, except in their own city. And lastly, there were the Roman colonies, military outposts to guard the frontiers and coasts, some of which had the Roman and some the Latin rights. There were also some outlying places in which there was no organized government, and to these Rome sent prefects whose duty it was to administer justice and to see that peace and order prevailed.

To all who were her allies and colonies Rome granted as much local independence as was possible. Within their own borders they could manage their own affairs. They had their local assemblies, their senates and their magistrates, but these were all subject to the higher power of Rome. In most cases Rome herself directly controlled the administration of justice, and it was Rome who settled all questions connected with the relationship of city with city. It was Rome alone who could make war or peace; it was Rome who defended the coasts and frontiers of Italy. The Italians were not always content with what Rome gave them, but it is a tribute to the Roman government as a whole, that when quarrels arose, it was not because the Italians desired their independence, but because they demanded fuller citizenship with Rome.

The great roads built during the early Republic all went out from Rome. North and South, East and West they went, connecting the cities and colonies, not with each other, but with Rome. Along these roads went, not only Roman armies, but also all those who in one way or another carried the spirit of Roman law and order into distant places. That Roman policy succeeded at last in creating the sense of citizenship and patriotism in the cities belonging to Rome is shown in the words written by Cicero in the last century B.C.:

Every citizen of a corporate town has, I take it, two fatherlands, that of which he is a native, and that of which he is a citizen. I will never deny my allegiance to my native town, only I will never forget that Rome is my greater Fatherland, and that my native town is but a portion of Rome.

CHAPTER VIII

The Character and Religion of the Early Romans

CICERO, writing in the last century B.C., claimed for the ancient Romans "a sense of dignity, a resolution of purpose, a loftiness of spirit, a feeling of truth and honour," and these are qualities which will always be associated with those who best represented the early Romans. Life was not easy to these men, but hard and toilsome, for they had continually to fight, not only against their warlike neighbours, but sometimes against famine, and always against the ever present danger of fever and pestilence which haunted the plains that lay about them. The early Roman grew up without much love or pity in his heart for his fellow-man or his sorrows; he had little sense of the beauty of the world about him, but his training made him brave, energetic and practical; he was a man who kept his word; from his earliest youth he had been taught the duty of obedience; he was self-disciplined and self-controlled.

As the early Roman character was practical, so was the early Roman religion. The later Romans looked back to Numa as the founder of their religion and they spoke of it as the "Religion of Numa." This is in itself very characteristic of the Romans.

Most of the great religious teachers of the world
have been men full of the spirit of the prophet or
the poet, but the practical Roman looked back to
a King and Lawgiver as the founder of his religion.

The early Roman looked upon his gods as beings
who were able to bring good or evil to him. They
had not the strong personality of the Greek gods,
but they stood in a quite definite relation to man and
the Roman believed that there were duties and obligations to be fulfilled on both sides. Religion was
looked upon as a contract; if a god answered the
prayer of man, then man must make a thank-offering; but on the other hand, if man had done his duty,
the god must make his return in gifts of prosperity
and well-being. Great importance was attached
to the ritual of worship. Every detail connected
with the sacrifices and ceremonies had to be most
carefully attended to, for if through carelessness or
ignorance, mistakes were made or acts omitted, the
god was not considered obliged to fulfil his share of
the contract. If the omissions were caused through
ignorance, further offerings and ceremonies could
set things right, but for deliberate neglect of the
gods there was no remedy, and it was believed that
in this case the gods showed their displeasure by
signal punishment.[1]

When a man wanted some particular gift or blessing, he would make a special covenant or *votum* (a
vow) with the god, in which he promised that if
his prayer were answered, he would perform certain
acts in return. Over and over again on the inscrip-

[1] See p. 41.

tions which record these vows are the words: "I have paid my vow gladly, as it was due."

As time went on, the right performance of every detail of the ritual became the most important part of the Roman religion. It was believed that unless the sacrifices and prayers were offered in the right way, in the right place, at the right time, with the right persons present, the worship was of no avail and it had to be begun all over again.

There were three sides to the early Roman religion, each of which had its own importance and its own form of worship. These were the worship of the family or household, the worship of the fields, and the worship of the state.

To the Romans of the Republic the family was the most sacred and the most important of all their ties, but the Roman *familia* did not exactly correspond to what we mean by a *family*. Our word *household* partly expresses it, though the relationships in a Roman *familia* were not altogether those of a modern household. The Head of the Family was the Father, the Paterfamilias, and the law gave him absolute power over all the members of his household. His word was law, all the family property was held in his name, and he was the priest of the *familia*.

The worship of the family probably had more direct influence on the Roman character than any other form of Roman worship. Those parts of the house which were closely bound up with the life of the family were sacred, and a particular god was supposed to have each in his care. Every morning each member of the family went out through the door to begin his day's work, and at the end of the day, his work done, he returned and passed within it. So the door was sacred to and watched over by Janus, the God of Beginnings and Endings. The hearth, which gave warmth and cheer to all who dwelt in the house, was sacred to the Goddess Vesta. The store-cupboard, which contained the food which gave life and strength to all, was in the care of the Penates; and of the Lares, the spirits of the family fields, one special spirit, the Lar Familiaris, had the house and household in his keeping and was specially worshipped on all occasions connected with the family life: at births and deaths, at weddings, and on the departure on a journey and return from it of any member of the household.

The offerings on all family occasions were made by the Paterfamilias, but of more importance than these formal acts on special occasions, was the daily worship of the family. Every day began with prayer and an offering to the Lares and Penates, the gods of the household. At the chief meal of the day, part of the food was placed on a sacred dish and then thrown upon the hearth as an offering to the gods. This joining together in a daily act of worship was one of the influences that helped to form the Roman character. For though the Roman looked upon his religion chiefly as a contract between him and the gods, one side of it was closely bound up with that which was most sacred to him, his home, and the daily worship of the household gods emphasized the fact that, whatever were his relations to his gods, he was dependent on a higher power than man for his daily needs.

When a Roman youth reached the age of manhood he went up to the Capitol and offered sacrifices to Jupiter, the great god of the state. But his last act at home before this ceremony was to lay the garments of his childhood before the shrine of his household gods and make them a thank-offering for having protected him through all the days of his childhood and youth.

Numa had made a calendar on which were marked the days on which state business might be performed, the days which were to be holidays and on which no business of any kind might be done, and the yearly festivals of the state that were to be observed by the whole people. Of these festivals, some were those connected with the worship of the fields. The early Romans were an agricultural people, and their feasts and festivals were closely bound up with the work in the fields. In the spring they prayed that their crops might grow and their herds prosper, it was the season of hope and aspiration; in the summer they gave thanks for the harvest and for the fulfilment of the hopes of the spring; in the winter they celebrated the sowing of the seed, and their winter festivals were those of social pleasures and rejoicing.

The chief festival of the spring was the Ambarvalia, when prayers and sacrifices were offered for the purifying of the fields that they might bring forth their fruits in abundance. The festival was celebrated both in the city and the country, but it was above all a country festival. The day appointed was kept as a holiday, and early in the morning the girls of the place went out to gather blossoms from the fruit trees to strew later in the day before the images of the gods as they were borne in procession to the fields. Everyone belonging to the place walked in this procession. As it made its way to the fields, in order that no interruption might mar the sacredness of the rite, no word was spoken except by the priests who chanted an old Latin liturgy as they went along. The maidens strewed the flowers before the images of the gods carried by the youths clad in white, and the cattle for the sacrifice were led to the altars on which their blood was to be shed as a symbol of the purifying of the fields. When the sacrifice had been made, this prayer was offered to Mars, who in the early days of Rome was the god who watched over agriculture:

Father Mars, I pray and beseech thee, that thou mayest be gracious and favourable to me, to my home and my household, for which cause I have ordained that the offering of pig, sheep and ox be carried round my fields, my land, and my farm: that thou mayest avert, ward off, and keep aloof all disease, visible and invisible, all barrenness, waste, misfortune, and ill weather: that thou mayest suffer our crops, our vines and bushes to grow and come to prosperity: that thou mayest preserve the shepherds and the flocks in safety, and grant health and strength to me, to my home, and my household.

Then a hymn was sung and everyone returned to the house, and feasting and merrymaking ended the day.

The great winter festival was the Saturnalia, a social, merry feast. Presents were exchanged, candles were lit, and it is very probable that some of our own Christmas festivities and customs had their origin in this ancient Roman festival.

The worship of the state grew out of the worship of the family. In the earliest times Janus was the chief god, and the gate of his temple which was closed in peace and open in war, was regarded as the door of the state.

As the hearth of the family was the most important spot in the house, so in the most ancient times was the King's hearth the most important spot in the state. Later, every village kept a public hearth always burning, so that at any time one could get fire from it. The care of this hearth was given to young girls, because they stayed at home and did not go off, as did the men, to the distant pastures, or to hunt and fish. By degrees the King's hearth became not only the central hearth, but the symbol of the community, and as Rome grew to be a city and a state, the symbol of the state itself. It was sacred, as was the fire on every hearth, to the goddess Vesta, and the maidens whose duty it was to tend it, were the priestesses of the goddess and were called the Vestals. There were only six Vestals at a time, and their duties were to tend the sacred fire and to guard certain sacred and secret tokens, on the safekeeping of which it was believed depended the well-being and prosperity of the Roman commonwealth.

The Vestals were elected when a vacancy in their

number had been caused by death. The maiden chosen had to be between the ages of six and ten, it was required that both her parents should be living, and that she should remain unmarried during the time that she served the goddess. The Vestal spent the first ten years after her election in learning her duties, the next ten in practising them, and then ten years in teaching the novices. At the end of these thirty years a Vestal was free to return home if she wished, but very few did so, because a Vestal had far more honours, privileges and wealth than the world could offer her. From being a very simple group of women, the Vestals grew to be a powerful and important order, and in later times, when Rome had become an imperial city, they had privileges accorded to no other persons. They had seats of honour in the theatres and amphitheatres; they alone were allowed to drive in the streets of Rome and everyone had to make way for them; if a Vestal met a criminal condemned to death, provided the meeting were accidental, he was pardoned. But if they had privileges, there were also stern punishments for the Vestals who were disobedient. The least fault was punished with the rod, and a Vestal who broke her vows was put to the horrible death of being buried alive.

By degrees the god Jupiter took the place of Janus as the supreme god of the state. Jupiter was the Father of Gods and the Lord of Justice, and as time went on, he grew to symbolize the majesty and greatness of Rome. In his temple on the Capitol sacrifices were offered by all youths as they approached manhood, by magistrates about to take office, by victorious generals returning from war with their spoils, and on the walls were hung all treaties made by Rome with other nations.

To us, to whom Christianity has given other religious ideals, this early Roman religion may seem very formal and of little influence on character, but it was not so regarded by the Romans themselves. "If we wish," said Cicero, "to compare ourselves with other nations, we may be found in other respects equal or even inferior; in religion, that is in the worship of the gods, we are far superior," and he speaks of the early Roman religion as one of the chief causes of the greatness of Rome.

Early Roman religion was undoubtedly, however, very formal and had perhaps little to do with the spirit of man, but the strictness with which every detail of the worship had to be carried out, and the quiet regularity of the daily worship in the family, served as an excellent training for the conscientious carrying out of every duty; the belief that religion was a covenant between the gods and men and that the keeping of such a covenant was a religious duty, helped to make the early Roman a man who kept his word; and as his old fear of the gods disappeared, there grew up in its place what he called *pietas*, a sense of duty towards both God and man, a respect for authority, self-restraint and good order, virtues of the utmost importance in a state that was growing and learning to feel its strength.

These things may not have been the highest or

the greatest that religion can give to a nation, but in the training of citizens, they are qualities of discipline and order, without which no state can become great.

PART II

ROME THE MISTRESS OF THE MEDITERRANEAN

CHAPTER IX

THE STRUGGLE BETWEEN ROME AND CARTHAGE

I. CARTHAGE[1]

FOR more than two centuries after the founding of the Republic, Rome had struggled for the control of Italy, and she had won it. She had lived through days of darkness and disaster, days which would have utterly dismayed a race of a less steadfast character, but she had triumphed. Not only had Rome conquered Italy, but she had set herself to govern it, and her keen instincts for law and order had established her authority on a firm and sure foundation.

During these centuries of struggle Rome had only dimly realized that she was part of a larger world than that of Italy, but when she found herself the mistress of Italy and felt herself a nation, young

---

[1] See *The Book of the Ancient World*: The Phoenicians.

still, but firmly established and secure, she realized that there was a world outside her own borders, a world in which she had now to take her part. But when Rome looked beyond her own coasts, she found herself face to face with another power in the Mediterranean world. This power was Carthage, that great city of the Phoenicians which had become the capital of a great commercial empire.

Legend says that Carthage was founded by Dido, a Phoenician princess, who, fleeing from the cruelty of her brother who ruled in Tyre, came to Carthage, where she established a new kingdom of her own and reigned over it as Queen. The land belonged to the Libyans, and it is said that Dido bargained with them for as much as could be enclosed by an ox-hide. The Libyans laughed at such a request, for they could not see how a town could be built on so narrow a space, but as that was all the land asked for, they gave it. The Phoenicians then cut the hide round and round in a long narrow strip and laid it on the ground, enclosing a space on which later a citadel was built, and a city soon grew up round it.

Another tale of early Carthage tells how Aeneas, sailing across the sea in his search for a new home, was driven by a storm into the harbour of Carthage. Dido received him hospitably and he spent some time at her court. And Dido loved Aeneas and would have had him stay always in Carthage, but the gods commanded him to leave Africa and to sail on to Italy where his destiny awaited him, and so in spite of the entreaties of the Queen, he left her and sailed on to Italy. Then Dido cursed Aeneas and all his race, and she said to the men of Carthage:

"This heritage be yours; no truce nor trust
'Twixt theirs and ours, no union or accord.
Arise, unknown Avenger from our dust;
With fire and steel upon the Dardan horde
Mete out the measure of their crimes' reward.
Today, tomorrow, for eternity
Fight, oft as ye are able—sword with sword,
Shore with opposing shore, and sea with sea;
Fight, Tyrians, all that are, and all that e'er shall be."[1]

Originally Tyre had been the chief Phoenician city, but when it was conquered by Alexander the Great, many of its inhabitants fled and some of them went as far as Carthage, where they made new homes for themselves, until gradually Carthage, growing in wealth and importance, took the place of Tyre as the leading Phoenician city. The situation of Carthage was admirably suited for the capital of a commercial empire. The Greeks had established colonies all over the Eastern Mediterranean, but the Phoenician power prevented them from expanding very far in the West, and by the beginning of the third century B.C. Carthage controlled the trade not only of African territory which reached almost to the great desert, but also that of the coasts of practically the whole of the Western Mediterranean, both of Africa and Spain, the islands of Sardinia and Corsica and the greater part of Sicily.

The Carthaginians preferred trading to fighting,

[1] Virgil: Aeneid, IV.

but they could fight well when occasion arose, and
necessity had made them warlike. They had not
been allowed to enlarge the territory which was
under their control without opposition, and for centuries they had fought with the Mediterranean
peoples for the control of the trade-routes. Their
chief enemies had been, first the Etruscans and then
the Greeks in Sicily, and this constant warfare had
made them build up their army and develop their
navy. A Carthaginian army consisted almost entirely of mercenaries, men of many races and many
tongues, and it was therefore neither very patriotic
nor very trustworthy, but Carthage believed that
such qualities could be bought like anything else.
The Carthaginian army, however, possessed great
military possibilities and under commanders of
genius became a formidable fighting force.

One very important part of the Carthaginian
army was the Numidian cavalry. The riders, carrying shields of elephant's hide and wearing a lion's
skin thrown over the shoulder, used neither saddle
nor bridle, and were fearless and splendid riders.
But the real strength of Carthage lay on the sea, and
had she done more to develop her navy, she might,
for a time perhaps, have become the mistress of the
civilized world.

Soon after the establishment of the Republic,
Rome had made a commercial treaty with Car-
thage, by which the greater part of the Western
Mediterranean had been recognized as Carthaginian
and only the coast of western Sicily was open to all.
The port of Rome was free to all honest seafarers,

and at that time Rome made no attempt to gain the control of any of the trade-routes. In 509 B.C. her interests were all in Italy, and Carthage had no great rivals in the Western Mediterranean. So completely did the Carthaginians control all this region, that they declared it was a Carthaginian lake and that no one might even wash his hands in it without their permission.

The rule of Carthage over this empire was a harsh and exacting one. She had little genius for law and order and none of the qualities which would have fitted her to become a ruler of men. She lived for trade, and believing there was nothing that money could not buy, was willing to sacrifice everything to her love of gain. It never entered the mind of Carthage or her rulers that commerce could open a door for the service of mankind, that the wealth they carried from place to place could minister in any way to those to whom they brought it, or that the civilization they helped to spread could be a means of setting free the spirit of man in his never-ceasing quest of learning how to live. The ideals of the Phoenicians were sordid and mean, but they could not have attained their supremacy without possessing certain qualities of a very high order. No matter what was their aim in setting out, only men of extraordinary courage and perseverance could have braved as they did the perils of the uncharted ocean, the hardships of the pathless desert, or the dangers of exploring unknown regions.

Such was the power which, when as mistress of Italy, she looked beyond her own borders, Rome

found confronting her, and the question which was
to be decided by the great conflicts of the next hundred years was whether the Phoenician, or as the
Romans called it, the Punic power, or the power of
Rome was to have the supremacy of the Mediterranean.

II. THE FIRST PUNIC WAR

264–241 B.C.

It is said that when Pyrrhus left Sicily he exclaimed
to those about him: "How brave a field of war do
we leave, my friends, for the Romans and Carthaginians to fight in,"[1] and it was in Sicily that the conflict between these states began. At the time it
seemed as if this struggle were merely between the
conflicting interests of two powers, but looking
back to it across the centuries we can see that
something much greater was involved. The chief
strength of Rome lay in the character of her citizens, a character which was honest, manly, law-abiding and god-fearing, a character which showed at
its best in times of trial and disaster, a character
distinguished by rare powers of steadfastness and
endurance. The chief strength of Carthage was in
her wealth; she oppressed those whom she governed,
and her citizens were corrupt, greedy, lacking in
discipline and could only be relied on in the days of
success. The real importance to history of the
struggle between Rome and Carthage is not the
question of which of them was to control the trade-

[1] Plutarch: *Life of Pyrrhus.*

routes of the Mediterranean, but which of the two civilizations was to endure.

Although the ancient world had so many of the same questions to answer and of the same problems to solve, that the world of today is still trying to answer and to solve, there was one great difference between ancient and modern times. One of the greatest problems that the world today is trying to solve is how great and powerful nations can live side by side in peace and friendship. The ancient world had not discovered that such a state of affairs was even possible. To the statesmen and thinkers of those days it seemed natural and right that one great and powerful state should have dominion over those that were weaker, and so when Rome and Carthage found that their interests were in conflict with one another, there was only one question between them to be settled: one must rule, the other obey, and such a question could only be settled by war.

The immediate cause of the outbreak of war was the occupation by some Campanian mercenaries who called themselves Mamertines or Sons of Mars, of Messana, a city in Sicily immediately opposite the southernmost point of Italy. These Mamertines gave so much trouble in Sicily by their overbearing and aggressive conduct, that Hiero, King of Syracuse, at length attacked them. But they were not strong enough to resist and appealed to Rome for help. The Roman Senate would have liked to refuse, but it was clear that the Mamertines were determined to keep what they had taken and that if Rome did not help them, they would turn to Carthage.

The Romans were in a difficult position, for Syracuse was their ally and the old commercial treaty with Carthage was still in existence. But they saw quite clearly that if the Mamertines turned to Carthage, then the Carthaginians would very soon control the whole of Sicily, for they would be certain to crush Syracuse. The Carthaginians already occupied Sardinia and Corsica; were they to take the whole of Sicily too, their next step would be into Italy, and this the Romans could not allow. The Roman Senate, therefore, though it was not the most honourable thing to do, voted to send aid to the Mamertines.

It was a fateful decision. Only the narrowest of straits separated Italy from Messana, yet it was for Rome a crossing of the sea, a stepping out for the first time in her history from the mainland into a new world. It was an entirely new adventure, the outcome of which was hidden in the future.

When the Romans arrived in Sicily, they found that Carthage had already interfered and had made friends with Syracuse. The alliance did not last long, however, and Syracuse made a treaty with the Romans, promising to provide them with food as long as they were in Sicily.

Rome now set herself to drive the Carthaginians out of Sicily. It was not very difficult for Rome to gain control of the interior of the island, for the inhabitants preferred her rule to that of either Carthage or Syracuse, but the coast towns were a very difficult matter, for Carthage protected them by her powerful navy. The Carthaginian ships were quinqueremes, whereas the Romans had only a few triremes which were quite unfit to meet the enemy. The result was that not only were the coast towns of Sicily protected, but the Carthaginians made constant raids on the Italian coast, and hardly a Roman ship dared leave her harbour. It seemed as if the Carthaginian boast of completely controlling the sea were justified.

The Romans saw that they must have a navy and have it with as little delay as possible, so with their characteristic energy and indomitable courage they set themselves to build a fleet. A Carthaginian ship had been wrecked on the coast of Italy, and taking it for a model, the Romans, who up to this time had known but little of the sea, performed the extraordinary feat of building a hundred and twenty warships in sixty days. Whilst trees were being cut down and transformed with amazing speed into ships, benches were set up on the shore and day after day soldiers took their places on them and practised rowing. At length the fleet was ready. Four years had passed since the beginning of the war, and though to a certain extent the Romans had been successful in Sicily, no great decisive battle had yet been fought. Now, in 260 B.C. Rome met Carthage in a sea battle off Mylae, and Rome was victorious.

This victory made the Romans more enthusiastic for the war, and it was determined to build a still larger fleet and carry the war into the enemy's country. A great army set sail under the Consul Regulus. They landed in Africa and Regulus took a large number of towns, which surrendered to him chiefly because of their hatred of the Carthaginians. Regulus then advanced further into the country, laying it waste as he passed. The Carthaginians, attributing their misfortunes to bad generalship, sent to Sparta asking for a commander. The Spartans sent them a general, who, coming in the hot season, attacked the Romans just after they had made a long march and were suffering from the dust, from thirst and exhaustion. The Romans were defeated, and of the thirty thousand led by Regulus, only a few escaped. The rest were either killed or taken prisoner and amongst the captives was the Consul Regulus himself.

During the first years of the war the Romans had taken prisoner a number of Carthaginians, and it was now suggested that these should be exchanged for some of the Romans. The Carthaginians made certain definite conditions concerning this exchange and sent Regulus to Rome to make the arrangements, promising him that if he succeeded in his mission, he should be amongst those set at liberty, but making him promise, on his side, that if he failed he would return to Carthage.

Now Regulus did not believe that it would be to the advantage of Rome either to exchange the prisoners or to make any treaty with Carthage, and he urged the Senate to reject the offers made. When this decision had been arrived at, Regulus announced his intention of returning to Carthage. He knew that a cruel death awaited him there, but neither the remonstrances of the Senators and his friends, nor the tears and pleading of his wife availed to change his mind. He was a Roman, and he had given his plighted word that if he failed in his mission, he would return. He had failed, for he had not secured what the Carthaginians demanded, but he was too honourable to break his word, and though he knew what was in store for him, he preferred to endure the cruelty and torture than to suffer any stain to fall upon the honour of a Roman.

> So, like a man outcasted, runs
>   The tale—he thrust away from him
> His loving wife and little sons
>   And bent on earth his visage grim;
>
> Till with such words as none e'er spoke
>   He braced the Senate's doubts at last,
> Then from his grieving friends he broke
>   And to immortal exile passed. [1]

In the meantime the war was still going on in Sicily. Rome had begun by a number of successes; but since the victory at Mylae all had not been going well. Year after year went by and no decisive victories were gained by either side, but in 249 B.C., seven years after the defeat and death of Regulus, another catastrophe overwhelmed the Romans. The Consul Publius Claudius was defeated in a naval battle in which he lost more than ninety ships. It was believed that this defeat was due to the impiety

[1] Horace: Odes, III, 5.

of the Consul. The augurs told him that the sacred
chickens refused to eat, an unfavourable omen in
war-time, but the Consul had replied angrily that
if they would not eat, then they should drink, and
he had ordered them thrown into the sea.

Rome was now in a very serious position. Disaster upon disaster had fallen upon her: she had lost
nearly all her ships; she had sent an army to Africa
and had struck a blow at the very heart of the
enemy, but the result had been a great catastrophe
and her men had perished. The years of warfare
in Sicily had drained all her resources, the nation
seemed exhausted, the money in the treasury had all
been spent. Carthage, on the other hand, was
still rich, both in men and gold, and, above all, she
possessed a general of genius, Hamilcar, surnamed
Barca, the *man of lightning*, who was now given command of the Carthaginian army in Sicily. There
seemed nothing before Rome but disaster and
defeat.   Only one thing could save her, and that was
a fleet, but the treasury was empty and ships could
not be built without money. Rome had lost much:
men, money, great quantities of material, ships, but
she had kept the greatest thing of all that she
possessed, the spirit of her people. Stern, resolved,
refusing to despair, they held on, whilst for three
long years Hamilcar Barca kept up a ceaseless petty
warfare, which would have worn out any nation
less determined than Rome. The state could not
build another fleet, but at this dark hour, by tremendous efforts, the Roman citizens of their own
free-will provided enough money to build no less

than two hundred ships, which they manned and presented as a gift to the state. Once more Rome could face the enemy, and once more a great sea-battle was fought off the coast of Sicily. It was the year 241 B.C., twenty-three years since the beginning of the war, and Rome was victorious. She defeated the Carthaginian fleet so completely that though Hamilcar, the general, was himself unconquered, he was forced to sue for peace on behalf of his country.

Carthage was forced to restore all Roman prisoners without any ransom, and to pay to Rome a large sum of money, but most important of all, she had to give up Sicily, and for the first time Rome ruled territory beyond the mainland. Three years later Rome seized Sardinia and Corsica. Carthage protested, but Rome threatened war if she made any objections, and both islands were given up to Rome. The possession of these islands gave Rome the control of that part of the Mediterranean, but it did also more than that. It definitely committed her to a policy that was to carry Roman influence far beyond the coasts of Italy. No longer could Rome remain a purely Italian state. She had already waged war on the sea and far beyond her coasts; her battle-line had even reached another continent. She had begun a greater undertaking than she had dreamed of in the beginning, but she had shown herself great under difficulties and defeats, and in the end the spirit of Roman determination had conquered.

The struggle was not yet ended, for Hamilcar Barca was still alive, and he himself had not yet been conquered, but for the time Carthage was subdued and there was an interval of peace.

III. THE SECOND PUNIC WAR

218–201 B.C.

The First Punic War ended in 241 B.C. and for twenty-three years there was peace between Rome and Carthage; but it was a peace that was really little more than a truce, for both sides knew that nothing finally decisive had yet been accomplished and that until some such decision was reached, the struggle would not end.

After the surrender of Sicily, Hamilcar had returned to Carthage. He was filled with a burning hatred for Rome and with anger at what she had taken from Carthage, and he was determined to avenge this humiliation. But now, as at all times during the Punic Wars, the Carthaginian government, ever slow, unpatriotic and incapable, refused to support Hamilcar or to find means either for raising or equipping an army. But Hamilcar was a patriot, determined to serve his country whether he was helped or hindered by his government, and he was resolved that Carthage should be avenged. He saw that nothing could be gained by remaining in Carthage, so he set out for Spain, where he planned to develop the wealth of the country, to increase the Carthaginian power, and to raise and train an army that should conquer Rome.

Hamilcar took with him to Spain his little son,

destined to be one of the greatest commanders the world has known, Hannibal, and long years afterwards Hannibal told the story of what his father did just before leaving Carthage.

My father Hamilcar [he said] when I was a very little boy, only some nine years old, offered sacrifices at Carthage, when he was going to take command in Spain, to Jupiter Optimus Maximus, and while these rites were going on, he asked me "Whether I should like to go with him to camp?" As I expressed extreme willingness to go, and begged him not to delay taking me, he replied, "I will do so, if you will give me the promise which I ask." Thereupon he led me to the altar at which he had begun to sacrifice, and, sending the rest of the company away, required me, taking hold of the altar, to swear "That I would never hold friendship with the Romans."[1]

And the oath made by the child was kept to his dying day.

Arrived in Spain, Hamilcar set himself to establish the Carthaginian power and to make the army strong. He succeeded in all that he undertook and when, nine years later, he fell in battle, he left behind him the memory of a statesman, a fearless soldier and a good general.

The three sons of Hamilcar had all been brought up by their father in the camp. He called them the "lion's brood" and they all inherited his genius, his hatred for Rome, and his resolve for her complete

[1] Cornelius Nepos: *Life of Hannibal.*

defeat. Even in his youth Hannibal had shown himself the greatest of the three, and it was prophesied that he would be greater even than his father. But at Hamilcar's death he was only nineteen and was considered too young to take supreme command of the army. This was given to his brother-in-law, but he was killed in battle seven years later, and then, at the age of only twenty-six, Hannibal became Commander-in-Chief of the Carthaginian army.

Hannibal was one of the great generals of history. He had been brought up in his father's camp and shared the fortunes of that father who had himself never been conquered. But he had learnt more than military matters; he was well educated and could both speak and write Greek. He was an unselfish patriot, devoted to a selfish and ungrateful country; a great warrior and a born leader of men; but he was also a statesman whose counsels were as valuable in the senate-chamber as in the camp. All through his career Hannibal was inspired by one motive, that of burning hate of Rome and the determination that Carthage should triumph over her. The only history we have of Hannibal was written by his deadly enemies, and they accused him of many wrong deeds: of great cruelty, and of deceit and treachery which the Romans called *Punic Faith*. They said he had no truth, no reverence towards the gods, no respect for an oath, no religion. Much of this was probably exaggerated. It is doubtful if he used any more cruelty than the warfare of those times recognized, and his Punic Faith was probably in large measure the genius he possessed for stratagem and ambushes, for taking unexpected routes and for making sudden and unexpected decisions. It is not surprising that his enemies spoke some evil of him, what is amazing is that in spite of the envy and hatred that wrote his history, the personality of Hannibal shines out through the ages as that of a great and noble man.

Livy, the Roman historian, writes of the arrival of Hannibal in Spain to take command, that

no sooner had he landed than he became a favourite with the whole army. The veterans thought they saw Hamilcar restored to them as he was in his youth; they saw the same determined expression, the same piercing eyes, the same cast of features. He soon showed, however, that it was not his father's memory that helped him most to win the affections of the army, there was no other leader in whom the soldiers placed more confidence or under whom they showed more daring. He was fearless in exposing himself to danger, and perfectly self-possessed in the presence of it. No amount of exertion could cause him either bodily or mental fatigue; he was equally indifferent to heat and cold; his eating and drinking were measured by the needs of nature, not by appetite; his hours of sleep were not determined by day or night, whatever time was not taken up with active duties was given to sleep and rest, but that rest was not wooed on a soft couch or in silence, men often saw him lying on the ground amongst the sentinels and outposts, wrapped in his military cloak. His dress was in no way superior to that of his comrades; what did make him conspicuous were his arms and his horses. He was by far the foremost both of the cavalry and the infantry, the first to enter the fight and the last to leave the field.[1]

This was the man who was to lead the armies of Carthage against Rome for the next seventeen years.

The Carthaginians controlled the greater part of Spain, but Saguntum, a Greek colony in Spain, was allied by treaty with Rome. Hannibal, ignoring this, besieged Saguntum, but when the Romans heard of it they sent ambassadors, men of age and experience, to Carthage, demanding that unless Hannibal should be delivered into their hands, they would consider his action as a breaking of the peace between Rome and Carthage and a direct declaration of war. But the Roman mission failed and the Carthaginians refused to consider their demand

Then the Roman, gathering up his toga, said, "Here we bring you war and peace, take which you please." He was met by a defiant shout bidding him give whichever he preferred, and when, letting the folds of his toga fall, he said that he gave them war, they replied that they accepted war and would carry it on in the same spirit in which they accepted it.[2]

When the Romans returned home, they were met with the news that after a siege of eight months, Saguntum had fallen. This meant war in earnest, and preparations were at once begun.

Hannibal determined to invade Italy. He knew the full extent of the Roman resources and that as

[1] Livy, XXI, 4.   [2] Livy, XXI, 18.

long as Italy was in danger of an invasion which would threaten Rome itself, Carthage was safe from attack. It was in the spring of the year 218 B.C. and swiftly and suddenly did Hannibal now move. With an army of probably fifty thousand foot-soldiers, nine thousand horsemen and a large number of elephants, he crossed the Pyrenees and marched through the south of Gaul to the Rhone. The native Gauls gave them some trouble here, but they were soon overcome and Hannibal prepared to cross the Alps. Envoys then came to him from beyond the mountains, offering to act as guides and to take their share in the dangers of the expedition, and the offer was accepted.

The army was appalled at the prospect of the journey across the Alps, but Hannibal called a number of the men together and encouraged them, reminding them of the great difficulties they had already surmounted; how they had crossed the Pyrenees, defeated the Gauls in the valley of the Rhone and then crossed the river, until now they were at last facing the Alps on the other side of which lay Italy.

What do you imagine the Alps to be other than lofty mountains? [he said]. Suppose them to be higher than the peaks of the Pyrenees, surely no region in the world can touch the sky or be impassable to man. Even the Alps are inhabited and cultivated, animals are bred and reared there, their gorges and ravines can be traversed by armies. What can be inaccessible to the soldier who carries nothing with him but his weapons of war? What toils and perils you went through for eight months to effect the capture of Saguntum! And now that Rome, the capital of the world, is your goal, can you deem anything so difficult or so arduous that it should prevent you from reaching it? Many years ago the Gauls captured the place which Carthaginians despair of approaching; either you must confess yourselves inferior in courage and enterprise to a people whom you have conquered again and again, or else you must look forward to finishing your march on the ground between the Tiber and the walls of Rome.[1]

These words so roused the Carthaginians, that they prepared with good-will for the march. At first

Hannibal's route lay mostly through open level country, and he reached the Alps without meeting any opposition from the Gauls who inhabited the district. But the sight of the Alps revived the terrors in the minds of his men. Although rumour, which generally magnifies untried dangers, had filled them with gloomy forebodings, the nearer view proved much more fearful. The height of the mountains now so close, the snow which was almost lost in the sky, the wretched huts perched on the rocks, the flocks and herds shrivelled and stunted with the cold, the men wild and unkempt, everything animate and inanimate stiff with frost, all helped to increase their alarm.

As the head of the column began to climb the nearest slopes, the natives appeared on the heights above; had they concealed themselves in the ravines and then rushed down they would have caused frightful panic and bloodshed. Hannibal called a halt and sent on some Gauls to examine the ground, and when he learnt that advance

[1] Livy, XXI, 30.

was impossible in that direction he formed his camp in the widest part of the valley that he could find; everywhere around the ground was broken and precipitous. The Gauls who had been sent to reconnoitre got into conversation with the natives, as there was little difference between their speech or their manners, and they brought back word to Hannibal that the pass was only occupied in the daytime, at nightfall the natives all dispersed to their homes.

Accordingly, at early dawn he began the ascent as though determined to force the pass in broad daylight, and spent the day in movements designed to conceal his real intentions and in fortifying the camp on the spot where they had halted. As soon as he observed that the natives had left the heights and were no longer watching his movements, he gave orders, with the view of deceiving the enemy, for a large number of fires to be lighted, larger in fact than would be required by those remaining in camp. Then, leaving the baggage with the cavalry and the greater part of the infantry in camp, he himself with a specially selected body of troops in light marching order rapidly moved out of the defile and occupied the heights which the enemy had held.

The following day the rest of the army broke camp in the grey dawn and commenced its march. The natives were beginning to assemble at their customary post of observation when they suddenly became aware that some of the enemy were in possession of their stronghold right over their heads, whilst others were advancing on the path beneath. The double impression made on their eyes and imagination kept them for a few moments motionless, but when they saw the column falling into disorder mainly through the horses becoming frightened, they thought that if they increased the confusion and panic it would be sufficient to destroy it. So they charged down from rock to rock, careless as to whether there were paths or not, for they were familiar with the ground. The Carthaginians had to meet this attack at the same time that they were struggling with the difficulties of the way, and as each man was doing his best for himself to get out of the reach of danger, they were fighting more amongst themselves than against the natives. The horses did the most mischief; they were terrified at the wild shouts, which the echoing woods and valleys made all the louder, and when they happened to be struck or wounded they created terrible havoc amongst the men and the different baggage animals. The road was flanked by sheer precipices on each side, and in the crowding together many were pushed over the edge and fell an immense depth. Amongst these were some of the soldiers; the heavily laden baggage animals rolled over like falling houses. Horrible as the sight was, Hannibal remained quiet and kept his men back for some time, for fear of increasing the alarm and confusion, but when he saw that the column was broken and the army was in danger of losing all its baggage, in which case he would have brought them through to no purpose, he ran down from his higher ground and at once scattered the enemy. At the same time, however, he threw his own men into still greater disorder for the moment, but it was very quickly allayed now that the passage was cleared by the flight of the natives. In a short time the whole army had traversed the pass not only without any further disturbance, but almost in silence.

He then seized a fortified village, the head place of the district, together with some adjacent hamlets, and from the food and cattle thus secured he provided his army with rations for three days. As the natives, after their first defeat, no longer impeded their march, whilst the road presented little difficulty, they made considerable progress during those three days.

They now came to another canton which, considering that it was a mountain district, had a considerable population. Here he narrowly escaped destruction, not in fair and open fighting, but by the practices which he himself employed—falsehood and treachery. The head men from the fortified villages, men of advanced age, came as a deputation to the Carthaginian and told him that they had been taught by the salutary example of other people's misfortunes to seek the friendship of the Carthaginians rather than to feel their strength. They were accordingly prepared to carry out his orders; he would receive provisions and guides, and hostages as a guarantee of good faith. Hannibal felt that he ought not to trust them blindly nor to meet their offer with a flat refusal, in case they should become hostile. So he replied in friendly terms, accepted the hostages whom they placed in his hands, made use of the provisions with which they supplied him on the march, but followed their guides with his army prepared for action, not at all as though he were going through a peaceable or friendly country. The elephants and cavalry were in front, he himself followed with the main body of the infantry, keeping a sharp and anxious lookout in all directions.

Just as they reached a part of the pass where it narrowed and was overhung on one side by a wall of rock, the barbarians sprang up from ambush on all sides and assailed the column in front and rear, at close quarters, and at a distance by rolling huge stones down on it.

The heaviest attack was made in the rear, and as the infantry faced round to meet it, it became obvious that if the rear of the column had not been made exceptionally strong, a terrible disaster must have occurred in that pass. As it was, they were in the greatest danger, and within an ace of total destruction. For whilst Hannibal was hesitating whether to send his infantry on into the narrow part of the pass—for whilst protecting the rear of the cavalry they had no reserve to protect their own rear—the mountaineers, making a flank charge, burst through the middle of the column and held the pass so that Hannibal had to spend that one night without his cavalry or his baggage.

The next day, as the savages attacked with less vigour, the column closed up, and the pass was surmounted, not without loss, more, however, of baggage animals than of men. From that time the natives made their appearance in smaller numbers and behaved more like banditti than regular soldiers; they attacked either front or rear just as the ground gave them opportunity, or as the advance or halt of the column presented a chance of surprise. The elephants caused considerable delay, owing to the difficulty of getting them through narrow or precipitous places; on the other hand, they rendered that part of the column safe from attack where they were, for the natives were unaccustomed to the sight of them and had a great dread of going too near them.

Nine days from their commencing the ascent they arrived at the highest point of the Alps, after traversing a region mostly without roads and frequently losing their way either through the treachery of their guides or through their own mistakes in trying to find the way for themselves. For two days they remained in camp on the summit, whilst the troops enjoyed a respite from fatigue and fighting. Some of the baggage animals which had fallen amongst the rocks and had afterwards followed the track of the column came into camp. To add to the misfortunes of the worn-out troops, there was a heavy fall of snow, and this new experience created considerable alarm.

In the early morning of the third day the army recommenced its heavy march over ground everywhere deep in snow. Hannibal saw in all faces an expression of listlessness and despondency. He rode on in front to a height from which there was a wide and extensive view, and halting his men, he pointed out to them the land of Italy and the rich valley of the Po lying at the foot of the Alps. "You are now," he said, "crossing the barriers not only of Italy, but of Rome itself. Henceforth all will be smooth and easy for you; in one or, at the most, two battles, you will be masters of the capital and stronghold of Italy."

Then the army resumed its advance with no annoyance from the enemy beyond occasional attempts at plunder. The remainder of the march, however, was attended with much greater difficulty than they had experienced in the ascent, for the distance to the plains on the Italian side is shorter, and therefore the descent is necessarily steeper. Almost the whole of the way was precipitous, narrow, and slippery, so that they were unable to keep their footing, and if they slipped they could not recover themselves; they kept falling over each other, and the baggage animals rolled over on their drivers.[1]

Such was the way in which Hannibal and his army reached Italy. It was five months since they had

[1] Livy, XXI, 32-35.

left Spain, and fifteen days of that time had been spent in crossing the Alps. The army had suffered enormous losses, some authorities think that as many as half the men who started lost their lives, as well as large numbers of animals, including some of the elephants, and great quantities of baggage. Alexander the Great or Julius Caesar might have accomplished such a feat, but no other general of the ancient world, save Hannibal, could have achieved it. His skill and daring, his heroic and undaunted spirit, his genius for command, his caution and good judgment, his unceasing care for the welfare of his troops were unmatched by any other general of his time. Could Rome hope to defeat such an invader?

The Romans had never dreamed that Hannibal would attempt to invade Italy by crossing the Alps, and when the challenge to war was accepted, they did what seemed to be the most natural thing to do: they sent an army under the Consul Publius Cornelius Scipio to attack the Carthaginians in Spain. When, however, the news of Hannibal's unexpected march reached Rome, Scipio was at once recalled from Spain and he was sent with all haste to the valley of the Po. There he found Hannibal awaiting him.

Now for a long time the name of Hannibal had been on all men's lips in Rome, he was recognized as a greater general than any Roman of that generation had seen, and it was with feelings not unmixed with dread that the Roman army found itself on the eve of battle with this great commander.

There had been strange signs, too, which alarmed
the Romans. "A wolf had entered the camp and
after worrying all it met had got away unhurt. A
swam of bees, too, had settled on a tree which overhung the headquarters tent."[1] But Scipio offered
the necessary sacrifices and led his army to the
battle. He was utterly defeated, and "to make
matters worse he was wounded and in danger, but
he was rescued by his son who was just approaching
manhood,"[2] a son who was to win great glory in
later years. After this defeat the Roman army
withdrew to what seemed to Scipio to be a more
favourable spot, where he was joined by the other
Consul, Sempronius, with fresh reserves of men.
Sempronius took the chief command of the two
armies and another battle was fought against Hannibal, and again the Romans were defeated.

Winter was now approaching and Hannibal made
no move towards another battle. His men had had
no rest since leaving Spain in the spring; they had
crossed rivers, climbed mountains, performed deeds
that beforehand seemed to them impossible and
which, looking back to them, seem to us almost incredible; they had fought with unfriendly tribes in
the mountains and descended into the plain below
to meet the Romans; they had fought two battles
with them and had been victorious. They had well
earned the rest Hannibal gave them through the
winter.

It was an uneasy winter in Rome. Men's hearts

[1] Livy, XXI, 46.
[2] Ibid.

failed them because of strange sights that were seen, and when once superstitious fears take hold, any and every kind of omen is believed. The Senate, however, paid little attention to these signs and gradually the people regained their confidence. It was said of the Romans that "both in public and private they were most to be feared when they stood in real danger," and they were in very real danger now.

Preparations were made to resist any further advance of Hannibal when the spring came. The two Consuls were each to command an army and were to take their stand at important places on two of the great roads which connected Rome with Central Italy. By these means it was hoped that Hannibal would be prevented from advancing any further.

One of the Consuls was Caius Flaminius. He had been Tribune of the people and then Consul, and it was he who had built the Flaminian Way, the road which connected Rome and Ariminum. Flaminius was a fiery, impatient leader, apt to be overbearing, self-willed and headstrong, no match for the cool and cautious Hannibal, but he was determined at all costs to drive out the invader. Hannibal knew this, and fully understanding the character of Flaminius directed his next move against him.

In the spring of 217 B.C. Hannibal, making one of his unexpected marches, crossed the Apennines into Etruria. It was another dreadful march for the Carthaginians, for the melting snows were flooding the roads, and they half-waded and half-swam through the deep pools of water.

What distressed them most of all was want of sleep, from which they had been suffering for four days and three nights. As everything was covered with water and they had not a dry spot on which to lay their wearied bodies, they piled up the baggage in the water and lay on the top, whilst some snatched a few minutes needful rest by making couches of the heaps of baggage animals which were everywhere standing out of the water. Hannibal, himself, whose eyes were affected by the changeable and inclement spring weather, rode upon the only surviving elephant so that he might be a little higher above the water. Owing, however, to want of sleep and the night mists and the malaria from the marshes, and as neither place nor time admitted of any proper treatment, he completely lost the sight of one eye. After losing many men and beasts under these frightful circumstances, he at last got clear of the marshes, and as soon as he could find some dry ground he pitched his camp.[1]

By this march Hannibal had placed himself between Flaminius and Rome, and he now lured the Romans into an ambush near Lake Trasimene. Flaminius and his army, thinking that all was well, marched into a narrow pass between high mountains which led down to the lake. The Carthaginian foot-soldiers were concealed behind some low hills near the entrance to the pass. Flaminius reached the place at sunset, but he waited until the morning before entering the pass. Then, fearing nothing,

[1] Livy, XXII, 2, 3.

he gave the command to advance. A thick mist
hung over everything, hiding even the sides of the
mountains. When the last Roman had entered,
Hannibal ordered the attack. Nothing could save
the Romans. Unprepared, with the enemy attacking on every side at once, the army was soon cut to
pieces. Thousands of men were driven into the
lake and drowned, others managed to take flight
and to hide in the surrounding hills, others perished
in the battle fighting heroically to the last. Flaminius the Consul was slain and the massacre was
horrible. During the battle, a great earthquake
shook the whole region.

It destroyed several towns, altered the course of
rivers, and carried off parts of high cliffs, yet such was
the eagerness of the combatants, that they were entirely
insensible of it.[1]

As soon as the news of this disaster reached Rome the
people flocked into the Forum in a great state of panic
and confusion. Matrons were wandering about the
streets and asking those they met what recent disaster
had been reported or what news was there of the army.
The throng in the Forum, as numerous as a crowded
Assembly, flocked towards the Comitium and the Senate-
House and called for the magistrates. At last, shortly
before sunset, the praetor announced, "We have been
defeated in a great battle." Though nothing more definite was heard from him, the people, full of the reports
which they had heard from one another, carried back
to their homes the information that the consul had been

[1] Plutarch: *Life of Fabius.*

killed with the greater part of his army; only a few survived, and these were either dispersed in flight throughout Etruria or had been made prisoner by the enemy.[1]

As the days went by small groups of fugitives
began to return with the tale that all was lost and
that the enemy was even then close at hand. Every
day a crowd

stood at the gates waiting for some one of their friends
or for news about them, and they crowded round those
they met with eager and anxious enquiries, nor was it
possible to get them away, especially from those they
knew, until they had got all the details from first to last.[2]

For a short time horror prevailed in the city and
Rome bowed her head in dismay.

Hannibal had defeated the Consul Cornelius
Scipio and slain the Consul Flaminius, but he had
not defeated the Roman people, and after the first
horror of the news of the disaster at Lake Trasimene,
the people lifted up their heads and Roman steadfastness and constancy took the place of terror
and despondency. The Senate told the people the
truth and bade them take heart, for all was not yet
lost. In spite of disaster and defeat the strength of
the Republic was not broken, the city was well
fortified, and no state allied to Rome had yet gone
over to the enemy.

As one consul had been killed and the other was
absent from Rome with his army, it was thought
wisest to appoint a Dictator, and the choice fell

Livy, XXII, 7.   [2] Ibid.

upon Quintus Fabius Maximus, a man of experience and one who was greatly trusted. The first thing he did was to strengthen the walls and towers of the city and add to its defences, to cut down the bridges over the river, and to waste the country round Rome, so that the enemy might have difficulty in getting supplies.

Now Fabius knew that Hannibal was a greater general than any Roman general and that in a pitched battle his great skill would tell in favour of the Carthaginians, but he also knew that if the Carthaginians had the greater general, Rome had the greater spirit. The Roman spirit could not be worn out, but the Carthaginian was of a different quality, and so Fabius introduced the policy of avoiding battles, and of following, harassing, annoying, attacking here a little and there a little, of keeping the enemy in constant trouble, and of wasting the land so that he had to live on plunder, which would make the Italians hostile to him. Fabius wanted to weaken the enemy and gradually to wear him out. Later on, the Romans realized that this Fabian policy had saved the state, but at the time it was very much disliked and gave rise to the suspicion that Fabius lacked courage. He was called *Cunctator*, the Delayer, and his opponents did all that they could to hinder him, and some of them even called him a traitor. Hannibal, however, was not deceived. He recognized the skill of Fabius and saw that if his tactics were carried on for long, the Carthaginian power would suffer very severely. Hannibal was too great a general not to see that in spite of his great successes in the field, of the destruction of a Roman army, and of his apparent ability to march wherever he chose in Italy, he had really accomplished very little. This Fabian policy was checking him on all sides; the allies of Rome had so far remained loyal to her; with all his resources he did not attack Rome itself; and, a very serious thing for a general invading a foreign state, no reinforcements or supplies of any kind were sent to him from Carthage. And he knew that in spite of disaster and defeat, the spirit of Rome was as unbroken, as resolute, determined and steadfast as ever.

Two new Consuls were now elected in Rome, Aemilius Paulus, an experienced soldier, and Varro who belonged to the party eager for forcing a battle. These generals raised an army of eighty thousand men, the greatest single army Rome had ever sent out at one time. It was in the summer of 216 B.C. about a year after the disaster at Lake Trasimene, that the Roman Consuls marched to Apulia where Hannibal was encamped. The Roman army was much larger than the Carthaginian, and high hopes were entertained. The Romans fought Hannibal at Cannae, and never before and never again did they meet with such overwhelming disaster. The slaughter was appalling, no one asked for mercy and none was given. Of the eighty thousand men who had gone into battle, seventy thousand were left dead upon the field, and amongst these were the Consul Aemilius Paulus and eighty of the Senators.

When this news reached Rome, there prevailed a greater excitement and panic than had prevailed at the news of any other disaster. The Senate met this desperate crisis with manliness and resolution.

The praetors called a meeting of the Senate to take measures for the defence of the city, for no doubt was felt that after wiping out the armies the enemy would set about his one remaining task and advance to attack Rome. In the presence of evils the extent of which, great as they were, was still unknown, they were unable even to form any definite plans, and the cries of wailing women deafened their ears, for as the facts were not yet ascertained, the living and the dead were being indiscriminately bewailed in almost every house. Under these circumstances Q. Fabius Maximus gave it as his opinion that swift horsemen should be sent along the Appian and Latin roads to make enquiries of those they met, for there would be sure to be fugitives scattered about the country, and bring back tidings as to what had befallen the consuls and the armies, and if the gods out of compassion for the empire had left any remnant of the Roman nation, to find out where those forces were. And also they might ascertain whither Hannibal had repaired after the battle, what plans he was forming, what he was doing or likely to do. They must get some young and active men to find out these things, and as there were hardly any magistrates in the city, the senators must themselves take steps to calm the agitation and alarm which prevailed. They must keep the matrons out of the public streets and compel them to remain indoors; they must suppress the loud laments for the dead and impose silence on the city; they must see that all who brought tidings were taken to the praetors, and that the citizens should, each in his own house, wait for any news which affected them personally.   Moreover, they must station guards at the gates to prevent anyone from leaving the city, and they must make it clear to every man that the only safety he can hope for lies in the city and its walls.   When the tumult has once been hushed, then the Senate must be again convened and measures discussed for the defence of the city.[1]

Order was restored and the Roman spirit of unyielding constancy, of undaunted courage, of discipline and steadfastness once more prevailed.   Messengers were sent out for news, and they returned with a letter from the Consul Varro saying that

Aemilius was killed and his army cut to pieces; he himself was at Canusium collecting the wreckage that remained from this awful disaster; there were as many as ten thousand soldiers, irregular, disorganized; the Carthaginian was still at Cannae, bargaining about the prisoners' ransom and the plunder.[2]

Then there followed the list of the dead, which was published, and Rome bowed her head in the dust for heavy grief and sorrow.   But outwardly she did not show it, the daily tasks were fulfilled as usual, and in quiet, self-controlled dignity she prepared for the return of the defeated Consul and of the few who were left to come with him.

Yet, in spite of all their disasters no one anywhere in Rome mentioned the word "Peace," either before the

[1] Livy, XXII, 55.　　　[2] Livy, XXII, 56.

consul's return or after his arrival, when all the memories of their losses were renewed. Such a lofty spirit did the citizens exhibit in those days that though the consul was coming back from a terrible defeat for which they knew he was mainly responsible, he was met by a vast concourse drawn from every class of society, and thanks were formally voted to him because he "had not despaired of the republic." Had he been commander-in-chief of the Carthaginians there was no torture to which he would not have been subjected.[1]

The defeat had other and more disastrous results than any other defeat the Romans had yet sustained. Up to that time the allies of Rome had remained firm and loyal, but after Cannae some of them wavered in their allegiance. The Samnites joined Hannibal, Capua opened her gates to him, and except for the Latin colonies which remained faithful, other states weakened in their loyalty and Rome could not rely on them. Then Sicily joined the Carthaginians, and Macedonia made an alliance with them. Hannibal had hoped that more of the Italians would have joined him. In this he showed himself a true Carthaginian, for in reverse circumstances, Carthaginian allies would probably have forsaken their state for a victorious general long ere this. On the whole these new allies were a burden to Hannibal rather than a help, for instead of supplying him with various resources, they themselves needed protection and support. Hannibal had not carried on even a victorious war without losses, and after the battle of Cannae he was in great need

[1] Livy, XXII, 61.

both of more men and of more money. But as usual, Carthage sent nothing, and Hannibal was left to win or lose with what resources he had, alone in an enemy's country.

The battle of Cannae was fought in 216 B.C. and for twelve more years Hannibal remained in Italy. The Romans drove him further and further south, but were unable to conquer him. Capua, one of the fairest and richest of the Italian towns, was occupied by the Carthaginians, but in 211 B.C. after a long and relentless siege, during which she suffered all the horrors of a famine, the Romans recaptured her. The faithless city was punished pitilessly; her leading men were scourged and then beheaded, the people were sold into slavery, and, greatest degradation of all, the rights and liberties of the inhabitants as Roman citizens were taken away. The fate of Capua was a terrible warning to all who might contemplate disloyalty to Rome.

During the siege of Capua in order, if possible, to draw off some of the Roman troops, Hannibal made a march on Rome and encamped only three miles from the city. With a small force of horsemen he rode actually to the gates of Rome, but he did not attack the city, knowing that his force was not large enough to undertake such a risk, and soon after he withdrew. The friends of Hannibal could never understand why he did not follow up his victories by an attack on Rome, and one of them once said to him indignantly: "You know, Hannibal, how to gain a victory, but not how to use it."[1]

[1] Plutarch: *Life of Fabius.*

In the meantime the Romans under Marcellus had been besieging Syracuse. This general was held in great honour by later generations. Virgil looked back to him as to one, who in a time of strain and stress had raised up the Roman power and who had struck down both the Carthaginian and the Gaul. He was not the equal of Hannibal, yet he was not an unworthy antagonist. Marcellus and Fabius were the only two Roman generals whom Hannibal really feared.

Marcellus [we are told] was a man of action and high spirit, ready and bold with his own hand, and, as Homer describes his warriors, fierce, and delighting in fights. Boldness, enterprise, and daring to match those of Hannibal constituted his tactics, and marked his engagements. But Fabius believed that by following close and not fighting him, Hannibal and his army would be tired out and consumed, so that Hannibal found by experience that encountering the one, he met with a rapid, impetuous river, which drove him back; and by the other, though silently and quietly passing by him, he was insensibly washed away and consumed; and at last, was brought to this, that he dreaded Marcellus when he was in motion, and Fabius when he sat still.[1]

Hannibal recognized the indomitable will and courage of Marcellus and said of him:

What will you do with this man, who can bear neither good nor bad fortune? He is the only man who neither suffers us to rest when he is victor, nor rests himself

[1] Plutarch: *Life of Fabius.*

when he is overcome. We shall have, it seems, perpetually to fight with him; as in good success his confidence, and in ill success his shame, still urges him to some further enterprise.[1]

Though the Romans respected Fabius greatly for his high-mindedness and wisdom, they considered his war policy too cautious and prudent. They thought it would keep them out of danger, but that it would not lead them to decisive victory, and so they sought to combine his caution and prudence with the boldness and confidence of Marcellus. They called "Fabius the buckler and Marcellus the sword of Rome."

Marcellus besieged Syracuse for a long time, but in 212 B.C. the city surrendered and Sicily was once more under the rule of Rome. This was the siege during which Archimedes put his scientific knowledge at the disposal of the King and people of Syracuse and at the end of which he lost his life.[2] Syracuse was a very rich Greek city, full of all kinds of works of art. When the Romans captured the city most of these were taken to Rome. This was the beginning of the practice of despoiling conquered cities and of enriching Rome at their expense which became very common in later Roman conquests.

Hannibal had conquered several Roman generals, but he had conquered neither the city nor the people of Rome. The Romans were a people who did not know the meaning of defeat and in spite of every-

[1] Plutarch: *Life of Marcellus.*
[2] See *Book of the Ancient Greeks*, Chapter XX.

thing they had suffered, the Roman spirit was unbroken. But if Hannibal had failed to conquer either Rome or the Roman spirit, neither had the Romans succeeded in conquering, still less in driving out Hannibal. And the Roman resources were steadily growing less. The losses in battle had been so great that soon Rome would find it difficult to raise armies; every available man was already in camp, and all the work at home was being done by women; the fairest parts of Italy had been laid waste; food was scarce and prices high; Rome was suffering from all the evils which war brings in its train. Her spirit might remain unbroken to the end and her men die fighting heroically to the last, but without resources the day would have to come when she would perish, and the name of Rome remain only a memory.

And now news came to Hannibal that reinforcements were at length coming to him. The general Publius Cornelius Scipio, whom he had defeated in the first battle fought on Italian soil, had been in Spain with his brother attempting to conquer the country, in the hope that the loss of it would seriously weaken the position of Hannibal. But the two Scipios were defeated and slain by Hasdrubal, Hannibal's brother, and now Hasdrubal had set out for Italy with a large army and great quantities of treasure to aid Hannibal. He crossed the Alps in 207 B.C. in milder weather and by an easier route than Hannibal had chosen, and immediately on arriving in Italy, he sent messengers to his brother to tell him that he was on his way to aid him. But the messengers were captured by the Romans and taken before the consul. On hearing that Hasdrubal, who, if not the equal of Hannibal, was yet a very great general, was in Italy, an army was sent out under the two consuls, and a great battle was fought at the Metaurus River. The Carthaginian army was taken by surprise, defeated and destroyed, and Hasdrubal himself was slain.

Hannibal knew that his brother was to leave Spain and to bring more troops and supplies to Italy, but owing to the capture of Hasdrubal's messengers no further news had yet reached him. Day after day he waited for a messenger, but none came. Then, one day, a bleeding head was cruelly tossed into his camp. Silently a Carthaginian soldier picked it up and took it to the general. It was the head of Hasdrubal. At the same time two of the prisoners taken by the Romans, but released in order to report to Hannibal all that had happened, arrived, and the tale of the battle was told to him. Hannibal himself was still unconquered, but all was not well with the Carthaginian power in Italy. After Rome had recaptured Capua, there had been no more revolts on the part of the Italian allies, and it was on the uniting of her friends and allies against Rome that Hannibal had placed almost his last hopes. Now, Hasdrubal had been slain and his army destroyed.

Stunned by the blow which had fallen on his country and on his family, it is said that Hannibal recognized the doom which awaited Carthage.[1]

[1] Livy, XXVII, 51.

"Alas," he cried,

> "No heralds shall my deeds proclaim
>   To Carthage now: lost, lost is all:
> A nation's hope, a nation's name,
>   They died with dying Hasdrubal." [1]

The Romans now sent Publius Scipio, son of the defeated and slaughtered general, to Spain to avenge his father's death.   He was young, but had already distinguished himself.   In one battle he had saved his father's life, and after the battle of Cannae, when a small number of faint-hearted survivors were planning to escape to some other land, leaving Rome and Italy to their fate, he roused them to action, crying out: "Let those who want to save the Republic take their arms at once and follow me," and to prevent any falling away from their loyalty he made them take an oath to stand by Rome to the end.

"I solemnly swear," he made them say, "that I will not abandon the Republic of Rome, nor will I suffer any other Roman citizen to do so; if I knowingly break my oath, then do thou, O Jupiter Optimus Maximus, visit me, my house, my family, and my estate with utter destruction." [2]

After a brilliant campaign in Spain, Scipio conquered it and then returned to Rome, where he was made Consul.   Their recent successes had inspired the Romans with great hope and courage, and Scipio now proposed that the war should be carried into Africa, for he believed that only by attacking Car-

[1] Horace: Odes, IV, 4.   [2] Livy, XXII, 53.

thage itself, would the Carthaginian power be broken. His proposal was agreed to and he set sail for Africa. When he landed he found that at first he could not do much, as a very large Carthaginian army opposed him. But Scipio made an alliance with the King of Numidia, and in several battles they defeated Carthage. In their dismay, the Carthaginians sent messengers to Italy with the command of the government that Hannibal should return and save his country from the destruction that threatened her. More than thirty years before, Hannibal had left Carthage. He had landed, a child in his father's camp, on the western shore of that sea which his countrymen had so proudly called a Carthaginian lake. Grown to manhood, he had been given supreme command of the Carthaginian army, and in one magnificent campaign after another, he had swept round the coasts of the Mediterranean from the West to the East. He had needed men, money, food, supplies of all kinds, but his country had sent him nothing. In spite of all his difficulties, he had gone on winning victory after victory, but his most brilliant achievements were rendered fruitless by the complete absence of any support from his country. Yet now, when she was in deadly peril, she sent for him, bidding him leave his task in Italy unfinished. It is said that he gnashed his teeth, groaned and almost shed tears when the message reached him, but he went, unhesitatingly putting himself at the service of his country and answering her call.

Hannibal returned to Carthage, but not even his

genius could save his country now. When he arrived he did all that was in his power to create an army, but time was pressing, and he had to add to the small force of veterans that had returned with him many new and untrained recruits. Then he took his stand at Zama, a few miles south of Carthage, and in 202 B.C. Scipio met him in a long fierce battle. It was the last battle in a long war, and for the first time in his career Hannibal was defeated in the open field. The defeat was so complete, that there was nothing for Carthage to do after it but surrender and ask for terms. She had been defeated on her own soil, close to her own stronghold. Hannibal was summoned before the Carthaginian Senate, and "he told them frankly that he had lost not a battle merely but the whole war, and that their only chance of safety lay in obtaining peace."[1]

Carthage surrendered and peace was made. Carthage was to give up Spain and all the islands between Africa and Italy; the King of Numidia was to be recognized as an ally of Rome; Carthage was to pay an annual tribute to Rome of two hundred talents for fifty years; she was to give up all her elephants; she was to wage no war without the consent of Rome; and she was to give up all her ships of war except ten triremes. Five hundred vessels, the glory of Carthage, the symbol of her commercial power, were towed out into the harbour and burnt. But Carthage was left a nation, and she was left free.

Scipio returned to Italy and landed in the south.

[1] Livy, XXX, 35

He sent the greater part of his army on in the ships, whilst he himself travelled through Italy. The country was rejoicing quite as much over the restoration of peace as over the victory he had won, and he made his way to Rome through multitudes who poured out from the cities to do him honour, and crowds of peasants who blocked the roads in the country districts. The triumphal procession in which he rode into the City was the most brilliant that had ever been seen.[1]

In honour of his great victory, Scipio was given the surname of Africanus, the first commander-in-chief to whom the Romans gave the name of the people he had conquered.

Scipio Africanus was the only Roman general who had proved a match for Hannibal. In later years he met Hannibal at the court of the King of Syria, whither he had gone on an embassy from Rome and where Hannibal was living in exile, and one day when the two were talking, Scipio asked Hannibal

"whom he considered to be the greatest commander in the world"; "Alexander," was the reply. Africanus then asked whom he would put second, and Hannibal replied, "Pyrrhus." On Scipio's again asking whom he regarded as the third, Hannibal, without any hesitation, replied, "Myself." Scipio smiled and asked, "What would you say if you had vanquished me?" "In that case," replied Hannibal, "I should say that I surpassed Alexander and Pyrrhus, and all other commanders in the world."[2]

[1] Livy. XXX, 45.   [2] Livy, XXXV, 14.

Scipio had an extraordinary belief in himself and he possessed the gift of making others believe in him too. He believed that he was specially favoured by the gods, and all who came near him seem to have been fascinated by the charm of his personality. He was a gallant soldier, almost worshipped by his men. He was generous to his enemies, and amongst the sterner heroes of the Early Republic, Scipio stands out as a strangely romantic figure, representing Rome as she stood at the parting of the ways, for the conquest of Carthage had brought Rome to the threshold of a new period in her history.

IV. THE DESTRUCTION OF CARTHAGE

146 B.C.

After peace had been made with Rome, Hannibal remained in Carthage. The treasury was exhausted and the Carthaginians found it very difficult to raise enough money to pay the tribute demanded by Rome. Instead of exercising self-control and discipline and resolutely setting their faces to the hard task required of them, the people wept and complained, and even in the Senate there was lamentation. Hannibal was a far-sighted man, and he realized that there might be harder days yet in store for Carthage and he told the people so. He reproved them for weeping and lamenting and said to them:

The proper time to weep was when we were deprived of our arms, when our ships were burnt, when we were interdicted from all war beyond our frontiers. That is the wound that will prove fatal. Of course we only feel public calamities so far as they affect us personally, and nothing in them gives us a sharper pang than the loss of money. When the spoils of victory were being dragged away from Carthage, when you saw yourselves left naked and defenceless amidst an Africa in arms, nobody uttered a groan; now because you have to contribute to the indemnity from your private fortunes you lament as loudly as though you were present at your country's funeral. I greatly fear that you will soon find that it is the least of your misfortunes which you are shedding tears over today.[1]

Hannibal now set himself as far as was possible to restore to Carthage some measure of order and well-being, and as a result of his policy the state began to grow prosperous again. This alarmed the Romans who demanded that Hannibal should be given up to them. On hearing this, Hannibal fled from Carthage and went into exile, and as a reward for all he had done for them, the Carthaginians confiscated his property and razed his house to the ground.

Hannibal spent the rest of his life in exile, wandering from place to place, sometimes a fugitive, never at peace, always pursued by the Roman hatred and fear of him. At length, when he was on the point of being betrayed into the hands of his enemies, rather than fall into their hands, he killed himself by drinking a cup of poison. "Let us," he said as he prepared to drink the poison, "relieve the Romans from the anxiety they have so long experienced, since

[1] Livy, XXX, 44.

they think it tries their patience too much to wait for an old man's death."[1]

Hannibal died, as he had lived, hating Rome, and hating her with all the passion of the East. He was a great man, a noble single-minded patriot, of whom his country was not worthy. Yet the final victory of Hannibal would have been a disaster and a tragedy greater than the personal tragedy of his defeat, for the real importance of the outcome of these Punic Wars was the question of which civilization was to prevail, the Phoenician or the Roman: the Phoenician which interpreted everything in terms of money, or the Roman which interpreted life in terms of law, order and unity amongst the nations.

Fifty-two years after the defeat of Hannibal, Rome was once more at war with Carthage. Rome had watched her growing prosperity with increasing anxiety and jealousy and when Carthage, without asking the consent of Rome, made preparations to defend herself against the constant raids on her land made by the King of Numidia, Rome declared that she was violating the treaty made with her by Hannibal. A Roman commission was sent to Carthage to enquire into the matter, one of the members of which was Marcus Cato. On his return he told the Senate that, far from being poor and unarmed, the Carthaginians were rich and laying up stores of arms and ammunition, that their skirmishes with the Numidians were kept up not so much from hostility to the Numidians, as from an

[1] Livy, XXXIX, 51.

intention to practise warfare in order to be able one day to fight the Romans again, that the peace they had made was nothing but a truce, and that they were waiting for a good opportunity to break out into war again. Then,

shaking his gown, he took occasion to let drop some African figs before the Senate. And on their admiring the size and beauty of them, he presently added, that the place that bore them was but three days' sail from Rome. And he never spoke in the Senate after that without ending his speech, Carthage, methinks, ought utterly to be destroyed.[1]

Cato's advice was followed, and war was declared against Carthage on the grounds that she had broken the treaty. A Roman army sailed for Africa and besieged Carthage, but the city held out for two years. Then the Roman command was given to Scipio Aemilianus, an adopted son of Scipio Africanus, and under his generalship the siege was brought to an end. Rome showed neither mercy nor pity, and in 146 B.C. the cruel and unjustifiable order was given that Carthage should be utterly destroyed. The inhabitants were massacred or else sold as slaves; the city was plundered and then burned; the whole site was ploughed up and a solemn curse laid upon anyone who should ever attempt to rebuild the city.

At the sight of the city utterly perishing amid the flames, Scipio, who was watching, burst into tears and

[1] Plutarch: *Life of Marcus Cato.*

stood long reflecting on the inevitable change which awaits cities, nations and dynasties, one and all, as it does every one of us men. This, he thought, had befallen Ilium, once a powerful city, and the once mighty empires of the Assyrians, Medes, Persians, and that of Macedonia, lately so splendid. And unintentionally or purposely he quoted:

> "The day shall be when holy Troy shall fall,
> And Priam, lord of spears, and Priam's folk."

And then turning round to a friend who stood near him, he grasped his hand and said: "It is a wonderful sight, but I know not how, I feel a terror and dread lest some one should one day give the same order about my own native city."[1]

And so it came about that Carthage was destroyed from off the face of the earth, and in the Western Mediterranean Rome was left without a rival.

[1] Polybius, XXXIX, 5.

CHAPTER X

OTHER CONQUESTS IN THE MEDITERRANEAN WORLD

201–133 B.C.

FOR more than two centuries after the establishment of the Republic, Rome had struggled for the control of Italy, and she had won it. In 264 B.C. began the struggle between Rome and Carthage for the supremacy of the Mediterranean, and by the end of the century Rome had won that. In the interval between the First and Second Punic Wars, Rome had strengthened her hold on Italy by conquering Cis-Alpine Gaul, the territory on the Italian side of the Alps, which had been inhabited by tribes of Gauls who had come originally from beyond the mountains. The possession of this land gave Rome dominion not only over the peninsula but also over the rest of Italy as far as the Alps.

The power of Carthage had been supreme only in the Western Mediterranean, but within fifty years of the defeat of Hannibal, Rome was to be mistress of nearly the whole of the Mediterranean world.

After the death of Alexander the Great, his empire

was torn by strife and bloodshed for about fifty years. Then, a certain measure of peace and order having been restored, three kingdoms were established in the Eastern Mediterranean: the Kingdoms of Macedonia, Syria and Egypt. The Greeks were not strong enough to maintain their independence and some of the Greek cities fell under the rule of Macedonia. Whilst Rome was struggling with Carthage in the Western Mediterranean, these three kingdoms held sway in the eastern part of that sea.

History has shown us, both in ancient times as well as today, that it has always been impossible for any state to live for herself alone, and this is especially true of great states. History is more than the story of separate and isolated nations. Each nation and each civilization has had and still has its own particular history, its own characteristics and gifts, its own struggles and sacrifices, its days of suffering and its days of greatness: those things which make of it a nation and the common possession of which binds its citizens together in that devotion and loyalty which we call patriotism. But in proportion as a state grows in wealth and power, so is it taken out of itself and drawn into that greater world that lies beyond its own boundaries. A nation that has become great and powerful has no choice as to whether it will or will not be drawn into the world, but it has the choice as to whether its relation to the world shall be for good or evil. And this was the choice that lay before Rome as the second century B.C. dawned.

During the Second Punic War Hannibal, finding

that he could count on no supplies or reinforcements from Carthage, looked towards the East in the hope of finding allies who would join with him in the war against Rome. He made an alliance with Philip of Macedonia, but Rome, to prevent Philip being of any real assistance to her great enemy, sent an army against him and carried on what is known as the First Macedonian War. There were no very important battles fought, but the war succeeded in its main object, that of preventing any real co-operation between Hannibal and Macedonia.

After Rome had defeated Hannibal and peace had been made, her attention was again drawn to the East. Some time before, a few of the Greek cities had made a friendly alliance with Rome, and now Rome heard that Philip was plotting against their liberty. She also found out that Philip was plotting with Antiochus, the King of Syria, to seize Egypt and divide it between them. Again it was the question of two great states with conflicting interests, to which the ancient world saw but one answer: one must rule and the other obey. More, however, even than this lay in the relations between Rome and the East. For centuries Egypt and the region near the Black Sea had supplied the ancient world with grain, and it was essential to the life of a young and growing nation like that of Rome that the trade-routes to these places should be open to it. The aggressions of Philip of Macedonia were threatening the security of these trade-routes for Rome, and as underlying these causes of hostility was the Roman desire to punish Philip for his alliance with

Hannibal, in 200 B.C. a Second Macedonian War easily broke out.

A Roman army under Flamininus was sent to Greece, but during the first two years of the war nothing decisive was accomplished. Then, in 197 B.C. the two armies, Roman and Macedonian, met at Cynoscephalae in Thessaly, where the Macedonians were utterly defeated and Philip was forced to acknowledge that he was beaten.

Peace was then granted to Philip on the following terms: All the Greek communities in Europe and Asia were to be free and independent; Philip was to withdraw his garrisons from those which had been under his rule and after their evacuation hand them over to the Romans before the date fixed for the Isthmian Games. He was also to withdraw his garrisons from certain cities in Asia. The King was also to restore all prisoners to the Romans, and all his decked ships, save five, were to be surrendered, but he could retain his royal galley, which was all but unmanageable owing to its size. His army was never to exceed five thousand men and he was not allowed to have a single elephant, nor was he permitted to make war beyond his frontiers without the express sanction of the Senate. He was also required to pay a heavy indemnity.[1]

Almost all the Greek states welcomed peace on these terms and Flamininus then went to Corinth.

Here he and the commissioners who had come from Rome for the purpose, discussed for days the measures

[1] Livy, XXXIII, 30.

for securing the freedom of Greece. Again and again Flamininus urged that the whole of Greece must be declared free if they wanted to inspire all with a true affection for Rome and an appreciation of her greatness —if, in fact, they desired to convince the Greeks that they had crossed the seas for the sole purpose of winning their freedom and not of transferring Philip's dominion over them to themselves. The commissioners took no exception to his insistence on making the cities free, but they argued that it would be safer for the cities themselves to remain for a time under the protection of Roman garrisons, rather than to run the risk of the King of Syria seizing them in place of Philip.[1]

It was finally decided that the cities should be free but that a Roman garrison should be placed in three of them until all danger from Syria was over.

The date fixed for the Isthmian Games was now close at hand. These Games always drew vast crowds, owing partly to the love of the nation for a spectacle in which they watched contests of every kind, competitions of artistic skill, and trial of strength and speed, and partly owing to the fact that the situation between two seas made it the common market of Greece and Asia, where supplies were to be obtained of everything necessary or useful to man. But on this occasion it was not the usual attractions that drew people from every part of Greece; they were in a state of keen expectancy, wondering what would be the future position of the country, and what fortune awaited themselves. All sorts of conjectures were formed and openly expressed as to what the Romans would do, but hardly anybody persuaded

[1] Livy, XXXIII, 31.

himself that they would withdraw from Greece altogether.

When the spectators had taken their seats, a herald, accompanied by a trumpeter, stepped forward into the middle of the arena, where the Games are usually opened by the customary formalities, and after a blast from the trumpet had produced silence, made the following announcement: "The Senate of Rome and Flamininus their general, having conquered King Philip and the Macedonians, do now decree and ordain that these states shall be free, shall be released from the payment of tribute, and shall live under their own laws." Then followed the list of all those states which had been under the sway of Philip.

When the herald had finished his proclamation, the feeling of joy was too great for men to take it all in. They hardly ventured to trust their ears, and gazed wonderingly on one another, as though it were an empty dream. Not trusting their ears, they asked those nearest them how their own interests were affected, and as everyone was eager not only to hear but also to see the man who had proclaimed their freedom, the herald was recalled and repeated his message.[1] A shout of joy followed it, so loud that it was heard as far as the sea. The whole assembly rose; there was no further thought of the Games; all were only eager to leap up and salute and address their thanks to the deliverer and champion of Greece.[2]

The universal rejoicing was not simply a temporary excitement; for many days it found expression in thoughts and words of gratitude. "There is," people said, "one nation which at its own cost, through its own exertions, at its own risk has gone to war on behalf of the liberty

[1] Livy, XXXIII, 32.   [2] Plutarch: *Life of Flamininus.*

of others. It renders this service not to those across
its frontiers, or to the peoples of neighbouring states, or
to those who dwell on the same mainland, but it crosses
the seas in order that nowhere in the wide world may
injustice and tyranny exist, but that right and equity
and law may be everywhere supreme.''[1]

Rome had defeated Philip and given Greece her
liberty, but Philip's ally, Antiochus the Great of
Syria, had made no terms with Rome and he now
interfered with the affairs of Greece on the grounds
that the Roman liberation of Greece was only hiding for a time the intention of Rome to rule all the
Greek states. He entered Greece with an army,
saying he had come to free the Greeks from Rome,
but he was driven out of Greece and pursued to Asia
Minor where in 190 B.C. he was defeated at Mag-
nesia by a Roman army under Lucius Scipio, the
brother of Africanus. The power of Syria had
always appeared much greater than it really was
and it never recovered from this defeat. Antiochus
was made to give up all the states he had ruled in
Asia Minor, and Rome exercised a kind of protec-
torate over them. The succeeding kings of Syria
were friendly to Rome but weak, and at length the
last king actually left his territory to Rome in his
will. At his death in 133 B.C. it became the Roman
province of Asia.

During the ten years 200–190 B.C. Rome had
gained great renown in the Eastern Mediterranean.
She had fought and won great battles against the

[1] Livy, XXXIII, 33.

Kings of the East, after which she had set dependent peoples free, but she had taken for herself none of the fruits of victory. The Greek states she had liberated, however, were unable to live at peace among themselves. They were just as jealous of their own independence and just as unable to unite for long, even though it were for their own welfare, as they had been in those earlier days when they were threatened by Persia. Rome was constantly called in to settle their disputes, and by degrees she became more and more their ruler. This state of affairs lasted until Philip died. He was succeeded by his son Perseus, who for a long time had been looking forward to a day when he would unite Greece and free her from the ever increasing power of Rome. The Romans opposed this policy and in consequence another war, the Third, broke out with Macedonia.

It did not last long. The Roman commander was the consul Aemilius Paulus, son of the consul bearing the same name who had been slain at Cannae. He was a man of great ability and a good general. In 168 B.C. he invaded Macedonia and pushed Persus north until they met in battle at Pydna. Perseus was defeated and fled, though he was taken prisoner soon after. It was the end of Macedonia. The state created by Philip II and brought to great renown by Alexander, perished, and a few years later became a Roman province. The Macedonian cities were full of treasures and these were brought by Aemilius to Rome: statues, pictures, magnificent armour, quantities of gold and silver. A great tri-

umph was accorded Aemilius and all these treasures
were borne before him in the procession.[1] In the
midst was drawn the chariot of Perseus, on which
was placed his armour and his crown. A little
behind it were his children, two sons and a daughter,
who were led captives with all their attendants.
Then came Perseus himself, in chains, and dressed in
black, looking as if he were stunned by his humiliation and misfortunes. At the end, accompanied by
troop after troop of cavalry, came Aemilius, seated
on a chariot magnificently adorned, dressed in a
purple and gold robe, and holding a laurel branch in
his right hand. Outwardly it seemed that Aemilius
rejoiced and triumphed, while only Perseus suffered.

He, it is true, was led in chains through the city
of his foes in front of his conqueror's chariot, but Aemilius, resplendent in gold and purple, was suffering too.
Two young sons should have been riding with him and
sharing his glory, but the younger, a boy of about twelve,
died five days before his father's triumph, and the elder,
a boy of about fourteen, died three days after it.[2]

The end of Greek freedom was near at hand.
Rome had to interfere once more in Greek affairs,
and once more there was war. Then in 146 B.C.
Corinth was besieged and captured. The gay,
rich, prosperous trading city shared the fate of
Carthage. It was plundered and burnt to the
ground, and ship after ship sailed out of the harbour

[1] For a full description of this triumph, see Plutarch: *Life of Aemilius Paulus.*
[2] Livy, XLV, 40.

bearing priceless treasures of every kind of Greek art to Rome.

Greece, Macedonia and Asia Minor had been conquered and were now Roman provinces. By 133 B.C. Rome, the Conqueror, was Mistress of the Mediterranean world. This world had known little or no peace during the two centuries that had passed since the death of Alexander the Great. Rome had shown herself great in the science of war. Her next task was to unite this world she had conquered and by bringing to it peace and law and order, show that she was great not only in war, but also in the arts of peace.

CHAPTER XI

How Rome United the Mediterranean World

THE beginning of the third century B.C. found Rome confronted with a difficulty she had not hitherto met: how was she to govern these new possessions of hers across the seas? The first overseas dominion that came to her was Sicily, which was only separated from the mainland by a narrow strait, but a hundred years later, Rome ruled over dominions that extended from the Atlantic Ocean in the West to the Taurus Mountains in the East. These dominions were not governed in the same way as Italy, and they were not placed on an equality with the Italian states. They were divided into provinces, each with its own governor, and were looked upon as being altogether outside Italy, for only the actual peninsula was considered Italy by the Romans.

The first province outside Italy was Sicily, acquired at the end of the First Punic War, and this was soon followed by the acquisition of Sardinia, which with Corsica became the next province. The conquests of the Younger Scipio in Spain, brought Spain under Roman rule and the country was divided into two provinces called Hither and

Farther Spain. Cis-Alpine Gaul was conquered in the interval between the First and Second Punic Wars and later was organized as a province. When Carthage was destroyed in 146 B.C. all the territory in Africa that had been ruled by Carthage became the Roman province of Africa. These were the Roman provinces in the Western Mediterranean, all of which had once been under the control of Carthage, but by becoming subject to Rome, they became Latin provinces, speaking the Latin tongue, and adopting Roman customs and habits of thought.

The Roman conquests in the East were at this time organized as two provinces, that of Macedonia, which included Greece, and that of Asia, which had formerly been the territory ruled over by the King of Syria. These eastern provinces never became Roman in language and thought as did those in the West. They were Greek and their civilization remained Greek both in language and in all their customs and habits of thought.

As each of these provinces was organized it was given a charter, drawn up as a rule by the general who had conquered it with the assistance of a special commission sent from Rome and approved by the Roman Senate. This charter clearly stated the extent and boundaries of the province, the number of towns included in it, the amount of taxation that was to be levied each year on the inhabitants, and other matters connected with the administration of justice in the province. As much self-government as was possible was granted to a province, but it was under the dominion of Rome, it was bound to have the same friends and foes as Rome, it might make no independent alliances with foreign powers, and it might neither declare war nor make peace without the consent of Rome.

Each province was ruled by a Roman magistrate appointed by the Senate, called at first a Praetor and later a Pro-Consul. These governors were bound to obey the constitution of the province as it was set forth in the charter, and they were supposed, like the magistrates in Rome itself, to consult the Senate on any difficult questions that might arise.

The first governors sent by Rome to the provinces were very much respected. They were men of worth and dignity, who impressed those whom they ruled by their able and just administration. But unfortunately, this state of affairs did not last. Though the charters given to the provinces were in the main just and fair, there were not sufficient measures taken to ensure that they would be carried out. The pro-consul was a very independent ruler. In Rome each consul had a colleague who had the right to veto his action did he so wish, but the pro-consul in the province had no such check on his actions, neither was there in a province any tribune of the people with the right of veto. In Rome public money could only be expended at the will of the Senate, whereas the taxes paid in a province could be spent as the pro-consul chose, and there were serious dangers in this lack of any real check on the actions of the governor. In the eyes of the provincials the pro-consul appeared as sole ruler. In the East he generally lived in the palace of the deposed king and he gradually surrounded himself with all the state of an eastern monarch. To keep up this state he often over-taxed the provincials, and it became a scandal of the time that a governor would go to his province a poor man and return rich.

This first attempt at provincial government made by Rome was not altogether successful. Rome was a city-state, and no city-state had yet succeeded in ruling well for any length of time a greater world beyond its shores. Unless Rome could overcome the limitations of a city-state and transform herself into an imperial city, she could not hope to endure. Unless she learned to govern her provinces in their interests and not in her own, unless she could make them feel they were part of one whole, each contributing its share to the common welfare, she could not expect to hold her empire together.

The task was a tremendous one, and on the success or failure of Rome depended the preservation of the great civilization we have inherited. The story of the next century is the story of how Rome succeeded in this task. Both within and without she was threatened by dangers so great that she nearly perished ere her task was done, but she succeeded in the end, and the ancient city-state on the seven hills by the Tiber, became the imperial city that for nearly five hundred years not only held together a great empire, but was the means for preserving for all time the civilization of the ancient world.

CHAPTER XII

THE CENTURY OF REVOLUTION WHICH MADE ROME AN EMPIRE

I. ROME IN 133 B. C.

IT has been said that up to this time the history of Rome had been the history of "great achievements done by men who were themselves not great." Looking back over the nearly four centuries which had passed since the Roman Republic was founded, we see great patriots, men who were ready to sacrifice all that made life dear to them for the good of the state, men of undaunted courage, of rare discipline, steadfastness and self-control, but no great generals who matched Hannibal, and no statesman of genius. But from the year 133 B.C. onwards, the history of Rome becomes the history not only of a great people, but also of great individuals through whose deeds and leadership that people achieved greatness.

No nation comes out of a war unscathed, and if the war is long, the wounds it leaves are very deep. Time will heal them, as it heals all wounds, but it depends on the wisdom of the leaders of a nation as to how they will heal, or what scars will be

left. War devastates fair lands, takes the lives
of men, and cruelly maims for all their days upon
earth those who were young and strong. These
things are evil, but there is one thing more evil still
which comes as a result of war, and that is not
the harm wrought to land, nor yet to life, but to
that which makes life itself worth living, to the
spirit of man. And this evil came to Rome.

The next hundred years were a dark period in
Roman history. At first, outwardly, all seemed
well. The East, Greece, Africa, Spain, all these
rich lands belonged to Rome, and they poured their
riches into the city of their conquerors. Wealth,
such as the early Roman had never dreamed of, and
luxuries of which he had had no conception, came to
Rome as a result of her conquest of the Mediterranean. But this wealth brought evils in its train.
In the early days of Rome the differences between
the patrician and the plebeian had been largely
those of birth and privilege, not of wealth or of standards of living. Now the differences were chiefly
those of wealth, and the great necessity for those
who were candidates for the highest offices of state
was unlimited money with which to provide spec-
tacular entertainments for the populace whose votes
they desired.

Before the Punic Wars Rome had been chiefly
an agricultural state, but the wars had almost
ruined the farmers. In the old days the land belonging to Rome had been divided into small farms, and
every freeman who lived in the country had owned
a piece of land which he cultivated and on which

he built his home. As the long years of war went by, these farmers had been called away to join the army. Many had never returned, no one was left to work the farms, and they were either ruined or else bought up by some rich man who employed large numbers of slaves to do the work.

This increase in the use of slave-labour was another result of the wars. The conquest of the Mediterranean had turned enormous numbers of the nations of the East into slaves, and the Roman land-owners found it cheaper to employ slaves than to pay wages to freemen. This sent large numbers of the latter into the city where they were attracted by the cheap food, the excitement of the shows and entertainments and the hope of making more money than was possible in the country.

These things, the increase of wealth and its use to purchase luxuries, the increase of slave-labour instead of that of freemen, the change from an agricultural to a city and commercial life, were changes in Rome brought about by the wars which had made her mistress of the Mediterranean. But of more far-reaching consequences than any of these was the great change which was taking place in the Roman character. The old Roman had been trained and disciplined in a school of the strictest obedience and loyalty. He had been taught to be stern and austere towards himself, and this had made him relentless in his severity towards others. He was upright and honourable, but narrow in his outlook and saw little beyond his own ancient traditions. To such men there had now come an extraordinary increase of power and responsibility. The conquest of the Mediterranean had brought with it new ways of looking at life, new ways of thinking, new ideas, new pleasures. The East with its charm, its mystery, its luxury, its wealth, lay open before them, and the old rugged Roman temperament was assailed by temptations it had never known before. When pleasures and luxuries are easy to possess, the sense of duty and of discipline may be weakened, and this happened in Rome. Pleasure became more important than duty, to live one's own life more important than the self-effacement required by the discipline of the early Republic.

One sturdy old Roman fought against the new spirit that was coming over Rome, Marcus Cato the Censor. He had been brought up as a farmer, and at the age of seventeen had entered the army to fight against Hannibal. He had served under all the great Roman generals of the time and had campaigned in Africa, Spain and the East as well as in Italy. It was he who had urged the destruction of Carthage, and he was as ceaseless and as insistent a foe of all the new ideas that came out of the East as he had been of the Carthaginian. Harsh, narrow, old-fashioned and holding in utter contempt everything that was new, he possessed, nevertheless, many of the sturdy, upright, honourable characteristics that had made Rome great.

II. THE REFORMERS: THE GRACCHI

The first serious troubles that now confronted Rome, were those connected with the land. Not only had the rich landowners bought up the smaller farms and employed slave labour instead of that of freemen, but they had even seized and occupied much of the public land, that according to the old Roman custom should have been distributed amongst the poorer people, so that a great deal of land was now owned by a few men.

The discontent created by these agrarian troubles had become very serious, when a young Roman noble came forward with plans for improving the state of affairs. This noble was Tiberius Gracchus. He was the son of a former consul and of Cornelia, the daughter of Scipio Africanus. His father had died when he and his younger brother Caius were children, but Cornelia brought them up and educated them with such care that they became two of the most distinguished young nobles of the time. Cornelia was proud of her sons, and it is said that once when a friend was visiting her, and displaying her jewels before her, asked her to bring out hers that she might see them, Cornelia sent for her sons, and proudly said to her friend: "These are my jewels." Cornelia was very ambitious that her sons should become distinguished in Rome. She herself was honoured wherever she went as the daughter of Scipio, but this did not satisfy her, and she used often to ask her sons when the time was coming that Romans would cease calling her the daughter of Scipio and would call her instead the "Mother of the Gracchi."

Tiberius was the older of the two brothers by nine years. He was able and accomplished, of

high character, and inspired by the old Roman
sense of duty, but he was young and inexperienced
and in his enthusiasm he was unwise in his methods
of attempting reform. In 133 B.C. he was elected
Tribune, and he at once proposed a law which would
first restore all the public land to the state, and then
divide it fairly amongst the people, but which would
limit the amount of land any one man might hold.
In pleading for the passing of this law he said:

" The savage beasts in Italy have their particular dens,
they have their places of repose and refuge; but the men
who bear arms, and expose their lives for the safety of
their country, enjoy in the meantime nothing more in
it but the air and light; and, having no houses or settlements of their own, are constrained to wander from
place to place with their wives and children." He told
them that the commanders were guilty of a ridiculous
error, when, at the head of their armies, they exhorted
the common soldiers to fight for their sepulchres and
altars; when not any amongst so many Romans is
possessed of either altar or monument, neither have
they any houses of their own, or hearths of their ancestors
to defend. They fought indeed and were slain, but it
was to maintain the luxury and the wealth of other men.
They were styled the masters of the world, but in the
meantime had not one foot of ground which they could
call their own.[1]

The law met with great opposition from the nobles
and the Senate. Some of the landowners maintained
that they had bought the land and that it was unjust
to deprive them of what they considered was honestly

[1] Plutarch: *Life of Tiberius Gracchus.*

theirs, and that in taking the land from them, their money also was being taken; others said that their forefathers had bought the land and that the graves of their ancestors were in the ground which was to be taken from them, and that this was an insult to the dead as well as a hardship to the living. On the other hand the poor complained that it was through their services in the army that the land had been won for Rome, yet they were robbed of their own lawful share in what should have been common property, and they were vehemently opposed to the wide use that was being made of slave-labour which threw so many freemen out of employment. There was great excitement in Rome when it came to voting on the law, some supporting it and some opposing it in every possible way. Tiberius Gracchus, himself, was convinced that nothing could do so much to improve the conditions in Rome as the passing of this law, and being young and inexperienced, he paid no attention to the difficulties in the way.

The opposition of the Senate was very great, and one of the tribunes was persuaded to veto the bill which would prevent it passing, as the unanimous consent of all the tribunes was required before a bill could become law. In his determination to get it passed, Tiberius forgot all prudence and if it could be done in no other way, he was even willing to use unconstitutional means rather than see it defeated. He brought in a bill, which actually became law, depriving of office the tribune who had vetoed the land bill, on the grounds that a man who could veto such a law was no friend to the people and was not fit to hold office. Then he worked to get himself re-elected as tribune, though this, too, was unconstitutional. This act brought him more enemies than he had already, for he was now accused of wanting to make himself master of the state. The nobles called him a traitor, the people who regarded him as their friend said he was a patriot. After a stormy meeting in the Senate, the nobles rushed out and a riot followed.

As the nobles

were persons of the greatest authority in the city, the common people did not venture to obstruct their passing, but were rather so eager to clear the way for them, that they tumbled over one another in haste. The attendants they brought with them had furnished themselves with clubs and staves from their houses, and they themselves picked up the feet and other fragments of stools and chairs, which were broken by the hasty flight of the common people. Thus armed, they made towards Tiberius, knocking down those whom they found in front of him, and those were soon wholly dispersed and many of them slain. Tiberius tried to save himself by flight. As he was running, he was stopped by one who caught hold of him by the gown; but he threw it off and fled in his under-garment only. And stumbling over those who before had been knocked down, as he was endeavouring to get up again, a tribune, one of his colleagues, was observed to give him the first fatal stroke, by hitting him on the head with the foot of a stool.[1]

[1] Plutarch: *Life of Tiberius Gracchus.*

Other blows followed and Tiberius was killed. The bitter feeling against him did not stop with his murder. Though his brother begged for his body that he might bury it, burial was denied by the Senators, who had the body thrown into the river together with the bodies of others who had been slain in the riot. Some of the murdered tribune's friends were slain and others were banished, and one was taken before the consuls to be examined as to what had happened and what part he had taken in the riot.

He freely confessed that he had done, without scruple, whatever Tiberius bade him. "What," cried one of the consuls, "if Tiberius had bidden you burn the Capitol, would you have burnt it?" His first answer was that Tiberius would never have ordered any such thing; but being pressed with the same question by several, he declared, "If Tiberius had commanded it, it would have been right for me to do it; for he never would have commanded it, if it had not been for the people's good."[1]

The murder of Tiberius Gracchus was the first time, since the kings had been driven out of Rome, that blood had been shed in any quarrel amongst the Romans. Other difficulties had been settled peaceably, each side giving up something, but never before had men tried to bring about changes by illegal means. Tiberius had acted from the highest motives, but he broke the law, and attempting to gain his ends by violence, he was met by violence in

[1] Plutarch: *Life of Tiberius Gracchus.*

return. He passionately desired to bring back content to the people and well-being to the state, but
the methods he used, instead of reform, brought
revolution.

Eight years passed, and in 123 B.C. Caius Gracchus, the brother of Tiberius, was made Tribune. He
would have preferred to spend his life more quietly
than was possible for a tribune or for anyone who
accepted public office, but it is said that after he had
expressed a wish to live privately,

his brother appeared to him in a dream, and calling him
by his name, said, "Why do you tarry, Caius? There
is no escape; one life and one death is appointed for us
both, to spend the one and to meet the other in the
service of the people." [1]

Caius Gracchus was a greater man than his
brother. He was more experienced when he took
office, a reformer, but practical, and a leader of
men. Having once accepted office he threw himself with all his heart into work for Rome, and he
amazed everyone by his capacity for work and by
his ceaseless energy.

He at once proposed certain laws which he considered were necessary for the welfare of the state.

The first was concerning the public lands, which were
to be divided amongst the poor citizens; another was
concerning the common soldiers, that they should be
clothed at the public charge, without any diminution
of their pay, and that none should be obliged to serve

[1] Plutarch: *Life of Caius Gracchus.*

in the army who was not full seventeen years old,
another gave the same right to all the Italians in general, of voting at elections, as was enjoyed by the
citizens of Rome; a fourth related to the price of corn,
which was to be sold at a lower rate than formerly to
the poor; and a fifth regulated the courts of justice,
greatly reducing the power of the senators. For hitherto, in all causes, senators only sat as judges and were,
therefore, much dreaded by the Roman knights and
people. But Caius joined three hundred ordinary citizens of equestrian rank with the senators, who were
three hundred likewise in number, and ordained that the
judicial authority should be equally invested in the six
hundred.[1]

The knights, men of the equestrian order, were
originally the Roman citizens rich enough to provide
war-horses; at this time they had become the rich
business men of Rome.

Caius Gracchus met with a great deal of opposition
and he did not succeed in carrying all these laws,
but they show his aims and how he recognized the
things which most needed reform. The law regu-
lating the price of corn was passed, but it had an
unfortunate result, which Caius had not foreseen.
The corn was sold at less than its proper value, so
that the state was partly feeding the people, which
tended to make them paupers rather than self-
respecting citizens. The law requiring half the
judges to be men belonging to the equestrian order
was also passed. Caius would have liked to have
increased the numbers of the senators for all their

[1] Plutarch: *Life of Caius Gracchus.*

duties, and not only when they sat as judges, for
he believed the Senate needed wider interests and
new ideas. He was not successful in this, but what
he did achieve very much weakened its prestige and
power. Caius was not successful in giving the Italians full share in Roman citizenship. This measure shows him at his best, perhaps, as a statesman,
but he was ahead of his time. Public opinion was
not ready for such a change and the prejudices
against admitting all Italians to the same privileges
as Romans were still so strong, that the proposal of
such a law raised up many enemies for Caius. Another proposal of his which met with opposition, was
that for founding colonies of farmers in various
places, especially one which he wanted to establish
at Carthage. These were all wise measures. It
would have been a good thing to get some of the
poorer people away from Rome to other places,
where they would have found the means to become
prosperous and self-respecting, and by giving equal
rights to all Italians, the day would have been
hastened when they all would have felt themselves
united as Roman citizens, all a part of one Italian
empire. But the time was not yet ripe. Romans
were not ready to share their citizenship with others,
and when the day came for voting on the bill, there
was tumult and rioting in the streets. Caius was
going out as usual, unarmed, except for a sharp
dagger, and fearless. His wife knew how high was
the feeling against him and entreated him to stay
at home, but he would not be kept back and went
out to meet his fate, the death that awaited him,

as it had awaited Tiberius, in the service of the people. A price had been set upon his head, and finding himself in the utmost danger, he fled to the Aventine, but he was pursued and slain, his head cut off and his body, like that of Tiberius his brother, thrown into the river.

So perished the Gracchi. Their mother, Cornelia, bore the loss of her two sons nobly and courageously, and she would speak of them "without any tears or signs of grief, and give the full account of all their deeds and misfortunes, as if she had been relating the history of some ancient heroes,"[1] so nobly did her spirit conquer her sorrow.

As for the people of Rome, they soon realized that they had deserted and slain the two men who might have saved them,

and they did not fail before long to let everyone see what respect and veneration they had for the memory of the Gracchi. They ordered their statues to be made and set up in public view; they consecrated the places where they were slain, and thither brought the first fruits of everything, according to the season of the year, to make their offerings. Many came likewise thither to their devotions, and daily worshipped there, as at the temple of the gods.[2]

III. MILITARY RULE

(a) *Marius*

The Gracchi were dead, and for a long time it seemed as if Rome were given over to all that was

---

[1] Plutarch: *Life of Caius Gracchus.*   [2] Ibid.

corrupt, unjust and evil. The government was neither just nor able. The land troubles had not been settled, and the cheap corn filled Rome with people who made little or no effort to do any work and who were a source of danger to the state, for they were ready to follow any popular leader who promised for the moment to give them what they wanted.

If Rome could not govern herself at this time, still less could she govern her distant dominions. She had not found it very difficult to govern her first overseas provinces. Sicily was separated from the mainland by only the narrowest of straits and on a clear day the headlands of Sardinia and Corsica could be seen from the shores of Italy. But now Rome had conquered lands that reached to the length and breadth of the Mediterranean. Long sea voyages were necessary to reach some of these lands, and no true Roman liked the sea. Cato once said, that one of the things he most regretted in his life was that he had ever travelled by water when he might have gone by land. These sea voyages were not only long, but perilous, for the Romans had no real fleet, and the sea swarmed with pirates. Rome was beset by dangers, both within and without. Could she survive? and if she survived, would there be enough of the old spirit left to make her great?

It has already been said that the history of Rome during these perilous hundred years was determined by the leadership of individual men. Their power was not always used for good, but through their deeds Rome learnt lessons, often bitter ones, which made her realize that she was an imperial city, the capital no longer of a city-state, but of an empire.

Rome was now confronted with three grave perils. The first concerned her frontiers. Italy was in great danger of being overrun by barbarian invaders, who were coming down from the Eastern Alps and threatening the destruction of some of the fairest lands under Roman dominion. If the frontiers broke down, Roman civilization was doomed. The answer to this peril was the career of Marius.

The next danger came from the East, where Mithridates, King of Pontus, was inciting the Greek states to revolt and threatening the creation in the East of a rival power to Rome. Could Rome survive if her empire were thus cut in two? The answer to this peril was the career first of Sulla and then of Pompey.

But greater than these external dangers, was that which threatened Rome from within. There were now two distinct parties in Rome, that of the Senate, and that of the people. From the foundation of the Republic down to the beginning of the last century B.C. the Senate had been the only permanent governing body in Rome and all the more important questions were settled by the Senate. It determined not only all domestic but also all foreign policy, and though war was actually declared and treaties ratified by the people, it was the Senate who presented these measures to them. It was the Senate that controlled the government of conquered lands, that ratified the charters of newly-formed provinces, that received foreign ambassadors, and made alliances with foreign powers, and above all, it was the Senate that controlled the finances of the state. The history of the Senate was rooted and grounded in that of the early Republic, and down to the end of the Punic Wars, a Roman Senator represented the best ideals of the early Roman: he was a man with a stern sense of duty, of upright and honourable character, of devoted patriotism, of ripe wisdom.

As the Senate was a small body, resident in Rome, it could easily be summoned. The assemblies of the people, on the other hand, were not so easily brought together. Large numbers of the citizens were away in camp, after the conquest of the Mediterranean many of them were away from Rome on business in the provinces, and even when they did meet in their assemblies, they had neither the knowledge nor the experience that were required to decide on the important matters brought before them. This had resulted in the steady increase in the power of the Senate, a power which it began to use for its own advantage, and which by the last century of the Republic had become the selfish rule in its own interests of one class.

In opposition to this narrow and selfish rule of the Senate was the popular party, the party of the people, and the third danger which now confronted Rome was the growing strife between these two parties. In governing the city and the Roman dominions, whose voice was to be supreme? that of the Senate or of the people? and if of the people, how was that voice to be made known and what form was the government to take? How was this question to be settled, and how much Roman blood was to be shed before the struggle was over? The answer to this peril was the career of Julius Caesar and his struggle with Pompey.

A few years after the murder of Caius Gracchus, Rome found herself with a war on her hands in Africa, which lasted from 111–105 B.C. The throne of Numidia had been seized by Jugurtha, a brave, able soldier, but a corrupt, crafty, treacherous man. With no sense of honour himself, he expected none in others, and wherever he went, he either corrupted men by bribes, or if that means failed, he prevented them from harming him by having them assassinated. He murdered his kinsman, who should by right have been King, and seized the kingdom. The Numidians, allies of the Romans, appealed to Rome for help, and ambassadors were sent to Africa to inquire into the matter. But they accomplished nothing and returned to Rome, bribed, probably, by Jugurtha not to interfere. When Jugurtha next murdered another of the rightful heirs, Rome was roused to more vigorous action. War was declared and an army sent to Africa. But Jugurtha pretended to surrender and bribed the generals to make peace, whereupon the consul and his army returned to Rome. When the means by which peace had been made were known in Rome, there was great indignation amongst the people, but what the Senators would do was a matter of doubt. At this time a man named Memmius was one of the tribunes. He was eloquent and had great influence when he spoke, and he pleaded now with the people to turn from their corrupt leaders and to refuse acquiescence in base and dishonourable acts, that were unworthy of their ancient faith and honour. He reminded them how they had allowed those who might have helped them to be murdered, and that their deaths had never been avenged, and of how, through sloth and indolence, they had permitted a few men to rule without honour or justice. He advised the people to summon Jugurtha to Rome, and to find out whether it were true that Roman honour had been sacrificed to the love of gold.

This advice was followed and Jugurtha was summoned to Rome. He came, but in spite of more bribery, he did not succeed in justifying himself before the Senate, and when news came to Rome that he had caused his last rival for the throne to be assassinated, the Senate ordered him to leave Italy. He departed, but "after going out of the gates, it is said that he often looked back at Rome in silence and finally said, 'A city for sale and doomed to speedy destruction if it finds a purchaser.'"[1]

Metellus was now consul in Rome, and in 109 B.C. he was sent to Numidia to wage war against Jugurtha. He had some successes, but was unable to subdue him entirely. There was in the army of Metellus a young officer called Caius Marius. He was of peasant birth and had served in the Roman army in Spain under Scipio Africanus as a common soldier, but his great ability soon made him

[1] Sallust: *War with Jugurtha*, XXXV,

noticed by his general. He became an officer and rose high in Scipio's favour. It is said that

once when at an entertainment a question arose about commanders, and one of the company asked Scipio where the Romans, after him, should obtain such another general, Scipio, gently clapping Marius on the shoulder as he sat next him, replied, "Here, perhaps." So promising was his early youth of greatness, and so discerning was Scipio to detect the distant future in the present first beginnings.[1]

This was the officer, young and ambitious, who was now in Africa with Metellus. Marius soon became very popular with the soldiers, for he was not only a brave and capable officer, but he gained their affections by sharing all their hardships, eating the same bread, lying on the same ordinary bed, assisting in the hard work of digging trenches. "Before long both Africa and Rome were filled with his fame, and some wrote home from the army that the war with Africa would never be brought to a conclusion unless they chose Caius Marius consul."[2] All this was unpleasing to Metellus and he grew very jealous of Marius.

The war was still dragging on, and it was very clear that only one thing would end it: the capture or the death of Jugurtha. Marius asked Metellus for leave to go to Rome and stand for the consulship, to which request he got the scoffing answer:

"You, Sir, design to leave us to go home and stand for the consulship, and will not be content to wait and

[1] Plutarch: *Life of Caius Marius.*   [2] Ibid.

be consul with this boy of mine?" Metellus's son being a mere boy at the time. Yet for all this, Marius
being very importunate to be gone, after several delays,
he was dismissed about twelve days before the election
of consuls; and performed that long journey from the
camp to the seaport of Utica in two days and a night,
and there doing sacrifice before he went on shipboard,
it is said the augur told him that heaven promised him
some incredible good fortune, and such as was beyond
all expectation. Marius, not a little elated with this
good omen, began his voyage, and in four days, with a
favourable wind, passed the sea; he was welcomed with
great joy by the people, and being brought into the
Assembly by one of the tribunes, sued for the consulship, inveighing in all ways against Metellus, and promising either to slay Jugurtha or take him alive.[1]

Marius was elected consul, and he returned to
Africa where he took command of the army. He
captured town after town until at last Jugurtha, the
crafty, treacherous King, was himself entrapped by
craft by Sulla, a young noble serving in the army
under Marius, and taken prisoner. The war was
over. Marius returned to Rome, where he was
given a great triumph and Jugurtha, clad in his
royal robes, was led captive before his conqueror's
chariot. Then he was thrown into prison, his
clothes torn off him, and naked and alone, he was
left to die of starvation. Romans had no pity for
their enemies.

The election of Marius as consul was a very
important act on the part of the Roman people.

[1] Plutarch: *Life of Caius Marius.*

For the first time in their history, the people had taken charge of a foreign war. Hitherto all foreign affairs had been determined by the Senate and the magistrates, but by deliberately electing Marius to take the place of Metellus, the people themselves had made their voice supreme in the city. And further, by electing Marius as consul in order that he, and he only, might be chief general, the people had taken over the control of the army. By this act, the leader of the army became a popular leader. If he were a strong man, he might gain extraordinary power, and there were tremendous possibilities, both for good and for evil, in this state of affairs.

After the war with Jugurtha, Marius set himself to re-organize and to train the army, and in a very short time he had completely changed its character. Up to this time the Roman army, like all the earlier armies of the ancient world, had been a citizen army, made up of men who served when there was a war and at the close of it went back to their farms or their business. Such soldiers often had no pay, they served because their country was in peril and the only reward for which they asked, was to be allowed to take their full share of danger in defending their country and their homes from the invader. But all this had changed now. Rome waged wars far away from her own shores. The land troubles had reduced the number of farmers and of freemen work·ing on their own land, and the men who lived in the city had lost that sense of loyalty to the state which had characterized the early Roman. The government, fallen into the hands of a few rich men, had become unscrupulous and corrupt and inspired neither confidence nor loyalty. Such being the state of affairs, Marius set himself to create a professional army, one that, serving for pay and having no other occupation, would always be ready and would follow its general wherever he should lead it. Men from all over the Roman world were taken into this army, and Marius

disciplined and trained them, giving them practice in long marches, and running of every sort, and compelling every man to carry his own baggage and prepare his own food; insomuch that thenceforward laborious soldiers, who did their work silently without grumbling, had the name of "Marius's mules." [1]

As a result of this training and discipline, the army became a magnificent human defence against the enemies of Rome.

Rome needed such a defence. During the years when Marius had been in Africa, barbarian tribes from beyond the Alps had been threatening the safety of the northern frontiers of Italy. There was grave danger that unless the frontiers could be defended, these tribes would invade Italy. The Romans of the time thought chiefly of the devastation of their land and of the menace to their dominion, but there was more than that. If the frontiers held, the civilization of the Greek and Roman world would have time to strike deeper roots, to develop, to become sturdy and strong; if they did not hold, that great civilization might perish.

[1] Plutarch: *Life of Caius Marius.*

The chief of these tribes were the Cimbri and Teutones, nomad peoples who had been wandering near the Roman borders for some time. They travelled from place to place with their wives and children and all their belongings. They were tall, fierce, fair-haired warriors, brave fighters, but savage and brutal after a victory. When these tribes came down from the North, they approached Italy by the Eastern Alps, but instead of crossing the mountains they marched to the west and entered Gaul. Rome sent out a consul with an army to drive them away from the Italian frontiers, but the Romans were defeated and the barbarians stayed in Gaul. Army after army went out to meet the barbarians, and five times were the Romans defeated with appalling losses. Then it was that Marius returned triumphantly to Rome, bringing with him Jugurtha in chains, and he was at once re-elected consul.

For some reason or other the barbarians, feeling, perhaps, secure after their victories, made no more warlike moves for a time, and it was in this breathing-space that Marius trained his army. Year after year, though contrary to all Roman law and tradition, he was re-elected consul. The chief power in Rome had passed to the army, and whoever had the army behind him was now the most powerful man in Rome.

At length the barbarians showed signs of preparing again for war. Marius marched to meet them and to prevent them, if possible, from crossing the Alps. He met the Teutones first. The Roman camp was strongly fortified, and Marius made the soldiers take turns in guarding it, so that they might become accustomed to the sight of the enemy, to the harsh sound of their voices, and to their weapons and the way in which they used them. They grew accustomed, too, to the strange sight of the barbarian women who fought as well as the men. This not only took away from the soldiers any fear they may have had of the barbarians, but it increased their enthusiasm to fight them, for the barbarians were not only plundering the country round, but attacking the outposts of the Roman camp itself, and calling out taunts and insults to the Roman soldiers. One body marched about the camp for six days, the men calling out that they were setting out for Rome, which they intended to capture, and they asked the Romans if they had any messages to send to their wives.

At length Marius was ready and he gave battle. The Teutones were utterly defeated and their army destroyed.

After the battle, Marius chose out from amongst the barbarians' spoils and arms those that were whole and handsome, and that would make the greatest show in his triumph; the rest he heaped upon a large pile and offered a very splendid sacrifice. Whilst the army stood round about with their arms and garlands, himself attired (as the fashion is on such occasions) in the purple-bordered robe, and taking a lighted torch, and with both hands lifting it up towards heaven, he was then going to put it to the pile, when some friends were espied with all haste coming to him on horseback. Upon which everyone remained in silence and expectation. They, upon their coming up, leapt off and saluted Marius, bringing him the news of his fifth consulship, and delivered his letters to that effect. This gave the addition of no small joy to the solemnity; and whilst the soldiers clashed their arms and shouted, the officers again crowned Marius with a large laurel wreath, and he thus set fire to the pile, and finished his sacrifice.[1]

A year went by and Marius, ever on the watch for any movement of the barbarians, found that the Cimbri were now trying to pass into Italy. These barbarians sent ambassadors to Marius demanding that he should give them

some part of the country for themselves and their brethren, and cities for them to inhabit. When Marius inquired of the ambassadors who their brethren were, upon their saying, the Teutones, all that were present began to laugh; and Marius scoffingly answered them, "Do not trouble yourselves for your brethren, for we have already provided lands for them, which they shall possess for ever." The ambassadors, understanding the mockery, broke into insults, and threatened that the Cimbri would make him pay for this.[2]

During this year the Cimbri had been living in a rich and fertile country which had not been invaded for long years, and they had been living on good food and sweet wines. The climate was softer and milder than that to which they had been accustomed, and so these barbarians were in no very good fighting condition. Marius knew this, and

[1] Plutarch: *Life of Caius Marius.*   [2] Ibid.

knowing, too, that his own men were in perfect condition, he gave battle to the Cimbri, feeling certain of victory. It was a hard battle, the barbarian women fighting as fiercely as the men, but the Roman victory was complete, and the Cimbri were destroyed as the Teutones had been. Marius had saved the frontiers of Italy and Rome was safe, as far as danger from the barbarians of the North was concerned. They were to come again, but not until five hundred years had passed were they to be any serious menace to Rome. It was Marius who had driven them back, and when he returned to the city, he was hailed as the saviour of Rome. "Everyone in their feasts and rejoicings with their wives and children made offerings and libations in honour of 'The Gods and Marius,'"[1] and so great was the enthusiasm for him that in 100 B.C. in defiance of all law, he was elected consul for the sixth time.

Marius was a good general, but he was not as good a statesman. Up to the time of his sixth consulship all his work for Rome had been as a general in the field, but he now found himself confronted with political difficulties in Rome, with which he was not capable of dealing. At the beginning of his career he seems to have been a rough, honest soldier, honest, in that in a corrupt age he never took bribes and never himself descended to acts of treachery, though he did not refuse to make use of men whose methods were less honourable than his. But Marius was not a great enough man to

[1] Plutarch: *Life of Caius Marius.*

stand the test of success. His ability as general brought him the loyal obedience of those who served under him, and the very fact that he knew he was needed

gave him power and dignity; but in civil affairs, when he despaired of getting the first place, he was forced to betake himself to the favour of the people, never caring to be a good man so that he were but a great one.[1]

Success had turned his head, and from now to the end of his career he seems to have thought more of his own ambition than of any service he could render the state.

One of the tests of greatness is the power to seize and use rightly opportunities when they come. Rome was torn by political strife. Who was to have the supreme voice in affairs? The Senate, corrupt, incapable of inspiring loyalty, or the people, powerful enough to elect a general as consul in spite of the Senate, yet weak and helpless without a leader? Marius had saved Rome from her external enemies and her frontiers were safe. The opportunity to save Rome from the greater enemies of corruption and injustice that were threatening the life of her spirit was now his. The opportunity came to Marius, but he was not great enough to take it, and he let it pass. From being worshipped almost as a god, he grew more and more unpopular, for during his sixth consulship riots and disturbances increased in the city, some of them resulting in mur-

[1] Plutarch: *Life of Caius Marius.*

der in the streets, and for all this Marius was blamed. At the end of the year he decided to leave Rome for a time and he withdrew to Asia. Marius had failed when his country was in most need of a leader, and because of his failure Rome was brought into the gravest peril.

(b) *The Struggle between Marius and Sulla*

Marius had withdrawn for a time from Rome, but his absence did not settle the question that was uppermost in the minds of the Romans, the question as to whose voice was to be supreme in Rome. Not only was this question not yet answered, but another was pressing for an answer. For a long time the Italian allies had been growing more and more discontented and had been demanding that they be given equal rights with the Romans. The Roman was proud of his citizenship, and in whatever part of the Roman world he found himself, a Roman citizen had definite privileges and rights. A Roman citizen condemned to death or to be flogged had the right, under the old Roman law, of appealing to the people, and by the same law he could not be flogged until he had been condemned. This pride in Roman citizenship lasted long after the Roman Republic had come to an end, and as long as the Roman Empire itself lasted. When the apostle St. Paul had been taken prisoner by the Roman officer at Jerusalem, the chief captain, not knowing that he was a Roman citizen, gave orders that he should be flogged, the usual punishment for those who were supposed to have had any share in rioting. As St. Paul was being bound, he said to the centurion who was standing by: "Is it lawful for you to scourge a man that is a Roman and uncondemned?" When the centurion heard that, he went and told the chief captain, saying: "Take heed what thou doest; for this man is a Roman." Then the chief captain came, and said unto him: "Tell me, art thou a Roman?" He said, "Yea." And the chief captain answered, "With a great sum obtained I this freedom." And Paul said, "But I was free born."[1]

The Romans were not only proud, but also very jealous of their citizenship and they were not at all willing to grant it to those who lived in other parts of Italy. The Italians, however, spoke the same language as the Romans, and were subjects of the same dominion, they paid taxes like the Romans, they fought in the same armies. They were as well educated and as well fitted to share in the responsibilities and privileges of Roman citizenship as those who lived in Rome.

The Italians had also been very faithful allies of Rome. Many a time had they been tempted to desert her, but their loyalty held firm, and even during the days when Hannibal occupied Italy, very few of them had deserted Rome. Their allegiance had not wavered when Rome was in danger, but now they felt that as they had fought in the armies of Rome, and had helped to save Rome from the enemies that had threatened her, they had the right

[1] Acts XXII, 25-28.

to share in the government and in all the privileges of Roman citizens. The Italians found a champion in Marcus Livius Drusus, who in 91 B.C. proposed a law which would have given all Italians equal rights with Romans, the power to vote in Rome and other privileges. All Rome was indignant at such a suggestion and Drusus, like the Gracchi, was murdered. Again the Romans, by their own act, got rid of a man who might have helped them.

The murder of Drusus was the signal for an outbreak on the part of the Italians, and for two years (90–88 B.C.) Rome was engaged in what was called the Social War or the War of the Allies. As Rome would not give them the full rights of Roman citizens, the Italians of Central Italy determined to set up a republic for themselves, one that should be a rival power to Rome. It seemed at first as if the Italians might be successful, and at the end of a year, realizing that it was essential that those allies who had remained faithful to Rome should still be loyal, a law was passed giving equal rights to all Italians who had not taken up arms against Rome. Not long after the law was extended to include all Italians who would lay down their arms within sixty days. This measure so weakened the Italians, that by the end of another year their power was broken and the war was ended.

Marius had returned to Rome on the outbreak of the Social War and had fought in it, but he was growing older and it was Sulla, the patrician officer by whose craft Jugurtha had been finally entrapped and captured, who gained most of the successes.

Sulla was in all ways the opposite of Marius and from the beginning there had been jealousy between the two, a jealousy that now brought the two men into direct conflict with each other.

When the war was over, Rome found herself at the mercy of these two leaders, who were now struggling for the chief power in the state. And who were these leaders, and by what authority did they intend to gain their power, and having gained it, to rule? They were generals, and their sole support was the army. Both men sought to make friends and to gain adherents. Marius declared himself the champion of the Italians and the friend of the plebeians, Sulla, on the other hand, sought his supporters among the old patrician families and the Senate. Marius was on the side of right and justice, but he upheld it by bloodshed and violence and he was defeated.

The first open conflict between Marius and Sulla came in 88 B.C. After his successes in the Social War, Sulla had been made consul. The revolution in Italy had been brought to an end, but war was now threatening in another part of the Roman world. Mithridates, King of Pontus, had secured for himself the control of Asia Minor and was successfully persuading the Greek cities to join him. Rome did not hesitate in sending out an army, but who was to lead it? The Senate appointed Sulla, the Assembly of the people, Marius.

Marius immediately made preparations to start and sent two tribunes to Sulla, demanding that he hand over to him the chief command of the army, and then there happened what had never happened in Rome before. Sulla, at the head of an army, marched to Rome and settled the question between him and Marius by force. This act meant that the supreme power in the state was with neither the Senate nor the people, but with a military master who had complete control of the army. Henceforward, the struggle for power was to be between men and not parties, and for good or for ill, Rome was to be ruled by successful commanders.

Sulla was successful in his struggle with Marius. He was given the command in the East and Marius was banished. He fled from Rome to the coast and escaped in a small boat. But no sooner had it set sail, than the sailors declared they would have nothing to do with him and they put him ashore. Then they

weighed anchor and departed, as thinking it neither honourable to deliver Marius into the hands of those that sought him, nor safe to protect him.

He, thus deserted by all, lay a good while silently on the shore; at length collecting himself, he advanced with pain and difficulty, without any path, till, wading through deep bogs and ditches full of water and mud, he came upon the hut of an old man that worked in the fens, and falling at his feet besought him to assist and preserve one who, if he escaped the present danger, would make him returns beyond his expectation. The poor man, whether he had formerly known him, or were then moved with his superior aspect, told him that if he wanted only rest, his cottage would be convenient; but if he were flying from anybody's search, he would hide him in a more retired place. Marius desiring him to do so, he carried him into the fens and bade him hide himself in a hollow place by the river side.[1]

But this did not prove a secure hiding place, and soon he heard soldiers who were pursuing him, for "there had been orders sent through all the towns to make public search for Marius, and if they found him to kill him."[2] He stripped himself of his clothes and plunged into the swamp, but he was seized and taken prisoner to the nearest town, for those who took him thought it better not to kill him at once.

Marius was placed in a house in a quiet part of the town, and the magistrates took counsel together as to what should be done with him.

Their fears were excited by the proclamation of the Roman people, but they hesitated to be the murderers of a man who had been six times consul and had performed so many brilliant exploits. So they sent a Gaul who was living in the place to kill him with a sword.[3]

The room where he lay was not very light, and it is said that

Marius's eyes seemed to the Gaul to dart out flames at him and he heard a loud voice say out of the dark, "Fellow, darest thou kill Caius Marius?" The barbarian hereupon immediately fled, and leaving his sword in the place, rushed out of doors, crying only this, "I

[1] Plutarch: *Life of Caius Marius.*   [2] Ibid.
[3] Appian: *Civil Wars,* I, 61.

cannot kill Caius Marius." At which they were all at
first astonished, and presently began to feel pity and
remorse, and anger at themselves for making so unjust
and ungrateful a decree against one who had preserved
Italy, and whom it was bad enough not to assist. "Let
him go," said they, "where he please to banishment,
and find his fate somewhere else; we only entreat pardon
of the gods for thrusting Marius distressed and deserted
out of our city." [1]

Once more Marius embarked on a ship and sailed
away seeking a refuge. This time he sailed for
Africa, and he landed near the place where Carthage had once stood. The Roman governor of
Africa at this time was

one that had never received either any injury or any
kindness from Marius; but who from compassion, it was
hoped, might lend him some help. But he was scarce
got ashore with a small retinue when an officer met him
and said, "The governor forbids you, Marius, to set
foot in Africa; if you do, he says he will put the decree
of the senate in execution and treat you as an enemy to
the Romans." When Marius heard this, he wanted words
to express his grief and resentment, and for a good while
held his peace, looking sternly upon the messenger, who
asked him what he should say, or what answer he should
return to the governor? Marius answered him with a
deep sigh; "Go, tell him that you have seen Caius
Marius sitting in exile among the ruins of Carthage." [2]

In the meantime the two consuls in Rome were
Octavius, leader of the nobles, and Cinna who led

[1] Plutarch: *Life of Caius Marius.*   [2] Ibid.

the people. A sharp conflict arose between the two over the enrolling of the Italians who had recently been enfranchised. They took to arms and Cinna was driven out, but not before the streets of Rome had run with the blood of Roman citizens. Marius now succeeded in returning to Italy, and joining Cinna, together they collected a number of followers and entered Rome. Octavius was murdered and there followed days of horror. Marius seems to have given himself up to revenge, and the citizens of Rome were murdered in cold blood. Anyone who was in any way suspected of being opposed to him was killed.

Every road and every town was filled with those that pursued and hunted them that fled and hid themselves; and it was remarkable that there was no confidence to be placed, as things stood, either in hospitality or friendship; for there were found but a very few that did not betray those that fled to them for shelter.

In the meantime, as if the wind were changing, there came news from all parts that Sulla, having put an end to the war in the East and taken possession of the provinces, was returning into Italy with a great army. This gave some small respite and intermission to these unspeakable calamities.[1]

Believing that war was nearing Rome, Marius was once again, for the seventh time, elected consul.

But he was worn out with labour and sinking under the burden of anxieties, and he could not sustain his

[1] Plutarch: *Life of Caius Marius*.

spirit which shook within him with the apprehension
of a new war and fresh encounters and dangers, the
formidable character of which he knew by his own experience. He was not now to risk war with Octavius
commanding an inexperienced multitude; but Sulla himself was approaching, the same who had formerly banished him, and since that had driven Mithridates as
far as the Euxine Sea.

Perplexed with such thoughts as these, and calling
to mind his banishment, and the tedious wanderings
and dangers he underwent, both by sea and land, he
fell into despondency. He could not sleep, and fearing
to lie awake he took to drinking, until at length on the
arrival of a messenger from the sea, he was seized with
new alarms and so fell into a sickness from which he did
not recover. Thus died Marius on the seventeenth day
of his seventh consulship.[1]

(c) *The Rule of Sulla*

Marius had secured the frontiers of Rome. The
next danger had come from the East, where Mithridates, King of Pontus, was creating a state in Asia
Minor that threatened to cut the Roman dominions
in two.

Mithridates was a brilliant, able and extraordinary man. His father was assassinated when he
himself was only eleven years old, and for seven
years he is said to have led a wandering life, pursued by those who would have liked to see him share
his father's fate, and amongst these pursuers were
not only his guardians, but also his own mother.

[1] Plutarch: *Life of Caius Marius.*

It is said that during these years he never slept under a roof, and that he became like the wild beasts he hunted for strength and cunning. His exploits were the talk of all the East and legend has been busy with his name. It was believed that he could run faster than the deer, shoot down flying game with unerring aim, that no horse was so wild that he could not tame it, and that he could ride a hundred and twenty miles a day without fatigue. Mithridates had all the cunning and cruelty of the Oriental, though to some extent it was hidden under the polish of a Greek education. He ruled over many lands and called himself the King of Kings. He could speak the various dialects of these lands and he collected rich and rare curiosities from Greece and Persia. He was also highly skilled in the art of poisoning, and by his orders several of his sons and daughters, his brother, his sister and his mother are said to have died mysterious deaths in prison. This was the man who for more than twenty years was to give the Romans trouble.

In 88 B.C. Sulla, having won a victory over his rival Marius, started for the East. Mithridates had brought all Asia Minor under his control, he had crossed into Greece where the Greek cities welcomed him, and he had sent one of his generals to occupy Athens. This was serious enough, but shortly before, with no provocation, he had given orders for a general massacre of all the Italians in the Roman province of Asia, a deed which Rome now intended to avenge.

Sulla first determined to capture Athens, and after

a long siege the city fell. He entered Athens about midnight

with all the terrors of trumpets and cornets sounding, with the triumphant shout and cry of an army let loose to spoil and slaughter, and scouring through the streets with swords drawn. There was no numbering the slain.[1]

At length, having completely humbled the Athenians, whom he called "the most ungrateful of men," Sulla agreed to pardon the survivors. He did this because of the pleading of two men who threw themselves on the ground before him and entreated him to have mercy for the sake of the memory of the ancient Athenians. "I forgive," he said, "the many for the sake of the few, the living for the dead."[2]

Athens was taken at the end of the first year of the war, and

within less than three years more Sulla had killed a hundred and sixty thousand men, recovered Greece, Macedonia, Ionia, Asia, and many other countries that Mithridates had previously occupied, taken the king's fleet away from him, and from such vast possessions restricted him to his paternal kingdom alone.[3]

Peace was made and the First Mithridatic War was over.

Sulla returned to Italy. After the death of

[1] Plutarch: *Life of Sulla.*   [2] Ibid.
[3] Appian: *Civil Wars*, I, 76.

Marius, Cinna had again been made consul, **and** he now opposed the return of Sulla.   But Sulla was at the head of a victorious army, entirely devoted to him and nothing could stay him.   A Civil War broke out (83 B.C.), the champion of the people resisting every advance of Sulla on Rome, but he fought his way, winning battle after battle, until he completely defeated his enemies outside the Colline Gate and he entered the city as its master.

And now followed a reign of terror more fearful than anything Rome had yet known.   Sulla's first act on entering the city was to give orders for the killing of everyone in Rome who had in any way opposed his entrance.   This massacre was carried out in the most brutal and cold-blooded fashion.   As there seemed no end to this slaughter and cruelty, one of the younger senators asked him one day

what end there was of these evils, and at what point he might be expected to stop?   "We do not ask you," said he, "to pardon any whom you have resolved to destroy, but to free from doubt those whom you are pleased to save."   Sulla answering that he knew not as yet whom to spare, "Why then," said he, "tell us whom you will punish."   This Sulla said he would do.[1]

He did, and every day a list of the proscribed was posted where all could see it.   The first day Sulla

proscribed eighty persons, and notwithstanding the general indignation, after one day's respite, he posted two hundred and twenty more, and on the third, again as many.   In an address to the people on this occasion, he

[1] Plutarch: *Life of Sulla.*

told them he had put as many names as he could think of; those which had escaped his memory, he would publish at a future time. He issued an edict likewise, making death the punishment of humanity, proscribing any who should dare to receive and cherish a proscribed person without exception to brother, son, or parents. And to him who should slay any one proscribed person, he ordained two talents reward, even were it a slave who had killed his master, or a son his father. And what was thought most unjust of all, he caused the attainder to pass upon their sons, and sons' sons, and made open sale of all their property. Nor did the proscription prevail only at Rome, but throughout all the cities of Italy the effusion of blood was such, that neither sanctuary of the gods, nor hearth of hospitality, nor ancestral home escaped. Men were butchered in the embraces of their wives, children in the arms of their mothers. Those who perished through public animosity or private enmity were nothing in comparison of the numbers of those who suffered for their riches. Even the murderers began to say, that "his fine house killed this man, a garden that, a third, his hot baths." One quiet peaceable man, who thought all his part in the common calamity consisted in condoling with the misfortunes of others, coming into the forum to read the list, and finding himself among the proscribed, cried out, "Woe is me, my Alban farm has informed against me." He had not gone far before he was despatched by a ruffian, sent on that errand.[1]

When this reign of terror was over, Sulla forced the people to make him Dictator, and he then set himself to reform the government. Some of the

[1] Plutarch: *Life of Sulla.*

laws he made were not lasting, for they were in the interests of the nobles alone and aimed at making the Senate supreme in the state, a policy that could no longer last, but some of his laws were good. He increased the number of courts and magistrates so that the business of the government could be more capably carried out, and some of his reforms became part of the constitution of the state.

Sulla as Dictator was the ruler of Rome, and he maintained his power because he was the commander of the army. More than four hundred years before, Rome, the small city-state, had driven out her kings and had established the rule of the people in their stead. Now, Rome, the chief city of a dominion that extended North and East and West of the Mediterranean, finding the old city-state government incapable of ruling such a vast territory, and not knowing what to put in its place, through strife and bloodshed and violence had gone back to the rule of one man, and this time to a man whose power was based on force. The statesmen who might have shown Rome the path to wiser government had been murdered. Order and peace were needed, but neither Marius nor Sulla had understood how to bring it about. The only real order and discipline in the state was in the army, but the army was the servant of its commander and not of the state. Not until a leader should arise who would understand that he who would lead the state must be its servant, would the state be saved. Leaders had arisen by whom the frontiers had been secured and the Roman Republic kept whole. But to restore order it was not enough to crush rebellions, the cause of rebellion must itself be rooted out. Not yet had a leader arisen who by his loyalty to the state would himself symbolize the state, so that not only the army, but also the whole people, in serving him, would be serving Rome.

When Sulla had finished his reform of the government, he retired into private life, and the next year, in 78 B.C., he died, died as he had lived, brave and brilliant, cold and cruel, asking of life nothing but that it should give him enjoyment, believing that he was favoured of the gods, calling himself Sulla the Fortunate. He was given a public funeral of great splendour and magnificence, and the funeral fire was lit in the Campus Martius where before him only kings had been buried.

IV. THE STRUGGLE BETWEEN POMPEY AND CAESAR

The death of Sulla left Rome without a military leader, and the people of Rome soon realized that if any kind of order were to be preserved, they must have one. Not only was a strong hand needed in Rome itself, but there was unrest in some parts of the Roman dominion. Western Spain, known then as Lusitania, now as Portugal, was growing very strong and independent under its governor Sertorius. This general belonged to the party of the people and had not regarded Sulla as the rightful ruler.

Before going to Lusitania, Sertorius had been in Africa, where he had distinguished himself, not only as a general, but as a ruler. He was a man of chivalrous nature, he was just and fair, and when the Lusitanians found themselves in need of an able leader, they sent messengers to Sertorius asking him to come and be their general. He accepted their offer and

left Africa, and being made general with absolute authority, he put all in order amongst them, and brought the neighbouring parts of Spain under subjection.

He was also highly honoured for his introducing discipline and good order amongst them, for he altered their furious savage manner of fighting, and brought them to make use of the Roman armour, taught them to keep their ranks, and observe signals and watchwords; and out of a confused number of thieves and robbers he constituted a regular well-disciplined army. He bestowed silver and gold upon them liberally to gild and adorn their helmets, he had their shields worked with various figures and designs, he brought them into the mode of wearing flowered and embroidered cloaks and coats, and by supplying money for these purposes, and joining with them in all improvements, he won the hearts of all. That, however, which delighted them most was the care that he took of their children. He sent for all the boys of noblest parentage out of all their tribes, and appointed masters to instruct them in the Greek and Roman learning, that when they came to be men, they might, as he professed, be fitted to share with him in authority, and in conducting government.[1]

Sertorius was one of the first to recognize that a province should be ruled as part of the whole domin-

[1] Plutarch: *Life of Sertorius.*

ion and not merely as a territory which would enrich Romans by paying taxes. He began that which later became the regular Roman policy, the romanizing of a conquered people by education. Sertorius ruled in the interests of the people and he became very popular. But the Romans were afraid that he would grow so strong that he might set up a rival state to Rome and to prevent this, they sent an army into Spain under the command of Pompey, a young officer who had already gained some distinction in the army under Sulla, and who had served both in Sicily and in Africa. At first Pompey could gain no successes in Spain, for Sertorius won battle after battle and seemed unconquerable, but at last, a conspiracy having been made against Sertorius, he was treacherously murdered at a banquet. Without a leader, the Spaniards were helpless and soon submitted to Pompey, who re-established the Roman rule more firmly than before and then returned to Italy.

Pompey had gained great popularity by his exploits and he now changed sides, and instead of upholding the rights of the Senate and the nobles, he came forward as the declared champion of the people. Rome badly needed a strong leader, for two dangers were threatening her near home. One was an uprising of slaves and gladiators.

Spartacus, a Thracian by birth, who had once served as a soldier with the Romans. but had since become a prisoner, and had been sold for a gladiator, was in the gladiatorial training-school at Capua. Here he persuaded about seventy of his comrades to strike for their own freedom rather than for the amusement of spectators. They overcame the guards and ran away, arming themselves with clubs and daggers that they took from people on the roads, and took refuge on Mount Vesuvius. There many fugitive slaves and even some freemen from the fields joined Spartacus, and he plundered the neighbouring country. As he divided the plunder impartially he soon had plenty of men.

A few skirmishes took place between Spartacus and the Romans and the Romans were defeated.

After this still greater numbers flocked to Spartacus till his army numbered seventy thousand men. For these he manufactured weapons and collected equipment, whereas Rome now sent out the consuls with two legions.[1]

For three years Spartacus defied the Romans and then the chief command of the army was given to Crassus. This commander forced an open battle with the rebels in which he was successful. Spartacus was slain and most of his army destroyed. Five thousand of the slaves, however, escaped from the battle, but Pompey, who had returned from Spain just in time, seized these five thousand and cut them down, and so completed the victory.

Crassus was a very rich man, the richest in Rome, but he wanted political power as well as money. He disliked Pompey, but he saw that Pompey was so popular amongst the people, that unless he ap-

[1] Appian: *Civil War*, I, 116.

peared to be friendly with him, he would never gain his ends. The result of this policy was that when Crassus and Pompey returned victorious to Rome, they were both elected consuls (70 B.C.).

The slaves had been subdued, but Rome was still in danger, for the seas were swarming with pirates.

The power of the pirates first began in Cilicia, having in truth but a precarious and obscure beginning, but gained life and boldness afterwards in the wars of Mithridates, where they hired themselves out and took employment in the king's service. Afterwards, whilst the Romans were embroiled in their civil wars, being engaged against one another even before the very gates of Rome, the seas lay waste and unguarded, and by degrees enticed and drew them on not only to seize upon and spoil the merchants and ships upon the seas, but also to lay waste the islands and seaport towns. So that now there embarked with these pirates men of wealth and noble birth and superior abilities, as if it had been a natural occupation to gain distinction in. They had divers arsenals, or piratic harbours, as likewise watch-towers and beacons, all along the sea-coast; and fleets were here received that were well-manned with the finest mariners, and well served with the expertest pilots, and composed of swift-sailing and light-built vessels adapted for their especial purpose. Nor was it merely their being thus formidable that excited indignation; they were even more odious for their ostentation than they were feared for their force. Their ships had gilded masts at their stems; the sails woven of purple, and the oars plated with silver, as if their delight were to glory in their iniquity. There was nothing but music and dancing, banqueting and revels, all along the shore. Officers in command were taken prisoners, and cities put under contribution to the reproach and dishonour of the Roman supremacy.

This piratic power having got the dominion and control of all the Mediterranean, there was no place left for navigation or commerce. And this it was which most of all made the Romans, finding themselves to be extremely straitened in their markets, and considering that if it should continue, there would be a dearth and famine in the land, determine at last to send out Pompey to recover the seas from the pirates.[1]

He was given five hundred ships and absolute power over the whole Mediterranean from the Pillars of Hercules in the West to the coasts of Syria and Pontus in the East, and on land, he was given the supreme authority for fifty miles inland. This command was given to him for the space of three years. It was extraordinary power, for it meant that during this time he would practically control all the provinces. No Roman commander before him had ever been given such unlimited power, and it was not given to Pompey without some opposition, but the results justified it, for in forty days Pompey had cleared the seas of the pirates. It was an extraordinary achievement. Of the pirates' ships, four hundred were taken and thirteen hundred destroyed, and this was done without the loss of a single Roman ship. The seas were cleared and Romans could once more cross them in safety.

Whilst Pompey had been fighting in Spain, defeating the slaves and then clearing the seas of pirates,

[1] Plutarch: *Life of Pompey.*

the Romans had also been carrying on war in the East, for Mithridates had grown strong again and was once more menacing the power of Rome. Lucullus, an able general, had been sent against him. He gained some successes, but he was not liked by his men, and just as victory might have been his, he was recalled and another general sent in his place. Soon after he, too, was recalled and Pompey was sent as chief general in the East. He was given absolute power over the army, and authority to make peace or war as he chose. This was really nothing less than creating a monarchy, for though he was not given the title, Pompey was given all the powers of a king, but the law was passed, and Pompey set out for the East.

Lucullus had already very much weakened the power of Mithridates, and Pompey was able to bring the war to a victorious end. His exploits in this war were likened to those of Alexander, and he carried his conquests far into the mysterious East.

He had a great desire to occupy Syria and to march through Arabia to the Red Sea, that he might thus extend his conquests every way to the great ocean that encompasses the habitable earth; as in Africa he was the first Roman that advanced his victories to the ocean, and again in Spain he made the Atlantic Sea the limit of the empire.[1]

All this Pompey accomplished, and then in 61 B.C. he returned to Italy, having added four new prov-

[1] Plutarch: *Life of Pompey.*

inces to the dominions of the Roman Republic:
Bithynia with Pontus, Syria, Cilicia and Crete.

Rumours of every kind were scattered abroad about
Pompey, and were carried to Rome before him, so that
there was a great tumult and stir, as if he designed forthwith to march with his army into the city and establish
himself securely as sole ruler. Crassus withdrew himself, together with his children and property, out of the
city, either that he was really afraid, or that he counter-
feited rather, as is most probable, to give credit to the
calumny and exasperate the jealousy of the people.
Pompey, therefore, as soon as he entered Italy, called
a general muster of the army; and having made a suitable address and exchanged a kind farewell with his
soldiers, he commanded them to depart, every man to
his country and place of habitation, only taking care
that they should not fail to meet again at his triumph.
Thus the army being disbanded, and the news commonly
reported, a wonderful result ensued. For when the
cities saw Pompey the Great passing through the country unarmed, and with a small train of familiar friends
only, as if he was returning from a journey of pleasure,
not from his conquests, they came pouring out to display their affection for him, attending and conducting
him to Rome with far greater forces than he disbanded;
insomuch that if he had designed any movement or innovation in the state, he might have done it without
his army.[1]

Pompey was again accorded a triumph, as he
had been after his other victorious campaigns, but
this was probably the most magnificent of all. His

[1] Plutarch: *Life of Pompey.*

conquests in the East had seized upon the imagination of the Roman people, for he had conquered Mithridates and there was now no Great King left in the East to call himself the King of Kings, and he had extended the Roman boundary to the Euphrates itself. To Pompey himself

that which seemed to be his greatest glory, being one which no other Roman ever attained to, was this, that he made his third triumph over the third division of the world. For others among the Romans had the honour of triumphing thrice, but his first triumph was over Africa, his second over Europe, and this last over Asia; so that he seemed in these three triumphs to have led the whole world captive.[1]

Whilst in the East, Pompey had made treaties, settled frontiers and organized the provincial governments of the new provinces entirely on his own responsibility, exactly as a king would have done, but in accordance with the powers granted him, and he had now returned to Rome expecting that the Senate would at once ratify his decisions. But it refused to do so.

What had been happening in Rome during the absence of Pompey in the East? The strife between the people and the Senate had continued, and Rome was given over to turmoil and confusion. In 63 B.C. two men stood for the consulship, Cicero, the orator, and Catiline, a young noble of great gifts, but of a vicious and dissolute life. Catiline was defeated and Cicero elected, but Cicero was

[1] Plutarch: *Life of Pompey.*

certain that Catiline was forming some kind of
conspiracy to destroy the government. He did not
rest until he had discovered it and then, as consul,
he summoned the Senate to consult with it as to the
punishment to be inflicted on the conspirators.
The Senators in turn gave their opinion, most of
them urging that the conspirators be put to death.
Then a young noble arose, one of the magistrates,
on whom there rested some slight suspicion that,
if he were not actually an accomplice, at least he
knew something of what was going on. This magistrate was Caius Julius Caesar. He was one of the
good orators of the time and he urged in a statesmanlike way that the Senate should not use violence in
punishing these men. He urged that nothing should
be done while everyone was under the influence of
passion and excitement, and warned the Senators
that if they used violence now, they would be preparing the way for the people, should they become
masters, to use violence in their turn. But he did
not propose that the men should be pardoned.

Do I then recommend that the prisoners be allowed
to depart and swell Catiline's forces? By no means!
This, rather, is my advice: that their goods be confiscated
and that they themselves be kept imprisoned in the
strongest of the free towns; further, that no one here-
after shall refer their case to the Senate or bring it before the people, under pain of being considered by the
Senate to have designs against the welfare of the state
and the common safety.[1]

[1] Sallust: *War with Catiline*, 51.

Caesar was followed by Cicero, who in a great speech urged that the conspirators be put to death. Catiline had been bold enough to sit as usual in the Senate, and Cicero turned to him and denounced him in bitter and scathing words. The guilt of the conspirators was fully proved and they were condemned to death. Catiline fled, but his companions were seized and, according to the old Roman custom, accompanied by the consul and the other magistrates, were taken through the Forum to the state prison, the dungeon under the Capitol, where they were immediately put to death. As soon as the sentence had been executed, the consul went out before the people crowding near the prison door, and announced the death of the conspirators in one single word: *Vixerunt,* meaning *They have lived.*

Such was the end of the uprising of Catiline, yet what had been done was unconstitutional, for no time had been allowed to the culprits for any appeal to the people. In its determination to keep the upper hand, the Senate had met violence with violence. Caesar, on the other hand, knew that what Rome wanted more than anything else was order, peace and rest, and that these could not be obtained by the kind of violence the Senate advocated. He had the insight of a statesman, but the time had not yet come for such advice to be heeded, and for the moment Caesar was not very popular, and it was Cicero who was the hero and who was hailed as the deliverer of Rome.

It was in the year after the conspiracy of Catiline that Pompey returned from the East. He had disbanded his army, but he had then found that without that support, he was far less powerful than formerly. The Senate refused either to ratify his decisions concerning the provinces he had conquered in the East, or to give grants of land to the men who had fought under him. But Pompey was a great commander and should he wish to collect another army, men would answer his call and serve him with unquestioning obedience and devotion. Pompey was a man to be reckoned with, and there was no doubt that whatever fate lay in store for Rome, Pompey would have some share in it.

Pompey, however, was not the only leader. There was Crassus, who had defeated Spartacus, and who was the wealthiest man in Rome. He had not the ability of Pompey, but his wealth gave him influence and he was a man of considerable political importance.

There was in Rome yet a third leader, Caius Julius Caesar, a noble, but on the side of the people, and who in spite of his suspected connection with Catiline was now growing in popular favour. Caesar was the nephew of Marius who had married his father's sister. He was born in 100 B.C. and had been brought up in a simple old-fashioned Roman home, and he owed much to the discipline and training given him by his mother to whom he was deeply devoted. He was exiled during the Sullan proscriptions. As the price of his life, Sulla had demanded that he divorce his wife who was the daughter of Cinna, but Caesar had refused. For some reason or other Sulla did not put him to death, but he was exiled and all his property and that of his wife was confiscated. After the death of Sulla, Caesar returned to Rome where he held various public offices. It was the custom for the magistrates to provide certain amusements for the people and Caesar gave some of the most splendid Rome had ever seen. These entertainments were so costly that Caesar was obliged to borrow money and he got heavily into debt. He

provided such a number of gladiators that he entertained the people with three hundred and twenty single combats, and by his great liberality and magnificence in theatrical shows, in processions, and public feastings, he threw into the shade all the attempts that had been made before him, and gained so much upon the people, that everyone was eager to find out new offices and new honours for him in return for his munificence.[1]

Caesar looked back to Marius as the champion of the people, and

while he was in the height of repute with the people for the magnificent shows he was giving, he ordered images of Marius and figures of Victory, with trophies in their hands, to be carried privately in the night and placed in the Capitol. Next morning when some saw them bright with gold and beautifully made, with inscriptions upon them referring to Marius's exploits over the Cimbri, they were surprised at the boldness of him who had set them up, nor was it difficult to guess who it was. The fame of this soon spread and brought together a great concourse of people. Marius's party took courage, and it was incredible how numerous they were

[1] Plutarch: *Life of Caesar*.

suddenly seen to be, and what a multitude of them appeared and came shouting into the Capitol. Many, when they saw Marius's likeness, cried for joy, and Caesar was highly extolled as the one man, in the place of all others, who was a relation worthy of Marius. Upon this the senate met, and one of the most eminent Romans of the time stood up and inveighed against Caesar, closing his speech with the remarkable saying that Caesar was now not working mines, but planting batteries to overthrow the state. But when Caesar had made an apology for himself, and satisfied the senate, his admirers were very much animated, and advised him not to depart from his own thoughts for anyone, since with the people's good favour he would ere long get the better of them all, and be the first man in the commonwealth.[1]

Caesar now rose rapidly in popular favour, and held one important office after another, including that of Pontifex Maximus, one of the most coveted of all the state offices. There were a number of competitors, men of influence and great reputation, but the choice of the people fell upon Caesar.

Upon the day of election, as his mother conducted him out of doors with tears, after embracing her, "My mother," he said, "today you will see me either high priest or an exile,"[2]

and he returned to her as Pontifex Maximus

Two years later, in 61 B.C., the year of Pompey's return from the East, Caesar was sent as Praetor to Spain. He showed there that he was not only

---

[1] Plutarch: *Life of Caesar.*   [2] Ibid.

a good general but also a good administrator in times of peace, but Spain did not offer enough scope for the power he felt within him.

It is said that once, after reading some part of the history of Alexander, he sat a great while thoughtful, and at last burst out into tears. His friends were surprised and asked him the reason of it. "Do you think," said he, "I have not just cause to weep, when I consider that Alexander at my age had conquered so many nations, and I have all this time done nothing that is memorable?" [1]

After a year in Spain, Caesar returned to Rome and stood for the consulship. He did not want to be second to any one. He had once said, when crossing the Alps and passing through a small, poor, and sparsely-inhabited village, that he would rather be the first man among those people than the second in Rome. Pompey, Crassus and Caesar were now the three most powerful men in Rome, each with his own ambitions, each desirous of power. Caesar saw that if they worked together nothing in Rome could withstand them, so he and Crassus planned with Pompey, that if Pompey would give all his influence and support in getting Caesar elected as consul, Caesar, in return, would secure from the Senate the ratification of all that Pompey wanted in the East. Pompey consented, and in 59 B.C. Julius Caesar was elected. He kept his word, and all that Pompey had requested was granted.

Pompey, Crassus and Caesar now worked to-

[1] Plutarch: *Life of Caesar.*

gether, unofficially, but none the less in combination. The union of these three leaders is known as the First Triumvirate, and nothing could resist the three. The military fame of Pompey, the wealth of Crassus, and the brilliant genius of Caesar, beginning to be felt in various directions more and more every day, carried all before them. At the end of his year as consul, Caesar was given what he had longed for, the office of Pro-consul of Gaul.

Roman influence had already extended beyond the Alps. Gaul possessed a good climate, the land was fertile and there were trading possibilities with the natives. This had attracted a number of Romans who had settled in the South. Caesar believed that Gaul would offer new and prosperous homes and wide opportunities to Italians, but for that to be possible, Gaul must be conquered and the boundaries made secure.

Caesar knew, too, the kind of power a great commander could wield, if he were able to make the army his devoted servant, and this command beyond the Alps which took with it so much independence of action, both in military and civil matters, gave him the opportunity he desired. So Caesar departed from Rome, leaving Pompey and Crassus in power.

Caesar spent nine years altogether in Gaul. In his campaigns there he showed himself as one of the great generals of the world. He fought and conquered, Gallic chiefs submitted to him and their towns and villages surrendered. The last and greatest of the Gallic chiefs to surrender was Vercingetorix, a hero who possessed the finest characteristics of his race, a love of liberty, devotion to his country, and who also had greater powers of discipline and organization than any other Gallic chief had shown. He was conquered in the end by Caesar in a great battle near a Gallic stronghold and taken prisoner. Caesar returned to Rome after this campaign and Vercingetorix was made to walk before his conqueror's chariot in the triumph awarded to Caesar, and then he was led away and put to death in the same dungeon in which Jugurtha and other men, far less noble than he, had perished before him.

The conquest of Gaul is a long and romantic story, the tale of which has been told by Caesar himself in his Commentaries. It resulted not only in the addition of Gaul to the Roman dominion, but also of part of the island beyond the sea that washed the northern boundary of Gaul, the island of Britain. Caesar was not only a great general, he was also a statesman, and as he conquered, he governed. Good roads and bridges were built, Roman money and weights and measures were introduced, the country was organized, justice was administered. But Caesar was wise enough not to try and change the religion of the peoples he conquered or their ancient customs and habits. The result was that as he advanced, he left behind him an ordered, settled land, with communications always open, and his conquests were lasting. Gaul became one of the most prosperous of the Roman provinces and one in which Roman civilization took deep hold. To the Romans the conquest of Gaul was a new and

marvellous adventure. On the one hand it opened
a new world to them, a world of boundless horizons
lost in the dim and misty North; on the other, it
gave a new field to their practical organizing ability, it opened new channels of commerce, and above
all, it made the Rhine a secure boundary against the
Germanic tribes of the North-East of Europe.

In the meantime Pompey had become the only
leader left in Rome, for Crassus had been sent to
the East in command of an army and had been slain.
Pompey had never really liked Caesar, and he now
used all the means in his power to undermine his
influence. He had married Julia, the daughter of
Caesar. Both Pompey and Caesar had loved her
greatly, but she died about this time, and the only
real link there was between the two men broke.
Pompey now began openly to support the Senate,
whilst Caesar stood as the defender of the people
and their rights. It had been an understood thing
between Caesar and Pompey, that at the expiration
of ten years Caesar should stand again for the consulship. Caesar had returned to Gaul and at the
head of his army, trained and disciplined by him,
he was all-powerful and would have been elected,
but it was against the law for a commander to cross
the Rubicon, the stream which formed the northern
boundary of Italy, and to enter the country at the
head of an army. Pompey had so intrigued and
raised up enemies against Caesar in Rome itself,
that were he to return as a private citizen he would
have little chance of election. Pompey was at the
head of troops in Rome, and Caesar proposed that

they should both lay down their arms. This Pompey refused to do, and then the Senate, controlled by Pompey, sent orders to Caesar that he should disband his army or be declared an enemy to the Roman state. What was Caesar to do? To obey meant the ruin, not only of his own ambitions, but of all that he dreamed of doing for Rome; to refuse, meant war. It was a fateful moment, and on the decision of Caesar hung the fate of Rome. The days of the Republic were numbered, something new was being born, though men hardly realized it. For long years now Rome had been at the mercy of one man or other supported by the army. She was waiting for a man who, ruling as the servant of the state, would inspire the loyalty of the army, not only to himself personally, but to himself as the symbol of the state. Was Caesar the man for whom Rome had been waiting? How would he decide?

Caesar was at Ravenna when the last message from the Senate reached him. He immediately sent forward some troops and then spent the day as he had planned, attending some public games, examining the plan of a fencing-school which he proposed to build, and then he dined with a number of friends. About sunset his carriage was brought out and with only a small escort he started on his journey. It grew dark and he lost his way. About dawn he met a guide who showed him the way

back to the road on foot by narrow by-paths. Then, overtaking his cohorts at the river Rubicon, which was the boundary of his province, he paused for a while, and realizing what a step he was taking, he turned to those about him and said: "Even yet we may turn back; but once cross yon little bridge, and the whole issue is with the sword."

As he stood in doubt, the sign was given him. On a sudden there appeared hard by a being of wondrous stature and beauty, who sat and played upon a reed; and when not only the shepherds flocked to hear him, but many of the soldiers left their posts, and among them some of the trumpeters, the apparition snatched a trumpet from one of them, rushed to the river, and sounding the war-note with mighty blast, strode to the opposite bank. Then Caesar cried: "Take we the course which the signs of the gods and the false dealing of our foes point out. The die is cast !" [1]

And Caesar crossed the Rubicon.

[1] Suetonius: *Julius Caesar*, 31, 32.

CHAPTER XIII

Julius Caesar

I. JULIUS CAESAR

As soon as it was known in Rome that Caesar had left Gaul, there began to be rumours that he might march with his army against the city. Some people believed it very probable that he would do so, and they said to Pompey that

if Caesar should march against the city, they could not see what forces there were to resist him, to which Pompey replied with a smile that they need have no concern, "for," said he, "whenever I stamp with my foot in any part of Italy, there will rise up forces enough in an instant, both horse and foot."[1]

As a matter of fact, Pompey had a much larger army at his disposal than Caesar, but Caesar had gained such renown in his campaigns in Gaul, that the mere idea that he might come as an enemy to Rome filled men's hearts with fear. No one knew what he would do. Had he definitely broken with Pompey? Was it the intention of each of these generals to be sole ruler of Rome and if so, would

[1] Plutarch: *Life of Pompey.*

the question be decided only by war? Caesar was a greater general than Pompey, but the deeds of Pompey in the East had won him great renown, and if there were to be a struggle, men knew it would be no easy one, and that if it were war between them, it would be war to the death.

Then Caesar crossed the Rubicon, and all Italy knew that war had come. For the moment terror spread through the land, and the inhabitants of the smaller towns fled to Rome. It was said that not only were

men and women fleeing from one town of Italy to another in their consternation, but that the very towns themselves left their sites and fled for succour to each other. The city of Rome was overwhelmed by the rush of people flying in from all the neighbouring places. All this caused so much disturbance that those who lived in Rome, seeing such confusion and disorder, began to leave the city as fast as the others came in. It was impossible to get any accurate news, for what each man heard by chance upon a flying rumour he would report for truth.[1]

In the midst of this confusion Pompey left Rome. He fled first to Brundusium and then set sail for Greece, where he prepared an army that should meet and destroy Caesar.

It is very probable that Pompey had planned this flight before Caesar crossed the Rubicon. Powerful as he was in Italy, he was still more so in the East where the memories of his victories were still fresh

[1] Plutarch: *Lives of Pompey and Caesar.*

in men's minds. Pompey had more to gain by a
victory in the East. A victory over Caesar in Italy
would definitely establish the supremacy of the
Senate of which Pompey was still nominally the
servant, whereas a victory over him in the East
would leave Pompey independent of the Senate
and without a rival anywhere in the Roman world.

In the meantime where was Caesar? this man at
the very sound of whose name Romans had fled,
leaving Italy and Rome at his mercy. Whatever
hesitation he may have shown as he stood on the
further side of the little river that formed the boundary of Italy, vanished when he had crossed it. The
die was cast and prompt action was needed. With
almost incredible swiftness he marched to Rome,
passing through cities which gave themselves up
to him without striking a blow, and without bloodshed in the space of sixty days he made himself the
master of Italy. Thirty years before, a victorious
general had marched at the head of his army on
Rome and had taken possession of the city, and
what had followed? A reign of terror which men
had not yet forgotten. Sulla had spared no one.
Now again a victorious general had entered Rome.
How would he treat his enemies and would the horror be repeated? This is one of the things that happened. Caesar was told that one of his old officers,
one who had been a trusted friend and who had
fought with him through the Gallic war, had deserted
him and had gone over to Pompey. All that Caesar
did was to send his money and belongings after him,
and he showed the same moderation and clemency

to everyone. There was no bitterness, no cruelty, no lives were taken, and gradually confidence was restored.

But matters had not been settled between Caesar and Pompey. Italy and Gaul were in the power of Caesar, but all the other Roman dominions were in the hands of Pompey. This was a serious matter for Caesar as nearly all the corn used by the Italians came from the lands controlled by Pompey, and unless Caesar could secure these lands and so be sure of a food supply, he could not hope to hold Italy for long.

Caesar went first to Spain, where he defeated two generals sent there by Pompey, and the country soon gave itself up to him. Large reinforcements were added to his army and he returned to Rome. While Caesar was in Spain, two of his generals had secured Sicily and Sardinia for him, and Italy was now sure of its food supply from the west. Caesar spent only eleven days in Rome, during which time he was made Dictator. These days were crowded even for a man of his tireless energy. He established order and relieved the fears of those who were still uncertain of his intentions, by passing some measures to relieve those who were in various ways suffering unjustly.

He called home the exiles, and gave back their rights as citizens to the children of those who had suffered under Sulla; he relieved the debtors by an act remitting some part of the interest on their debts,[1]

[1] Plutarch: *Life of Caesar.*

and he granted the much coveted privilege of Roman citizenship to the inhabitants of Cis-Alpine Gaul. Then he set out for Brundusium, whence he intended to follow Pompey to the East.

Caesar was not an easy general to follow, but he demanded no hardships that he was not himself willing to endure and he inspired his men with devotion and loyalty to him.

He now marched so fast that he left all his army behind him, except six hundred chosen horse and five legions, with which he put to sea in the very middle of winter, and having landed in Macedonia he sent the ships back to Brundusium to bring over the soldiers who were left behind in the march. They, while yet on the march, their bodies no longer in the full vigour of youth, and they themselves weary with such a multitude of wars, could not but exclaim against Caesar, "When at last, and where, will this Caesar let us be quiet? He carries us from place to place, and uses us as if we were not to be worn out, and had no sense of labour. Even our iron itself is spent by blows, and we ought to have some pity on our bucklers and breastplates, which have been used so long. Our wounds, if nothing else, should make him see that we are mortal men whom he commands, subject to the same pains and sufferings as other human beings. The very gods themselves cannot force the winter season, or hinder the storms in their time; yet he pushes forward, as if he were not pursuing, but flying from an enemy." So they talked as they marched leisurely towards Brundusium. But when they came thither, and found Caesar gone off before them, their feeling changed, and they blamed themselves as traitors to their general. They now railed at their officers for marching so slowly, and placing themselves on the heights overlooking the sea towards Epirus, they kept watch to see if they could espy the vessels which were to transport them to Caesar.[1]

When Caesar had landed all his troops he set up his camp not far from the shore. Pompey hoped that Caesar would suffer from lack of food, and so for some time he made no attempt to offer battle. He knew that everything depended on the struggle between them, whenever it should come, and he was afraid to risk a battle until he could feel certain of victory. As his camp was well provided with food and supplies for any length of time, he thought that by delaying action he would wear out the army of Caesar, which was not as well provided with food. There were a number of skirmishes and at last Pompey made a real attack which very nearly cost Caesar his army. There was a sharp fight and two thousand of Caesar's men were killed, but instead of forcing his way on into the camp, Pompey did not follow up his success, but retreated, so that Caesar, seeing what an advantage he had lost, said to his friends, "The victory today had been on the enemies' side if they had had a general who knew how to gain it."[2]

There was great rejoicing in the camp of Pompey over this success, especially when, almost immediately after, Caesar raised his camp and marched towards Thessaly. Some declared that the war was

[1] Plutarch: *Life of Caesar.*
[2] Ibid.

over and that Caesar had fled, others planned what public offices they would sue for when they should return in triumph to Rome, and what houses they would buy, and some even sailed off to tell Cornelia, the wife of Pompey, who was in Lesbos, that her husband would soon return in triumph. But some of Pompey's officers upbraided him for not pursuing Caesar and bringing the war to a decisive end; they told him that he was evidently reluctant to fight in order that he might keep his command of the army, and they asked if he were going to stay on where he was rather than fight and win and go home. "Good friends," said one of them who had spoken very frankly about Pompey's love of command, "you must not expect to gather any figs in Tusculum this year."[1]

At length Pompey decided to pursue Caesar and he followed him into Thessaly. They met at Pharsalia, and both generals knew that the hour of crisis had come. This battle was not a fight between nations, but a last struggle between two men, and it was the fate of Rome that hung in the balance. The spirit which had made the early Roman a man of a stern, upright and disciplined character, a man who put his duty before his pleasure, and who considered it his highest privilege to serve the state he loved, had passed away. Through a century of turmoil and bloodshed the chief power in the state had passed into the hands of one man, and out of the old Rome something new was rising. Pompey represented the spirit of that which was passing; though tradition

[1] Plutarch: *Life of Pompey.*

has handed down his name as that of a man just and honourable in himself, his aims were more for himself than for the state; his army was made up of men devoted to him, but not loyal to each other or to the state, men chiefly from the East with no strong feeling for Rome; that which he represented had been tried and found wanting.

Caesar, on the other hand, represented the new spirit that was awakening in Rome; his army was made up of men from the West and from Gaul, men of a more vigorous type than those in Pompey's army and united in loyalty and devotion to Caesar, and Caesar was loyal to the state. He represented order and progress, and he had realized long ago that, the Senate having lost the confidence and allegiance of the state, to restore Rome to her former greatness it was necessary to renew her old qualities of trust and loyalty and obedience to authority. The conditions of the past can never be brought back again, and it is not always desirable that they should be, but certain qualities of mind and character are undying, and it is when such qualities are strong enough to be the guiding principle of a state that progress is made. Caesar believed that these qualities would only be restored to Rome, when a man worthy of trust and loyalty and obedience should be a symbol to Romans of the state. It was for this end he had been working all the years that he was in Gaul, and now, in the year 48 B.C., at Pharsalia in Thessaly, the fate of Rome was to be decided.

The battle was just about to begin when Caesar

found one of his captains, a trusty and experienced soldier, encouraging his men to exert their utmost. Caesar called him by his name, and said, "What hopes, Caius Crassinius, and what grounds for encouragement?" Crassinius stretched out his hand, and cried in a loud voice, "We shall conquer nobly, Caesar; and I this day will deserve your praises, either alive or dead." So he said and was the first man to rush upon the enemy, followed by the soldiers about him.[1]

He earned the praise of Caesar, but at the cost of his life, for he was struck down and slain in the first encounter.

It was a terrific battle and Pompey was defeated. He had been sure of success, for Caesar's soldiers who took the camp found

all the tents and pavilions richly set out with garlands of myrtle, embroidered carpets and hangings, and tables laid and covered with goblets. There were large bowls of wine ready, and everything prepared and put in array, in the manner rather of people who had offered sacrifice and were going to celebrate a holiday, than of soldiers who had armed themselves to go out to battle, so possessed with the expectation of success and so full of empty confidence had they gone out that morning. Pompey fled from the camp, taken up altogether with thoughts, such as probably might possess a man that for the space of thirty-four years together had been accustomed to conquest and victory, and was then at last, in his old age, learning for the first time what defeat and flight were.[2]

[1] Plutarch: *Life of Caesar.*
[2] Plutarch: *Life of Pompey.*

Pompey fled to Egypt. The King of Egypt was Ptolemy, a boy, to whose father Pompey had once shown great kindness and it was therefore hoped that he would receive the fugitive with favour. But the counsellors of the young King were uncertain whether Pompey should be received or not; some advised sending him away, others wished him to come. Then one of their number, a crafty, cunning man, declared it was neither wise either to let him come or to send him away; for if they entertained him they would make Caesar their enemy and Pompey might become their master, and if they sent him away, it would make Pompey their enemy and might displease Caesar for allowing his escape. He advised, therefore, that he should be invited to come, and then put to death, for by that means they would please Caesar and have nothing to fear from Pompey, for he added, "a dead man cannot bite."

This base advice was followed, and when the ship on which Pompey had come to Egypt arrived, a boat was sent out to meet it. The harbour was dotted with small vessels full of soldiers, and all the shore was covered with armed men. Pompey was warned that he was in danger, but he paid no heed, and after bidding farewell to his wife who had fled with him, he stepped into the boat sent to meet him.

When the boat drew near to the shore, Cornelia, together with the rest of his friends in the galley, was very impatient to see the event, and began to take courage at last when she saw several of the royal escort coming to meet him, apparently to give him a more honourable reception; but as he rose from his seat in the boat, he was treacherously stabbed in the back. He, therefore, taking up his gown with both hands, drew it over his face, and neither saying nor doing anything unworthy of himself, only groaning a little, endured the wounds they gave him, and so ended his life.[1]

His head was cut off and his body thrown overboard, where it lay upon the shore, until Philip, his freedman who had accompanied him in the boat, took it up with care and reverence, and having found some old planks from a little fishing boat, he prepared a funeral pyre for his master.

As he was busy gathering and putting these planks together, an old Roman citizen, who in his youth had served in the wars under Pompey, came up to him and demanded who he was that was preparing the funeral of Pompey the Great. And Philip making answer that he was his freedman, "Nay then," said he, "you shall not have this honour alone; let even me, too, I pray you, have my share in such a pious office, that I may not altogether repent me of this pilgrimage in a strange land, but in compensation of many misfortunes may obtain this happiness at last, even with mine own hands to touch the body of Pompey, and do the last duties to the greatest general among the Romans." And in this manner was the funeral of Pompey performed.[2]

Caesar had pursued Pompey to Egypt, and he arrived in Alexandria soon after the murder. The Egyptian who had advised this cruel deed, think-

[1] Plutarch: *Life of Pompey.*   [2] Ibid.

ing that Caesar was as base as himself, brought him
the head of Pompey, expecting that he would rejoice
at the death of his enemy, but Caesar turned away
from him in horror as from a murderer, and when
he was given Pompey's signet ring, he wept. A
number of Pompey's friends who had also escaped
to Egypt were well treated by Caesar and

in a letter to his friends at Rome, he told them that the
greatest and most signal pleasure his victory had given
him was to be able continually to save the lives of fellow-
citizens who had fought against him.[1]

For the first time in this dark century of strife and
bloodshed did the conqueror spare his enemies, for
the first time, instead of revenge and cruelty, did he
think of peace and healing. After the battle of
Pharsalia some secret correspondence had been
found in Pompey's tent, in which men who had
pretended to be friends of Caesar had betrayed to
Pompey all that they knew of his plans. Caesar
knew that the names of these men were in the letters, but he threw the whole correspondence into
the fire unread.

One of Pompey's friends to whom Caesar showed
marked kindness was Marcus Brutus. He himself
was pardoned after Pompey's defeat at Pharsalia,
and he then procured from Caesar the same favour
for a number of his friends. Caesar treated him
with great confidence and later, when he had returned to Rome, made it possible for him to hold
several high offices.

[1] Plutarch: *Life of Caesar.*

Caesar did not leave Egypt immediately. The young King, Ptolemy, was fighting with his sister Cleopatra as to who should rule. Cleopatra was a very beautiful and enchanting queen and Caesar supported her against her brother. He spent some months in Alexandria helping to settle Egyptian affairs and to make the throne secure for Cleopatra. She was an ambitious woman and would have been well content had Caesar desired that she should rule in Rome as well as in Egypt, but in this she did not succeed. The Egyptians resented the interference of the Roman general and there was some fighting between the Romans and the Egyptians. It was during these disturbances that the great Library in Alexandria caught fire and was burned. The loss was an irreparable one, for priceless manuscripts were lost and the originals of many of the ancient classics.

In the spring of 47 B.C. Caesar left Egypt and went to Asia Minor, where he marched swiftly against the son of Mithridates who was stirring up revolt. He defeated him in battle, and settled affairs there in such a way that there was no further danger of rebellion. He then sent to Rome a despatch telling of his actions. Probably no general has ever sent home a shorter or more concise report than this sent by Caesar. It consisted of three words: *Veni, vidi, vici*, I came, I saw, I conquered.

The following year 46 B.C. found Caesar in Africa, where some of the remaining adherents of Pompey made a last stand against him, but they, too, were defeated and Africa was organized as a Roman

province. Caesar was now elected consul for the
fourth time and then he went to Spain where the
sons of Pompey, though

they were but young, had gathered together a very
numerous army, and showed they had courage and conduct to command it, so that Caesar was in extreme
danger. He fought a great battle and defeated them,
but it was not an easy victory and when he came back
from the fight, he told his friends that he had often
fought for victory, but that this was the first time he
had ever fought for life.[1]

This was the last war which Caesar undertook.
There was now no danger of disturbance, for the time
at least, in any part of the Roman world. He had
defeated his enemies, the civil wars were over, and
peace had been restored. Caesar now returned to
Rome, where one after the other all the great offices
of state were his. The Republic was ruled by one
man only, but by a man who desired to rule not only
for his own glory, though he was ambitious and loved
power, but by one who desired to use it in the interest of the state.

Caesar had been made Dictator for life, and now
that the supreme power was his, he set himself to use
it well. He had returned from Spain in the year
45 B.C. and immediately, almost as if he knew that
his time was short, he set himself to rule with far-
seeing wisdom. He pardoned his enemies; he made
no favourites; he increased the number of senators;
he made new laws for the distribution of corn, so

[1] Plutarch: *Life of Caesar.*

that it was not given freely to those who could afford to buy it, but only to those who were in real need; he encouraged the founding of colonies; he made new laws for the just settlement of debts; he extended the much-prized Roman citizenship to some of the conquered provinces; and he reformed the calendar.

These things Caesar accomplished, but he planned many more. He proposed to improve the port of Ostia, and to drain the Pontine marshes; to erect great buildings which would add to the beauty and dignity of Rome; to collect a great library of Greek and Roman books; to bring the vast body of Roman law together in a code; and to build roads and canals in provinces where they were needed. The conquests of Caesar had brought great wealth to Rome, and he intended that it should be spent on the state.

All this work was accomplished by Caesar in a year. He wielded the absolute power of a King, and had he wished, he might have had the title, but he always refused it. Once when he was addressed as King, he answered that his name was Caesar not King, and on another occasion when he was in the Forum, Mark Antony, who was consul at the time, came up to him and offered him a diadem wreathed with laurel. But Caesar refused it and the people approved of his refusal, for the name of King was still hated in Rome.

Julius Caesar refused the title of King, but he was surrounded by all the outward forms of monarchy. He was honoured and feared as no one had ever been before. All kinds of honours were devised for his gratification without stint, even such as were divine,—sacrifices, games, statues in all the temples and public places, by every tribe, by all the provinces, and by the kings in alliance with Rome. He was represented in different characters, and in some cases crowned with oak as the saviour of his country. He was proclaimed the Father of his Country and chosen dictator for life and consul for ten years and his person was declared sacred and inviolable. It was decreed that he should transact business on a throne of ivory and gold; that he should himself sacrifice in triumphal costume; that each year the city should celebrate the days on which he had won his victories; that every five years the priests and Vestal Virgins should offer up public prayers for his safety; and that the magistrates immediately upon their inauguration should take an oath not to oppose any of Caesar's decrees. In honour of his birth the name of the month Quintilis was changed to July. Many temples were decreed to him as to a god, and one was dedicated in common to him and the goddess Clemency, who were represented as clasping hands.[1]

Julius Caesar was one of the greatest of the Romans. A lesser man than he would probably have accepted the title of King, and have been spoiled and degraded by the flattery which was heaped upon him, but throughout it all, he preserved his self-control and dignity. His manner was courteous and gracious to all with whom he came in contact, and in the short space of time in which it was given him to rule Rome, he made for himself a place in the imagina-

[1] Appian: *Civil Wars*, II, 106.

tion of the people that no other Roman ruler ever occupied.

Such a personality, however, was bound to have enemies, and there were men in Rome who refused to believe that Caesar was ruling for the good of the state, and who were certain that sooner or later he would overthrow the ordered government he had established and make himself King. These men made a conspiracy and determined to kill Caesar. The leaders were Brutus, whom Caesar had pardoned after the defeat of Pompey and to whom he had shown great kindness, and Cassius, the friend of Brutus. The day was fixed for the deed; Caesar was to be assassinated on the Ides of March. It is said that about this time Caesar met a soothsayer who bade him beware of the Ides of March, for some great danger awaited him on that day. The night before, he was at supper with some friends and the conversation turned on death. Caesar declared that the fear of death was worse than death itself. "It is better to die once," he said, "than to be always in fear of death." "What kind of death is best?" asked one of his friends, and Caesar replied, "That which is least expected." That night Caesar's wife had a strange dream, which filled her with foreboding, and in the morning she begged Caesar not to go to the Senate that day, but to wait for another time. But he went forth, unafraid, as usual.

When Caesar entered the Senate, everyone present rose in respect to him and certain members came and stood near his chair. Then one of them came forward and petitioned Caesar for the recall of his

brother who had been exiled. Caesar answered that
the matter could not be settled then, whereupon the
conspirator seized hold of his purple robe as if he
would more strongly urge his petition, and then suddenly he called out: "Friends, what are you waiting
for?" It was the signal, and the conspirators rushed
upon Caesar, stabbing him with daggers. Whichever way he turned, he met blows. It is said that he
attempted to defend himself, until he received a blow
from Brutus, from the man whom he had befriended,
and that then, saying, "*Et tu, Brute!*" he drew his
robe up over his face and fell, and as he lay, helpless
and bleeding, the conspirators continued their attack
until there was no life left in him.

Caesar was dead, and the whole city was stunned
by the news. The Forum was deserted and silence
fell upon everyone. Then gradually the citizens collected and preparations were made for the funeral.
First, Caesar's will was opened and read to the
people. His gardens were given to the city for the
use of the Roman people, every citizen was to receive
a sum of money as a legacy, and his great-nephew,
Caius Julius Caesar Octavianus, generally known as
Octavius, was to be his heir.

After the will had been read, Mark Antony came
before the people and delivered a great funeral ora-
tion over the body of the dead Caesar. At the end
of it the people were so carried away by fury at
what had happened, that they rushed through the
city to set the houses of the murderers on fire.
Then they returned to the Forum and bore the body
of Caesar

to the Capitol in order to bury it in the temple and place it among the gods. Being prevented from doing so by the priests, they placed it again in the Forum, where stood the ancient palace of the Kings of Rome. There they collected together pieces of wood and benches of which there were many in the Forum, and anything else that they could find of that sort, for a funeral pile. Then they set fire to it and the entire people remained by it throughout the night.[1]

Caesar was dead, and we are told by the great Roman poet that the sun himself had pity for Rome:

He too, it was, when Caesar's light was quenched,
For Rome had pity, when his bright head he veiled
In iron-hued darkness, till a godless age
Trembled for night eternal.[2]

Caesar was soon

ranked among the gods, not only by a formal decree but also in the belief of the people. For during the first games which Augustus, his heir, consecrated to his memory, a comet shone for seven successive days together, rising about the eleventh hour, and it was believed to be the soul of Caesar who had been taken into heaven.[3]

II. THE END OF THE REPUBLIC

The murderers of Caesar fled from Rome, and for a moment all was confusion. Then Antony was

[1] Appian: *Civil Wars*, II, 148.　　[2] Virgil: *Georgic*, I.
[3] Suetonius: *Julius Caesar*.

recognized as leader of the army, and he determined to gain for himself the power which so lately had been Caesar's.

Octavius, whom Caesar had named as his heir, was at this time only eighteen years old, and he was at Apollonia in Illyria where Caesar had sent him to finish his education. He had been there for about six months, when one evening a messenger arrived with the news of the murder of Caesar. The friends of Octavius advised him to stay where he was, and some of them even thought it would be wiser of him to renounce his inheritance altogether, for the enemies of Caesar were very strong and Brutus and Cassius were still alive. But Octavius did not hesitate in making his decision. He announced his intention of going at once to Rome and of avenging his adopted father's death. Though young in years Octavius showed that he understood affairs, for as soon as he reached Rome, he tried to make friends with the leaders of the army. But Antony opposed him and joined with Antony was his friend Lepidus. Antony's opposition was so great, that he and Lepidus marched against Octavius and the soldiers who had gone over to him, and a battle followed in which Octavius was victorious. He was then elected consul, and he proposed to Antony that they should come to some understanding together. They met and decided that Octavius, Antony and Lepidus should form a Triumvirate and should rule the Roman world between them: Octavius was to rule the West, Antony the East, and Lepidus Africa.

The first thing this Second Triumvirate had to do

was to make themselves secure against their enemies, and once more the streets of Rome ran with
the blood of her citizens, of whom the greater number were guilty of no greater crime than that of
being the political opponents of the three rulers.
Octavius contented himself with being avenged on
those who had been in any way connected with the
death of Caesar, but the others were less scrupu-
lous. Cicero had made great speeches in the Senate against Antony, and for this he was hunted down
and killed, and Rome lost her greatest orator.

But Brutus and Cassius were still alive. They
had fled to Macedonia where they had collected an
army. In 42 B.C. Antony and Octavius pursued
them there and the two armies met in battle at
Philippi. Brutus and Cassius were defeated and
rather than be captured by their conquerors, they
took their own lives. Cassius, it is said, killed himself with the same dagger with which he had struck
Caesar. Tradition says that Brutus had expected
this defeat. Some time before, he was lying one
night awake in his tent, when

he heard a noise at the door, and looking that way, by
the light of his lamp, which was almost out, saw a terrible figure, like that of a man, but of unusual stature
and severe countenance. He was somewhat frightened
at first, but seeing it neither did nor spoke anything to
him, only stood silently by his bedside, he asked who
it was. The spectre answered him, "Thy evil genius,
Brutus, thou shalt see me at Philippi." Brutus answered courageously, "Well, I shall see you," and immediately the appearance vanished. The night before

the battle the same phantom appeared to him again, but spoke not a word. He presently understood his destiny was at hand, and exposed himself to all the danger of the battle. Yet he did not die in the fight, but seeing his men defeated, got up to the top of a rock and fell upon his sword and thus met his death.[1]

Antony and Octavius were now strong enough to rule without the help of Lepidus, who had not shown himself very capable, and on the grounds that he was suspected of plotting against them he was dropped from the Triumvirate, and Antony and Octavius were left to rule alone. Octavius returned to Rome, and Antony, as had been originally planned, went to the East.

When Julius Caesar was in Alexandria, he had taken the side of Cleopatra against her brother and had left her in possession of the throne of Egypt. When Antony arrived in the East he was told that in the late war Cleopatra had been giving help to Cassius, and he sent a messenger to her with the command that she should come herself to Cilicia, where Antony was, and answer the accusation made against her. She was advised to go, and

she made great preparations for her journey, of money, gifts, and ornaments of value, such as so wealthy a kingdom might afford, but she brought also her own beauty and fascination. She came sailing up the river in a barge with gilded stern and outspread sails of purple, while oars of silver beat time to the music of flutes and fifes and harps. She herself lay under a canopy of

[1] Plutarch: *Life of Caesar.*

cloth of gold, dressed as Venus in a picture, and beautiful young boys, like painted Cupids, stood on each side to fan her. Her maids were dressed like sea-nymphs and graces, some steering at the rudder, some working at the ropes. The perfumes diffused themselves from the vessel to the shore, which was covered with multitudes, part running out of the city to see the sight.

On her arrival Antony sent to invite her to supper. She thought it fitter that he should come to her; so, willing to show his good humour and courtesy, he complied and went. The enchanting queen captivated him. Her beauty joined with the charm of her conversation, and the character that attended all she said or did, was something bewitching. It was a pleasure merely to hear the sound of her voice, with which, like an instrument of many strings, she could pass from one language to another; so that she spoke to few strangers by an interpreter, which was all the more surprising because most of the kings, her predecessors, scarcely gave themselves the trouble to acquire the Egyptian tongue, and several of them quite abandoned the Macedonian.[1]

Antony loved luxury and a life of ease and pleasure, and he had all this to his heart's content at the court of Cleopatra. He went back with her to Alexandria, and there he seems to have forgotten that he was a Roman. He adopted eastern habits and dress and he even wore a diadem as if he were playing at being King. But if Antony, in this life of pleasure and feasting, had forgotten his ambitions, Cleopatra had not forgotten hers. She had once hoped to rule Rome as the Queen of Caesar, but she had not succeeded; now she hoped to rule it

[1] Plutarch: *Life of Antony.*

as the Queen of Antony, and she promised him her help on the sole condition that she should rule beside him. Rumours of all this reached Rome, where it was said that Antony intended not only to conquer Octavius and Rome, but to make Alexandria the capital of the Roman world.

At length matters had gone so far that Octavius declared war on Antony, and in 31 B.C. at Actium on the west coast of Greece, a naval battle was fought between them. In the middle of the battle Cleopatra, who had come herself to watch the fight, suddenly took flight and all the galleys she had brought with her followed. When Antony saw her gilded vessel with its purple sails making for the open sea, he disgracefully left the battle and followed her. The day was lost. Knowing that he was utterly defeated, Antony killed himself, but Cleopatra was taken prisoner. She heard that she was to be taken to Rome and that there, in the triumph, she, the Queen of Egypt, would be made to walk a captive, before her conqueror's chariot. Rather than submit to that humiliation she killed herself, tradition says by allowing a poisonous asp to bite her arm.

> Not hers to quail
> From steel as women do;
> To shores afar she bent no sail;
> A finer end she knew:
>
> She nerved herself unmoved to look
> Upon her wrecked domains;
> And gripped the asps and deeply took
> Their venom in her veins:

No brutal ships, no triumph high,
 With her should work their will;
Flushed with her dark resolve to die,
 Unqueened, but queenly still.[1]

Cleopatra was the last of the Ptolemies, those Kings who had ruled Egypt since the death of Alexander the Great. Egypt was no longer free. The battle of Actium had decided her fate, and she now became a Roman province.

The battle of Actium completed what the battle of Marathon had begun. For four hundred and fifty years the East had struggled with the West: the East with its charm, its mystery, its romance, but its lower ideals and its inability to understand what was meant by freedom and progress; and the West which represented youth and strength, sturdy independence and the spirit of the pioneer. Greece had conquered Persia, Rome had conquered Carthage, and now Octavius had conquered Antony. Great things had come and were still to come out of the East, but the centre of the world was in the West, and Octavius Caesar was its master.

[1] Horace: *Odes*, I, 37.

PART III

ROME THE MISTRESS OF THE WORLD

CHAPTER XIV

Augustus and the Golden Age of Rome

31 B.C.–14 A.D.

It is not always given to a great man to see the fruit of his labours. Julius Caesar had planned for the restoration of loyalty and of law and order in Rome, but it seemed as if his death had come before he had finished his task. It is interesting to wonder what he might have done, had he lived longer, but it is also worth while to wonder whether, after all, he were the man to carry to its completion that which he had begun. It sometimes happens that a great ideal is carried out better by a lesser man than he who gave it birth, and it is possible that this may have been the case with Julius Caesar. He was a man of genius, a man of great powers of vision and imagination. He belonged to a family that claimed descent from the gods, and the people thought both his personality and his exploits so god-like that even during his life-time he was given divine honours, and

after his death he was numbered with the gods.
Such a man was far removed from ordinary, conventional people, and so remarkable a personality
was bound to have enemies as well as devoted followers.

None of this glamour hung about the name of
Octavius. He was a young, able man, very much
more ordinary and conventional than his great uncle,
but possessed of keen political insight and a steady,
determined will. These gained for him the quiet
trust and confidence of the people, and because of
this he was able to finish what Julius Caesar had so
magnificently begun, and to restore such law and
order to Rome that she was able to enjoy two centuries of peace and prosperity.

Julius Caesar had ruled alone, supported by the
army, and he had ruled well, but there was no law
in Rome which gave such power to one man alone.
The first thing Octavius had to do was to give the
authority of the state to that power which had been
won by the sword. But though he was still young,
Octavius was wise, and he knew that in spite of all
the revolutions, civil wars and changes through which
Rome had passed, the Romans were conservative at
heart and did not want the outward form of the
state changed. Above all, the Romans wanted no
King. But Rome was no longer a Republic, she
was an Empire, a number of nations bound together
in allegiance to the mother-state of Rome, and in
fact, if not in name, she was ruled by one man.

Octavius had returned to Rome in 29 B.C. and had
celebrated a magnificent triumph which had lasted

three days, and the people had hailed him as their deliverer and bringer of peace. They called him *Imperator*, the military title which was given to every general who was allowed the honour of a triumph. In this year of his return to Rome there was such peace throughout the Empire that the gates of the Temple of Janus which had been open for two hundred years, were once more closed with solemn rejoicings.

Octavius made no effort to gain any title for himself. He held in turn all the great offices of state: he was Tribune, Consul, Censor, and Pontifex Maximus. At length, as a symbol of their gratitude to him for all that he had done to restore peace, the Senate gave him the title of *Augustus*, a word meaning Majesty or Honoured, and from that time on he has been called by that name. He had first been consul in the month Sextilis, and to do him yet more honour, the name of that month was changed to August.

In this way Augustus was at the head of all the political and religious affairs of the state. When he retired from the consulship the Senate allowed him to retain the *imperium*. He was given the official rank of a consul and granted certain rights which usually belonged only to the consuls: he could summon the Senate for business, he could nominate candidates for public offices, and he could issue decrees. The Senate next appointed him pro-consul of certain provinces, and then they gave him powers of authority over all the provincial governors. As the consul was always the commander-in-chief of the Roman army, so was the pro-consul the commander of the provincial army, so this authority made Augustus the commander-in-chief of all the armies of the Empire.

Though outwardly the Roman Empire seemed to be governed as of old by the Senate and the people, in fact it was now governed by Augustus. He held all the chief offices, and he took precedence of all Roman magistrates, whether in Rome itself or in the provinces. Augustus had gained this power not by force but by the vote of the Senate, and the power which Julius Caesar had won by the sword was now deliberately given by constitutional means to his successor. No one before had occupied such a position in Rome, and the people called Augustus *princeps*, a title meaning *first citizen*. When Augustus was given these titles, they were little more than expressions of honour and respect to one who had deserved well of the state, and though Augustus is now spoken of as the first Roman Emperor, it was not till long after his death that his successors assumed the title.

Julius Caesar had already brought about great reforms in Rome itself. Augustus continued these, and though it had less actual power than formerly, much of its ancient dignity was restored to the Senate. Augustus continued the regulations for the distribution of corn, the water-supply was improved, a fire-brigade was instituted and the police force made more efficient.

The most crying need for reform at this time was in the government of the provinces. In 133 B.C.

Rome had found herself the mistress of the Mediterranean. She had tried to rule her new dominions in the way she had ruled herself, but what had sufficed for a small city-state did not suffice for an empire, and the first experiments of Rome in provincial government were very unsatisfactory.[1] During the last century of the Republic, the provinces had suffered even more than Rome from misgovernment. Much of the fighting had been carried on in the provinces, the land had been plundered and wasted, and the inhabitants heavily taxed in order to pay for the wars. Barbarian tribes had come down upon the undefended frontier towns, and everywhere there was confusion, misgovernment and discontent.

Augustus set himself to remedy this and to govern the provinces as real parts of the Empire. He divided them into two classes: the older provinces which were left under the control of the Senate, and the newer provinces, especially those on the frontiers, which he kept under his own direct control. This division of authority had very good results, for each power acted as a check on the other. As the Senate had given Augustus general authority over all the provinces, he was able to exercise some control over its as well as his own; and he, on his part, was required from time to time to give an account to the Senate of the administration of his provinces, and as it was the Senate who had entrusted him with all this power, he was constitutionally responsible to it for all he did. This

[1] See Chapter XI.

resulted in a better and fairer government of the provinces, for no longer was it possible for the governors to misgovern them. They were responsible either to the Senate or to Augustus, and any governor who failed to administer the law justly was summoned to Rome and punished.

Much of the former discontent in the provinces had been caused by unjust and heavy taxation. Augustus had a thorough survey made of all the resources of the Empire and the taxes were regulated in accordance with the report made. Most of the money collected in taxes was spent by the government in building good roads and bridges, aqueducts, and public buildings in the cities.

Augustus had no ambitions of conquest. He believed that the Empire was as large as it was possible to govern well and that it was his task to make it loyal, peaceful and contented. It was not an easy thing to restore order and good government to all these lands that belonged to Rome. Some of them, like Greece and Egypt, had old and well-established forms of government; others, like the newly conquered province of Gaul, had hardly any. It was the task of Rome to weld all these different peoples into an empire, owning one allegiance only, and that to Rome.

In order to preserve peace throughout the Empire, it was necessary that the frontiers should be secure. Since the conquests of Marius over the Cimbri and Teutones, the boundaries of the Roman dominion had been greatly extended. Augustus believed that wherever it was possible, natural boundaries should form the frontiers, and to a great extent this was possible. The Empire extended in the East to the Euphrates, in the West to the Atlantic Ocean, in the South it was bounded by the great African desert, and only in the North and North-East were there difficulties in the way. The Rhine and the Danube were the natural frontiers, but the land beyond these rivers swarmed with fierce Germanic tribes, and Augustus believed that the Elbe would make a more secure boundary. The conquest of the country between the Rhine and the Elbe was accomplished, and in 9 A.D. Varus was sent as governor of the newly conquered territory. But the Germanic tribes rose in rebellion against the Roman government, and in a fierce battle the Romans were defeated, the army destroyed, and the prisoners mercilessly put to death. Rather than survive such a humiliation, Varus killed himself. When the news of the disaster reached Augustus, he was heart-broken, and he is said to have cried out many times in grief: "Varus, Varus, give me back my legions!" But it was on peace and not on conquest that the heart of Augustus was set, and seeing that it would only waste men's lives to try to force a settlement as far as the Elbe, he definitely fixed the Rhine and the Danube as the northern frontier.

Augustus himself was a man of simple tastes and habits, and he wanted to restore to Rome something of the older traditions of simple living. As peace and content increased throughout the Empire he tried to turn men's minds towards those things in the past which had helped to make Rome great.

He wanted to restore reverence and respect for the
gods and for the religion which from the earliest
days had been so closely bound up with the Roman
state.

In 17 B.C., fourteen years after Augustus had begun
to rule, when Rome was at the height of her prosperity under him, he gave orders for the celebration
of some public games. These were special games
known as the *Ludi Saeculares* or Secular Games,
from the Latin word meaning *end of a period*. This
festival was a very ancient one and was supposed
to have been first celebrated in the early days of
the Republic because of a pestilence that raged in
the country. In some way or other it was believed
that the festival brought with it some kind of purifying to the state, and tradition said that it had been
celebrated at certain long intervals whenever such a
purifying seemed necessary. The Sibylline Books
were now consulted, and everything seeming favourable, it was decreed that they should be celebrated
once again, as the outward sign that the Roman
world had been cleansed from the violence and bloodshed of the past and that under Augustus a new
reign of peace and prosperity had begun.

The Festival lasted for six days, the last three of
May and the first three of June in 17 B.C. Torches
were distributed to the entire population of Rome,
and during the last days of May the people made
offerings of all kinds to the gods. Except when sacrifices were being offered or special ceremonies taking place, the six days were given up to games and
amusements of every kind. On each of the last

three evenings of the festival, Augustus offered a sacrifice and made a public prayer to Jupiter for himself, his *familia*, his whole house and the state; he prayed that Jupiter would increase the power and majesty of Rome both in war and peace, that he would grant safety and health to all the Roman people, that he would protect the Latin name, and be favourable and gracious to himself and all his family. On the first two of these nights, the sacrifice was offered on the Capitol and on the third on the Palatine, where Augustus had built a temple to Apollo. Looking over the city from these hills, the scene must have been a very impressive one; every spot of standing ground was occupied by the crowds, bearing lighted torches in their hands. They pressed down to the river's bank, and the torchlight was reflected in the water.

After the sacrifice had been offered, two choirs of twenty-seven boys and twenty-seven girls, all of whose parents were still alive, sang a hymn called the *Carmen Saeculare* which had been specially composed for the day by the poet Horace. They sang it first on the Capitol and then on the Palatine.

> Phoebus and Dian, huntress fair,
> Today and always magnified,
> Bright lights of heaven, accord our prayer
> This holy tide,
> On which the Sibyl's volume wills
> That youths and maidens without stain
> To gods, who love the seven dear hills,
> Should chant the strain!

Sun, that unchanged, yet ever new,
    Lead'st out the day and bring'st it home,
May nought be present to thy view
    More great than Rome!

   .   .   .   .

Grant to our sons unblemish'd ways;
    Grant to our sires an age of peace;
Grant to our nation power and praise,
    And large increase.

   .   .   .   .   .   .

Faith, Honour, ancient Modesty,
    And Peace and Virtue, spite of scorn,
Come back to earth; and Plenty, see,
    With teeming horn.
Augur and lord of silver bow,
    Apollo, darling of the Nine,
Who heal'st our frame when languors slow
    Have made it pine;
Lov'st thou thine own Palatial hill,
    Prolong the glorious life of Rome
To other cycles, brightening still
    Through time to come!
From Algidus and Aventine
    List, goddess, to our grave Fifteen!
To praying youths thine ear incline,
    Diana queen!
Thus Jove and all the gods agree!
    So trusting, wend we home again,
Phoebus' and Dian's singers we,
    And this our strain.[1]

Augustus died in 14 A.D. He left an Empire
which extended from the Euphrates in the mysteri-

[1] Horace: *Carmen Saeculare.*

ous East, to the Atlantic on the western edge of the world, from the burning African desert in the South, to the forests and misty lands of the North. He had brought together peoples of many lands and of many tongues under one just and able government, he had brought peace and order to the world.

CHAPTER XV

ANCIENT ROME

I. THE CITY OF ROME

ACCORDING to the most ancient traditions Rome was founded by the descendants of Aeneas, though modern excavations have shown that there was a still older settlement there. Virgil tells us how Aeneas and his comrades sailed up the Tiber until in the distance they saw walls and a citadel and scattered house roofs, a settlement that was then but small, but which was destined to become a great city.[1] The first hill they must have seen was the Aventine, which sloped steeply to the river's edge, and as they rounded the bend, before them would have risen up the Palatine and to their left the Capitoline. All through her history the heart and life of Rome lay at the foot of these same three hills. On the opposite bank of the Tiber rose the Janiculum, the hill from which in ancient times, as now, the finest view over Rome was to be had.

In the last years of the Republic the Pons Sublicius still spanned the river from the Janiculum to

[1] See Aeneid, VIII, 90ff.

the foot of the Palatine. Crossing it, a Roman coming to the city found himself close to the Forum Bo-
arium or Cattle Market which was full of shops and
where a great deal of business in the way of buying
and selling was carried on. Leaving this to the
left, the Roman would find himself in the valley
between the Aventine and the Palatine. From the
very earliest times this had been the place where the
Romans amused themselves. It was known as the
Circus Maximus, and in the days of the early Kings
the country people had come here for their games.
In those days there was no shelter from either sun
or rain, and the seats were few and uncomfortable.
Old custom had always used this valley for the public games, but the first Tarquin King formally gave
it to the people as a circus. It had been much improved by the last century B.C. but it was made more
magnificent by the Caesars, who enlarged it so that
it could hold about a hundred and fifty thousand
spectators.

Leaving the Circus Maximus and keeping to the
road which wound round the base of the Palatine,
the Roman came to the beginning of the Sacra Via,
the road which ran through the very heart of ancient
Rome. It led from the high ground near the Palatine down through the Forum Romanum to the Capitol. It was not a straight road, but wound along
between important buildings, and in different places
it varied in width. At the entrance to the Forum
stood the round temple of Vesta, the House of the
Vestals, and that of the Pontifex Maximus; a little
further on was the Temple of Castor, built close

to the spring where the Twin Gods were said to have watered their horses when they brought the news of the victory at Lake Regillus to Rome. Then the road wound on and in front of him the Roman saw the Rostra[1] or platform from which leaders of the people and other great orators addressed the crowds assembled from time to time in the Forum. To the right of the Rostra was the Comitium, or assembly place of the people, with the ancient Senate House close by, and to the left was a great Basilica or Law Court. The Basilica was a large oblong building with a central nave divided from two side aisles by rows of pillars, above which there were sometimes galleries. At one end there was a semi-detached arched recess, called the apse, in which trials were conducted and in which the seat of the judge was placed. In the main part of the building were to be found business men who found it a convenient place in which to transact business, and groups of idlers who lounged about knowing they were sure to meet their acquaintances there.

At the foot of the Capitol was the Temple of Janus and in a dungeon beneath was the state prison. To the left was the Temple of Saturn used as the State Treasury, and just below the Temple on the Capitol was the Tabularium, the State Record Office. At each end, therefore, of the Sacra Via were the buildings which were the outward signs of those things which had endured through all the

---

[1] *Rostra* = beaks. The platform was so called because it was decorated at each end with the prows of ships captured from the people of Antium. See Livy, VIII, 14.

stormy days of the history of Rome. At one end were the symbols of the state religion, above all the Sacred Hearth of the City, sacred to Vesta and tended by the Vestals, and at the other were the places in which centred the political life, out of which was to develop the spirit of law and good government that was to be one of the great gifts of Rome to the world.

The whole Sacra Via was dominated by the hill of the Capitol which rose steeply up at one end. On the Capitol itself stood the Temple of Jupiter Optimus Maximus, symbol of the strength and majesty of the state. Here came the magistrates to offer sacrifices and to make their vows when they came into office; here did the consul offer prayers for victory before he departed for war, and on his return he brought his booty and placed it in the temple; it was along the Sacra Via that a victorious general crowned with laurel passed in triumph, and it was upon the knees of the statue of Jupiter that he placed the laurel wreath, emblem of his victory. Jupiter Optimus Maximus was the symbol to Romans of Rome and of all that Roman citizenship meant, and it was before his statue that Roman youths offered sacrifices on the day when they attained manhood.

The land between the Capitol and the river, which takes a bend there, consisted of a great open space called the Campus Martius. An old tradition told that this land had once belonged to the Tarquin Kings, and that after they had been driven out of Rome it was taken by the Senate, consecrated to Mars, and then given to the people for the drilling of soldiers and for games.

There happened at the time, it is said, to be a crop of corn there which was ripe for the harvest, and as it would have been sacrilege to consume what was growing on the Campus, a large body of men were sent to cut it. They carried it, straw and all, in baskets to the Tiber and threw it into the river. It was the height of the summer and the stream was low, consequently the corn stuck in the shallows, and heaps of it were covered with mud; and gradually as the débris which the river brought down collected there, an island was formed.[1]

Another tradition said that in the middle of the fifth century B.C. a pestilence broke out in Rome and both the city and the country round were ravaged. The Sibylline Books were consulted, and it was found that if Aesculapius, the God of Healing, were brought from Epidaurus to Rome, all would once more be well. This was done, and a temple was built to Aesculapius on this island in the Tiber and the sick were brought to it to be cured. The island is still there, but though the Temple and the statue have long since disappeared, the sick still go there to be healed and have done so ever since those early days. After the pagan temple had gone, Christian monks established a monastery on the island where they cared for the sick, and to this day there is still a hospital there.

Up to the time of Augustus, for its great build-

[1] Livy, II, ϰ.

ings and architecture, Alexandria had been the finest city in the Mediterranean world. But Alexandria was now part of the Roman Empire, and Augustus was determined that as Rome was the capital of the Roman world, so should no other city excel her in outward magnificence.

Julius Caesar had already begun great changes in the appearance of Rome. He had altered and enlarged the old Forum and he had planned new buildings, but he had not lived to complete his plans, and it was left to Augustus to carry them out. He built a palace on the Palatine, a very simple dwelling compared to those his successors were to build, but it was a larger house than had been built in Rome before, and close to his palace was a beautiful temple to Apollo and a library. Assisted by his minister Agrippa, Augustus built a new Senate House opposite the Basilica Julius Caesar had erected, and he also built at one end of the Forum a temple to the honour of Caesar. The old Rostra was replaced by a magnificent marble platform, and as the old Forum was too small for all the business that had to be transacted there, he built a new one near by known as the Forum of Augustus.

The plans of Augustus included temples and porticoes, a great stone theatre, baths and other public buildings, and he wrought such a transformation in the appearance of the city, that before his death he used to boast that he "found Rome of brick and left it of marble."

The successors of Augustus continued to enlarge Rome and beautified it with every kind of splendid

building. There were great government buildings,
basilicas and fora where the business of the law and
trade were carried on: circuses, stadia, theatres and
amphitheatres, of which the Flavian Amphitheatre
or Colosseum built by Vespasian was the greatest,
for amusement; baths, especially those of Caracalla
and Diocletian, for recreation and enjoyment;
temples and shrines, such as the Pantheon begun by
Augustus but rebuilt by Hadrian, for the worship
of the gods; triumphal arches and statues erected in
recognition of great deeds done for the state. On
the Palatine were the palaces of the Emperors,
on other hills, chiefly the Caelian, Esquiline and
Quirinal, were the houses of the rich, separated
from each other by gardens, and the air was sweet
with the fragrance of flowers and shrubs. To ensure an adequate supply of water for all these gardens and palaces and the great baths, mighty aqueducts were built which brought the water from great
distances to the city.

But there was another side to the splendour and
magnificence of Imperial Rome. So great an amount
of space was taken up by these public buildings and
large houses, that the dwellings of the poorer people,
who lived chiefly on the Aventine, were crowded
together in high and sunless buildings. Juvenal, a
severe critic of many things in Imperial Rome,
complained of the high rents in the city, and said
that it was possible to buy a house and garden in
the country for the amount of rent asked for a dark
room in Rome.

Walking in the streets and fora, or watching the

games and shows in the amphitheatres could have been seen men from every part of the Roman world. Great nobles and slaves, poets and scholars, mer-- chants and artisans were there, and mingling with the Romans and Italians were dark-complexioned men from the East, and Egyptians, always looked upon as having something mysterious about them; Greek teachers with their pupils; tall, fair-haired Germans of the Emperor's Guard; and Britons from the far north of the Empire, gazing in wonder at all the splendour of the city.

Visitors who came to Rome from all parts of the Empire found a city of amazing magnificence, and one of them, Strabo, a Greek from Asia Minor, gave an account of what he had seen:

The ancients of Republican times bestowed little attention upon the beautifying of Rome. But their successors, and especially those of our own day, have embellished the city with numerous and splendid objects. Pompey, the Divine Caesar, and Augustus, with his children, friends, wife and sister, have surpassed all others in their zeal and munificence in these decorations. The greater number of these may be seen in the Campus Martius which to the beauties of nature adds those of art. The size of the plain is remarkable, allowing chariot races and the equestrian sports without hindrance, and multitudes here exercise themselves with ball-games, in the Circus, and on the wrestling grounds. The structures that surround the Campus, the greensward covered with herbage all the year round, the summit of the hills beyond the Tiber, extending from its banks with panoramic effect, present a spectacle which the eye aban-

dons with regret. . . . If thence you proceed to visit
the ancient Forum, which is equally filled with basilicas,
porticoes and temples, you will there behold the Capitol,
the Palatine, and the noble works that adorn them, and
the palace of Livia, the wife of Augustus, each successive
work causing you speedily to forget that which you have
seen before.   Such then is Rome!

II. THE ROMAN HOUSE

What is more strictly protected by all religious feeling, than the house of each individual citizen?   Here is
his altar, his hearth, here are his Di Penates: here he
keeps all the objects of his worship and performs all
his religious rites: his house is a refuge so solemnly protected, that no one can be torn from it by force.

In this way did Cicero describe the feeling of the
Roman for his home, for the house of a Roman was
a real home, not as with the Greek a place where
he did little more than sleep and have his meals and
where the women lived.

The earliest form of Roman house was very simple.
It consisted of an oblong room, called the *atrium*,
with an opening in the middle of the roof through
which the rain water fell into a basin specially built
into the floor beneath, which was called the *impluvium*.   This atrium was the living-room for the whole
family; the meals were cooked and then eaten in it,
all indoor work was done in it, in the atrium the
daily offerings were made to the Lares and Penates,
and at night the family slept there.   There was
only one door, and the hearth was generally oppo-

site it. Near the hearth was kept the chest or strong box which contained the valuables of the family, and the mother sat beside the hearth when she was busy with her spinning or weaving.

This primitive room very soon began to be insufficient, and as standards of living were raised and more luxuries were introduced, a larger house was found to be necessary. The atrium was still the centre of the house, but a number of smaller rooms used for sleeping and as store-rooms were built round it and opening into it, and between two of them was a narrow passage serving as entrance-hall or *vestibulium*. In a larger house there was generally an open recess on each side of the atrium in which, if the family were noble, the images of the ancestors were kept. Beyond the atrium and separated from it only by a curtain, which was generally drawn back, was the *tablinum*. This was used by the master of the house, and in it he kept the chest with the family valuables, which in older times had stood beside the hearth, and all his papers. He could secure privacy by drawing the curtains, but if they were thrown back he could command a view of the greater part of the house. The tablinum opened into a court, open to the sky and surrounded by a colonnade. This was the *peristyle*. The *triclinium*, or dining-room, frequently opened out of the peristyle and the kitchen was beyond it.

This was in the main the plan of a Roman house during the later Republic, and the general plan changed very little in the days of the Empire. Each house varied, naturally, with the wealth and taste of the owner, but whatever the size of the house, the atrium was the centre round which it was built. When the peristyle was added, it became the centre of the domestic life of the family, and the atrium was used as a reception room or for more formal entertainments. Some of the largest houses had two peristyles, with a number of smaller rooms opening from them: a sun-room, libraries, rooms similar to our drawing-rooms, and nearly always a private chapel in which stood images of the gods.

To the Roman his house was a place to be lived in, not merely to be looked at from the outside, and from the houses that still exist and a few wall pictures, the exterior seems to have been plain and undecorated. But standing in the vestibulium the view of the interior must have been very beautiful. One looked first into the atrium with its mosaic floor, in the centre of which was the impluvium, a marble basin with sometimes a fountain in the middle. The pillars of the atrium were of marble, and along the walls stood statues and other rare works of art. The walls themselves were painted or panelled in marble and the ceilings were covered with decorations in ivory and gilt. If the curtains were drawn back, one looked beyond the atrium through the tablinum into the peristyle, with its marble columns, its fountain and beautiful plants and flowers. Now that the city of Pompeii has been excavated, it does not require much imagination to think oneself back into the time of the ancient Romans, for so many of the houses are well preserved, and the peristyles as beautifully planted with flowers and shrubs as they were more than two thousand years ago.

The rooms all opened either into the atrium or the peristyle and many of them must have been very cold in the winter. A few houses had furnaces from which hot air was taken through pipes to the floors of some of the rooms, but this was not always done, and probably the chief method of keeping warm was that of putting on warmer clothes and keeping as much as possible in the rooms warmed by the sun. Sometimes charcoal braziers were used. These were metal boxes into which hot charcoal was put; they stood on legs so that they did not damage the floors, and handles were attached to them by means of which they were carried about.

The Roman, like the Greek, did not like his rooms filled with furniture. The principal articles of furniture used in a Roman house were chests, couches, chairs, tables and lamps, most of which were of beautiful form and artistic workmanship.

Life in Rome during the last years of the Republic became more and more feverish and restless. Cicero complained that life there gave him no quiet, for "in Rome," he said, "there is not time to breathe." The result of this was that well-to-do Romans began to build country houses for themselves outside Rome, where they could go during the summer months when the heat of Rome made life in the city very trying. During the last years of the Republic many of these country houses were the old farm-houses, enlarged to meet the requirements of the Roman who wanted a retreat from city life.

Sometimes they were the old homes of their forefathers, and as such they felt for them a great love
and reverence.

Here [said Cicero] is the ancient stock from which
we are sprung, here are our sacred rites, here our kindred, here countless traces of our ancestors. Just look
at this country-house; you see it, as it is now, enlarged
by the care of my father, who having weak health passed
almost all his life here in literary pursuits; but in this
very house, I must tell you, when it was a little old-
fashioned cottage, I was born. And so there is a something, some sort of lurking feeling and fancy, which seems
to make me take a peculiar pleasure in it. And why
not? when we remember that the wise man of old is
said to have rejected immortality that he might see
Ithaca once more.

Under the Empire the country house became a
villa, a large house built with all the conveniences
of the town in country surroundings. The Roman
took great delight in this country life. He enjoyed the quiet beauty of rich plains and fertile valleys, he took pleasure in the song of the birds and in
the rippling of the streams.

Picture to yourself [wrote Pliny in a letter describing
the district in which he had built himself a country
villa] an immense amphitheatre such as only nature can
create, with a wide-spreading plain ringed with hills,
and the summits of the hills themselves covered with
tall and ancient forests. Down the mountain slopes
there are stretches of underwoods, and among these are
rich, deep-soiled hillocks, where if you look for a stone

you will have hard work to find one, which are just as fertile as the most level plains, and ripen just as rich harvests, though later in the season. Below these, along the whole hillsides, stretch the vineyards which present an unbroken line far and wide, on the borders and lowest level of which comes a fringe of trees. Then you reach the meadows and the fields. The meadows are jewelled with flowers, and produce trefoil and other herbs, always tender and soft, and looking as though they were always fresh, for all parts are well nourished by never-failing streams. You would be delighted if you could obtain a view of the district from the mountain height, for you would think you were looking not so much at earth and fields as at a beautiful landscape picture of wonderful loveliness.[1]

The immediate neighbourhood of the city of Rome was full of small country villas. Further off in the Alban and Sabine hills and at such places as Praeneste and Tibur, there were larger estates, and the sea-coast of the Bay of Naples from Cumae to Salerno was dotted with beautiful houses. On the coast Baiae was particularly liked and the place became very fashionable.

The large Roman villa had two parts, the house of the master with its gardens, and the farmer's house with the stables, barns, orchards and fields. The country house was built somewhat differently from the town house. It was more varied in plan and did not as a rule have a peristyle, the gardens taking its place. The Roman garden, like the modern Italian garden, was very carefully laid out, with

[1] Pliny the Younger, V, 6.

trees and shrubs cut into prescribed and sometimes fantastic forms, and stiff flower-beds full of the crocus, violet, narcissus and rose.

Most Roman gentlemen of the Empire had several country villas. One, perhaps, would be near Rome, a place to which they could escape for a day or two from the business and noise of the city; another would be further off in the real country; and another, probably, by the sea.

You will cease to wonder [wrote Pliny to a friend] of my love for my estate, when you are told the charms of the villa, the handiness of the site, and the stretch of shore it commands.

The villa is large enough for all requirements, and is not expensive to keep in repair. At its entrance there is a modest but by no means mean-looking hall; then come the cloisters, which are rounded into the likeness of the letter D, and these enclose a smallish but handsome courtyard. They make a fine place of refuge in a storm, for they are protected by glazed windows and deep overhanging eaves. Facing the middle of the cloisters is a cheerful inner court, then comes a dining-room running down toward the shore, which is handsome enough for anyone, and when the sea is disturbed by the south-west wind the room is just flecked by the spray of the spent waves. There are folding doors on all sides of it, or windows that are quite as large as such doors, and so from the two sides and the front it commands a prospect as it were of three seas, while at the back one can see through the inner court, the cloisters, the courtyard, then more cloisters and the hall, and through them the woods and the distant hills. . . . Adjoining one of the rooms is a chamber with one wall rounded like a bay, which catches the sun on all its windows as he moves through the heavens. In the wall of this room I have had shelves placed like a library, which contains the volumes which I not only read, but read over and over again. Next to it is a sleeping-chamber. . . . On the other side of the building there is a nicely decorated chamber, then another room which would serve either as a large bed-chamber or a moderate sized dining-room, as it enjoys plenty of sunshine and an extensive sea-view. Behind this is an apartment with an ante-room, suitable for summer because of its height, and for winter use owing to its sheltered position, for it is out of reach of all winds. . . . Close by is the tennis court, which receives the warmest rays of the afternoon sun; on one side a tower has been built with two sitting-rooms on the ground-floor commanding a wide expanse of sea, a long stretch of shore, and the pleasantest villas of the neighbourhood. There is also a second tower, containing a bedroom which gets the sun morning and evening. On the floor beneath is a sitting-room where, even when the sea is stormy, you hear the roar and thunder only in subdued and dying murmurs. It looks out upon the exercise ground, which runs round the garden.[1]

Life in the country could be and often was made as restless and extravagant as life in the city, but most Romans enjoyed the months they spent in the country as giving them a simpler, quieter, more peaceful and health-giving life than that in the city.

I prefer my Tuscan house [writes Pliny again] to my other places, because in addition to all its beauties,

[1] Pliny the Younger, II, 17.

my repose here is more profound and more comfortable, and therefore all the freer from anxiety. There is no necessity to don the toga; no neighbour ever calls to drag me out; everything is placid and quiet; and this peace adds to the healthiness of the place, by giving it, so to speak, a purer sky and a more liquid air. I enjoy better health both in mind and body here than anywhere else, for I exercise the former by study and the latter by hunting. Besides, there is no place where my household keep in better trim, and up to the present I have not lost a single one of all whom I brought with me. I hope Heaven will forgive the boast, and that the gods will continue my happiness to me and preserve this place in all its beauty.[1]

III. ROMAN DRESS

The Romans, lords of the world, the race that wears the toga.[2]

The toga was the most ancient and the most characteristic dress of the Roman gentleman. It was a long white woollen robe, covering the figure down to the feet, and when properly put on was a very dignified and graceful garment. Under it was worn a tunic, generally without sleeves. When he was at home or at work in the country, the Roman might wear only the tunic, but whenever he appeared in public, and on all ceremonious occasions, he had to put on his toga. When the messengers from the Senate went out to tell Cincinnatus that he had been appointed Dictator, we are told "that he was re-

[1] Pliny the Younger, V, 6.   [2] Aeneid, I.

quested to put on his toga that he might hear the commands of the Senate."[1] It would not have been considered fitting that he should receive such a message clad only in the tunic in which he was working.

The Roman boy wore a special toga with a purple hem until he reached manhood and was admitted to the duties and privileges of citizenship, when he wore the regular white toga of the Roman citizen. The toga had to be worn on all ceremonious occasions: when the Roman married, when he performed his duties as magistrate or governor, and by the general when he entered Rome in triumph. When a Roman died, his body lay in state in the atrium of his house, and there he lay wrapped for the last time in his toga. Only a free Roman citizen might wear the toga, and were he sent out from Rome into exile, he was obliged to leave it behind him. The toga was the outward symbol of Roman citizenship.

The toga was not easy to put on, for it seems to have had no pins or fastenings to keep it in place, and it was the work of a properly trained slave to adjust its folds and to see that it was properly put on. It was an oblong piece of cloth with rounded corners, so that spread out it looked oval. This was folded lengthwise, but not quite in the middle, which made one fold wider than the other. One end was then thrown over the left shoulder, so that one-third of the material hung down in front to the feet, the longer piece hanging down the back. This part was then brought forward under the right shoulder and again thrown over the left, with the loose end hang-

[1] See p. 78.

ing down the back. The toga of the ordinary citizen was white; consuls, censors and dictators wore a white toga with a purple border; that of a victorious general was purple.

On his feet the Roman gentleman wore sandals of various kinds and sometimes shoes; his head was generally bare. It was rare for a Roman gentleman to wear jewellery. He usually wore a signet ring, but to wear more than one ring was considered bad taste.

The Roman lady wore three garments: the tunic, the stola and the palla. The tunic was very similar to that worn by the man, except that it frequently had short sleeves, and it only came down to the knee. The stola was a long outer tunic, with short sleeves, a narrow flounce or hem at the bottom, and a girdle by means of which it was adjusted to the proper length and the folds kept in place. The stola was generally open from the shoulder to the waist, and it was fastened on the shoulders by brooches. The palla was a garment worn out of doors and arranged very much like the toga, though the lady often drew it up so as to form a hood for her head. Only a Roman matron might wear the stola. Girls and foreign women wore only the tunic and the palla, and sometimes the foreign women arranged their palla so that it was worn more like a Greek chiton than the toga.

Like the man, the woman wore sandals or slippers, only these were often more elaborately embroidered than those worn by the men.

The Roman lady of the Empire was very fond of

jewellery. She wore rings, brooches, pins, bracelets, necklaces and ear-rings. Cornelia, the mother of the Gracchi, represented an older and more austere spirit when, unable to bring out trinkets of gold and precious stones to display to her friend, she pointed to her sons, saying: "These are my jewels."

IV. ROMAN AMUSEMENTS

The Romans had no Sundays or other days in the week on which every day business was regularly stopped, but their calendar provided for a number of holidays. These amounted to about a hundred days a year, and on some great and unusual occasions there were additional holidays announced. These days were given up to public amusements, to the theatre, the circus, and the spectacles in the amphitheatre. The theatre did not appeal to the Romans as it did to the Greeks, and the Circus and the Amphitheatre are more characteristically Roman. All these public amusements were provided for the people by the state, but as they grew more elaborate and magnificent, the Emperor and private individuals used to help in providing them, and already at the end of the Republic, the providing of public amusements had become a favourite method of trying to win popular favour.

All through Roman history the Games of the Circus played a very important part in the life of the Roman people. They had begun in very early times, and as far as is known, they were a religious ceremony celebrated in honour of some god, whose favour it was in some way hoped to gain by the spectacle provided for him. Every year in September the *Ludi Romani* took place in the Circus Maximus, of which the chief attraction was the chariot race. Not a seat would be empty, and as the chariots raced seven times round the arena, the charioteers wearing special colours, red and white, green and blue, excitement ran very high as the vast audience favoured one or the other colour.

Seest how the chariots in mad rivalry
Poured from the barrier grip the course and go,
When youthful hope is highest, and every heart
Drained with each wild pulsation? How they ply
The circling lash, and reaching forward let
The reins hang free! Swift spins the glowing wheel:
And now they stoop, and now erect in air
Seem borne through space and towering to the sky:
No stop, no stay; the dun sand whirls aloft;
They reek with foam-flakes and pursuing breath;
So sweet is fame, so prized the victor's palm.[1]

It was in Imperial Rome that these public amusements were most splendidly celebrated, and their highest point of magnificence was reached in the building of the great Flavian Amphitheatre known later as the Colosseum.

It was in the Colosseum that the gladiatorial and other similar combats were held, the most popular of all the Roman amusements. It is difficult to imagine ourselves in the amphitheatre. Pity and mercy had never been special characteristics of

[1] Virgil: *Georgic*, III.

the Roman, and he had never been marked by any great delicacy or fineness of feeling. But he watched the combats in the arena not only with brutal callousness, but with actual enjoyment, and in so doing has left a stain on his character that no sternness or hardness alone would have left.

The origin of these combats goes back to very ancient times. It was always believed amongst primitive people that blood, without which no man could live, was the most valuable thing that could be offered to the gods, and hence came the custom of making human sacrifices. This was also partly the origin of the custom of slaying his slaves at the funeral of an important man. But slaves were valuable and were wanted by the heir, so this custom was in time looked upon as wasteful, and in Rome combats between slaves, in which invariably the stronger survived, seem to have become the custom. All this took place in primitive times, but it is thought that the training of the gladiator to fight in the arena had its origin in some such custom, and was one reason for the Roman indifference to the cruelty of it. These shows had always existed in Rome, but it was not until the period of the Empire that they became so extraordinarily popular.

In the gladiatorial shows there were different kinds of combatants. There were slaves, prisoners of war, condemned criminals and professional gladiators, as well as wild beasts. The gladiators were generally, though not always, freemen, thoroughly and severely trained in gladiatorial schools. The profession was looked upon as doubtful in character, but a successful gladiator was a popular hero. The condemned criminal was forced to fight, and whatever the outcome of the combat his life was forfeit.

The Emperors made the spectacle in the amphitheatre as magnificent as possible. The Colosseum held eighty-seven thousand people. The Emperor and his suite occupied special seats of honour; special places were reserved for the Vestals; the Senators sat together, recognized by the broad purple stripe on the tunic; citizens wore their holiday attire and had garlands on their heads; men of all nations and all tongues crowded together to see men and beasts fight. If the sun were very hot, a richly coloured awning was placed over the seats; perfumed water played into the air from fountains; music was played between the horrible combats.

The gladiators entered the arena in a procession, took their places and the fight began. As soon as one was wounded, the people cried out "Habet!" and the fate of the vanquished depended on their will. He appealed to their mercy by raising his forefinger. If they wished him to be killed, they turned their thumbs down and he was at once put to death by the victor, but if he had fought well, and the spectators desired that his life should be spared, they waved handkerchiefs.

When the turn came for the condemned criminals to fight, knowing that whatever happened they would not be allowed to live, they marched up before the Emperor and saluting him said: *Ave Caesar! morituri te salutant.* Hail Caesar! those about to die salute thee!

The insatiable appetite of the people for the arena was not satisfied with fights between man and man, and fights were arranged between men and wild beasts. The deserts in the north of Africa were searched for every kind of known and unknown and strange beast that would fight. Sometimes these animals were kept without food before the combat, so that they might be the more fierce. Men fought with beasts, and beasts fought with beasts, and sometimes criminals who had particularly roused popular indignation, were sent unarmed to fight with the wildest beasts. And all this was done to make a Roman holiday.

It was not until the sixth century that the combats of the arena were stopped by law. The Colosseum still stands, one of the great monuments left of Imperial Rome, a building in which every Roman of his time spent days in brutal amusement. The magnificence of the building was so impressive that a prophecy was made concerning it, and it was said:

> While stands the Colosseum, Rome shall stand;
> When falls the Colosseum, Rome shall fall;
> And when Rome falls, the world.

CHAPTER XVI

Roman Education

I. THE DEBT OF ROME TO GREECE

IT is not known when Greek influence was first felt in Italy, but before the founding of Rome there had been Greek colonies in Sicily and the south of Italy. In all kinds of ways Greek ideas began to spread. With their wares, wandering traders took also ideas and the language. From the earliest times the Keepers of the Sibylline Books must have known Greek, for these books were written in that language. In many Roman homes children grew up understanding Greek, for Delos in the Aegean Sea was the greatest slave market of the ancient world, and most of the house slaves bought there were Greeks. All this early use of Greek was for practical purposes, but interest in the language soon began to extend to its literature. Poetry was studied, and by the middle of the third century B.C. most educated Romans seem to have been able to speak and understand Greek. Towards the end of the third century B.C. Andronicus, a Greek slave who had been given his freedom, seeing the growing interest in Rome for Greek literature, translated the

317

Odyssey into Latin, in order that Roman children might read it. He also translated into Latin a number of Greek plays, chiefly comedies, which were acted in Rome, and by this means Greek ideas and Greek habits of thought were introduced.

This did not take place without protest and amongst others, Cato vigorously opposed the growing tendency to use Greek methods in education. These old-fashioned Romans particularly objected to the Greek methods of teaching rhetoric, for they thought that rhetoric dealt only with words and not with the development of character, and that it was a dangerous instrument to put into the hands of youth. But men like Cicero and Caesar did not despise it. Rhetoric could be abused like anything else, but in the hands of statesmen who knew how to put it to noble ends, it was a great instrument for the carrying out of their ideals.

After the Roman conquests in the East, Greek art began to flow towards Rome. On the occasion of one triumph "seven hundred and eighty brazen statues and two hundred and thirty marble statues"[1] were carried in the procession, and in the triumph of Aemilius Paulus it took two hundred and fifty chariots to carry all the statues, pictures and images brought from Greece.

All this necessarily influenced the taste of the Romans. They learnt to appreciate what was good, the fashion of collecting grew, and the original Greek statues were copied in large numbers. But as time went on, Rome developed her own art and

[1] Livy, XXXIX, 5.

literature, she did not merely copy. Nevertheless, like all succeeding generations, she owed an immeasurable debt to those who had gone before, and all that was most worth while in the things of the higher intellectual life she owed to Greece. In the words of her own poet:

> Greece, conquered Greece, her conqueror subdued,
> And Rome grew polished, who till then was rude.[1]

II. THE ROMAN SCHOOLBOY

The Paterfamilias was the Head of the Roman Family, and every member of it was subject to his will. His authority over his children began as soon as they were born, and he even decided whether they should be given the right to live or not. An ancient custom decreed that a new-born child should be laid at the feet of the father. If he took it up in his arms, it was a sign that the child should live and be brought up as a Roman citizen; but if he turned from it and left it lying on the ground, the child was an outcast. It was taken from the house by a slave, and unless some kindly person took pity on it and cared for it, the baby was left somewhere to die.

The first important ceremony in the life of a child was the giving of the name. Every Roman man had three names: his *praenomen*, *nomen* and *cognomen*. The nomen corresponded to our surname, though it was placed in the middle of the

[1] Horace: *Epistles*, II, 1.

three names, it was the name of the gens to which the person bearing it belonged; the cognomen which stood last was the name of the particular branch of the gens to which he belonged; and the praenomen, which stood first, was the special name given to him as an individual.

A child was given his praenomen on the ninth day after his birth. A sacrifice was offered, and it was a day of rejoicing, when relatives and friends came to the house, and in honour of the occasion they brought with them little toys for the baby. After the offering of the sacrifice, the father hung a small locket, of gold if he could afford it, otherwise of some less valuable material, containing an amulet round the child's neck. This was called the *bulla*, and it was worn by the boy until he attained manhood and by the girl until her marriage.

A boy was brought up at home by his mother until he was old enough either to go to school or to be taught by his father. In the early days of the Republic, the father generally gave the boy whatever instruction he had, but after the Punic Wars, when Rome had come into closer contact with other lands beside Italy, and especially with Greece, it was the custom for a boy to be taught by a Greek slave. But even if the boy went to school, the more important part of his early training was given him at home. It was there that he learnt his earliest lessons of obedience, that unquestioning and absolute obedience which was demanded of every Roman child, of truth and honour, of keeping his word, and of reverence for the gods. Roman children were with their parents more than most other children of the ancient world.

The old custom of Rome was for young people to learn from their elders the proper course of conduct, by watching their behaviour as well as by listening to their instructions. Each one took his parent for his guide, or, if he had no parent, he chose the noblest and most aged Senator to supply the place of one.[1]

The boy, when he was not at school, was constantly with his father. If he were a farmer, like Cincinnatus, the boy would help in the work of the fields; if the family lived in the city, the boy would be expected to stand gravely and respectfully at his father's side when he received his guests, and he would accompany him to the Forum when a distinguished orator was to address the people, in order that he might listen to what the great Romans of the time had to say. At one time the boys were allowed to go with their fathers to the Senate, but this was stopped, because it was said that their mothers tried to find out from them afterwards what had been discussed.

In the earlier days of the Republic one of the first things a boy had to learn was the Laws of the Twelve Tables. He generally learnt them at the time when he received his first lessons in reading, writing and arithmetic. Later there was less insistence on the Twelve Tables and Cicero remarks that "when we were boys we had to learn the

[1] Pliny the Younger, VIII, 14.

Twelve Tables by heart like a kind of hymn. Nobody does it now."

In the days of the later Republic, the Romans,
the conquerors of Greece, yet themselves conquered
by her spirit, began to adopt Greek methods of
education. Aemilius Paulus, the conqueror of Perseus, brought up his children not only

as he himself had been, in the Roman and ancient discipline, but also with unusual zeal in that of Greece.
To this purpose he not only procured masters to teach
them grammar, logic and rhetoric, but had for them also
preceptors in modelling and drawing, managers of horses
and dogs, and instructors in field sports, all from Greece.
And, if he was not hindered by public affairs, he himself
would be with them at their studies, and see them perform their exercises, being the most affectionate father
in Rome.[1]

But most of these Greek teachers were slaves,
well educated, it is true, yet they were not freemen, and Romans of the old school, like Cato, objected to the employment of slaves as teachers.

Cato was one of the last representatives of the
simple and austere standards of the earlier Republic,
and he refused to allow a slave to teach his son, and
instead, he taught him himself.

When he began to come to years of discretion, Cato
himself would teach him to read, although he had a
servant, a very good grammarian, who taught many

[1] Plutarch: *Life of Aemilius Paulus.*

others; but he thought it not fit, as he himself said, to have his son reprimanded by a slave, or pulled, it may be, by the ears when found tardy in his lesson; nor would he have him owe to a servant the obligation of so great a thing as his learning; he himself, therefore, taught him his grammar, law and his gymnastic exercises. Nor did he only show him, too, how to throw a dart, to fight in armour, and to ride, but to box also and to endure both heat and cold, and to swim over the most rapid and rough rivers. He says, likewise, that he wrote histories, in large characters, with his own hand, that so his son, without stirring out of the house, might learn to know about his countrymen and his forefathers.[1]

Most Roman boys, both of the later Republic and of the Empire, went to school. There were three kinds of schools for them to attend: the Elementary School, the Grammar School, and the School of Rhetoric. Such schools were found not only in Rome, but in most of the important provincial cities, for Roman education was of the same type in all parts of the Empire.

As soon as a boy was old enough to go to school, he was given a pedagogue, generally a well-educated slave, who took him to school every morning, waited for him until the lessons were over, and sometimes carried his books for him. Out of school hours the pedagogue was expected to look after the boy unless he was with his father, help him with his lessons, punish him, if necessary, and in general be his companion and friend.

The school building was a very simple affair.

[1] Plutarch: *Life of Marcus Cato.*

Often it was not much more than a kind of shed built on to the side of some public building, sheltered by a roof, but open at the sides so that the children were distracted by all the coming and going in the street. The school day began early, often before dawn, and it is said that the people who lived near a school found it a very noisy neighbour. They complained that there was no chance of sleep in the early morning hours, because even before cock-crow the streets were full of the sound of noisy schoolboys and the angry voice of the schoolmaster trying to keep order.[1]

In the Elementary School not much beyond reading, writing and arithmetic was taught. Great stress was laid from the very beginning on the careful and correct pronunciation of words. The pupils had to stand before the teacher and repeat them after him syllable by syllable until they had mastered both pronunciation and spelling. Writing was taught first by means of wax tablets on which the letters were scratched with a stilus, then, when the forms of the letters were familiar, the boy was allowed to write on papyrus. The Romans were a businesslike race and they insisted that their boys should be thoroughly grounded in arithmetic, especially in all forms of mental calculation. The work of the Elementary School included very little that was not strictly utilitarian in nature. On the whole it was the kind of education the early Romans desired for their sons, but occasionally such purely utilitarian aims met with sharp criticism.

[1] Martial.

To Greece, fair Greece, ambitious but of praise,
The Muse gave ready wit, and rounded phrase.
Our Roman boys, by puzzling days and nights,
Bring down a shilling to a hundred mites.
Come, young Albinus, tell us, if you take
A penny from a sixpence, what 'twill make.
Fivepence.   Good boy! you'll come to wealth one day.
Now add a penny.   Sevenpence, he will say.
O, when this cankering rust, this greed of gain,
Has touched the soul and wrought into its grain,
What hope that poets will produce such lines
As cedar-oil embalms and cypress shrines?[1]

When a boy knew how to read, write and do some
arithmetic, he left the Elementary School and went
to the Grammar School. Here, the chief subject
he learnt was literature. These schools became especially popular after the period of the Punic Wars,
when Greek teachers were much sought after. The
most important literature studied was poetry, and
that of Homer in particular. All kinds of subjects
were suggested by such study, history, mythology,
geography, language and style, but above all the
Greek teachers brought to the Roman mind something of the harmony at which the Greeks aimed
in the training of their youth. Subjects were not
kept apart and everything that was learnt con-
tributed to one harmonious whole. In order to
study Homer, the Roman boys learnt Greek, though
they often rebelled at being made to do so much
work in a foreign language. Though the Roman
boy had to learn Greek, it does not appear, however,

[1] Horace: *De Arte Poetica.*

that the Greek or other boys in the East had to learn Latin.

The Greek teachers in the Grammar Schools were sometimes freedmen but more often they were slaves, and though many of them earned the respect and affection of their pupils, as a class they were despised. The Roman admired Greek education and Greek culture and he wanted to give it to his son, but he despised the Greek. Some of the greatest gifts that have been given to civilization have come from the Greeks, but they lacked the one thing that the early Roman held to be the greatest, that which is best described as *character*. The Greek was unstable and not always to be trusted. It seems strange that the Romans should have been willing to entrust the education of their children to men whom, whatever they may have thought of their culture, they despised as persons, but possibly the Roman father believed that the lessons in character he gave his son himself, both by precept and example, were sufficient.

In thinking of these Greek slave teachers in Rome, it must, however, be remembered, that in those days slaves were nearly always prisoners of war, and that they were often well-born, well-educated and high-minded persons. If some of their ideals were different from those of the great Athenians of the fifth century B.C. it must also be remembered that great changes had come to Greece. The Greek had been conquered, and the loss of his freedom had hurt his soul. Nevertheless, slave as he was, he had great things to give to his Roman pupils. History has shown again and again that true greatness is born of suffering. If that wondrous civilization brought into being by the Greeks was to endure, it needed the discipline, the strength and sternness of the Roman character. It was because Greece was conquered by Rome that her civilization was able to gain that which at the time only Rome could give, and because she gave it, the Greek spirit has lived.

Roman boys were taught gymnastics; they went to the Campus Martius and the Tiber and learned to ride, to run, to jump and wrestle and to swim. But this training was for the sake of making them hardy and strong and fit to endure hardships, not as with the Greek, for the sake of making the body as beautiful as it could become.

The third school to which the Roman boy could go was the School of Rhetoric. Sometimes he went to it before he attained manhood and sometimes afterwards. These were the schools in which Greek influence was most deeply felt. Prose authors, rather than poetry, were studied here, and great attention was paid to the practice of composition and oratory. The aim of the study of rhetoric was to form the taste and judgment and to learn how to say the right thing in the right way, especially when speaking in public. To this end the pupils in these schools were given speeches to prepare on certain subjects, they argued with each other and debated. In studying the art of speaking in public, great importance was attached by the teacher to the arguments chosen, the order in which they were presented, the language used, the tones of the voice and the gestures employed. Because this teaching was of Greek origin when it was first introduced, some of the older Romans regretted it, thinking it would lead the youths astray. As usual, Cato voiced the opposition. At one time some Greek orators having come to Rome,

it began to be told that one of them, a Greek famous even to admiration, winning and carrying all before him, had impressed so strange a love upon the young men that quitting all their pleasures and pastimes, they ran mad, as it were, after philosophy; which indeed much pleased the Romans in general; nor could they but with much pleasure see the youth receive so welcomely the Greek literature, and frequent the company of learned men. But Cato, on the other hand, seeing the passion for words flowing into the city, from the beginning took it ill, fearing lest the youth should be diverted that way, and so should prefer the glory of speaking well before that of arms and doing well. He wanted the Greek philosophers to go home again to their own schools, and declaim to the Greek children, and leave the Roman youth to be obedient, as hitherto, to their own laws and governors.[1]

By the last century of the Republic, however, the Schools of Rhetoric were firmly established in Rome and they became increasingly important under the Empire. Treated as an end and not a means, oratory could become a very dangerous thing.

After much meditation [said Cicero, himself one of the greatest of Roman orators] I have been led to the

[1] Plutarch: *Life of Marcus Cato.*

conclusion that wisdom without eloquence is of little use to a state, while eloquence without wisdom is often positively harmful, and never of any value. Thus if a man, abandoning the study of reason and duty, which is always perfectly straight and honourable, spends his whole time in the practice of speaking, he is being brought up to be a hindrance to his own development, and a dangerous citizen.

The best Romans understood that real oratory required not only study and practice, but a wide knowledge of what great men of all ages had thought, and that for oratory to be used for the highest ends and for the good of the state, it must be joined to high ideals and honourable conduct.

The Roman youth generally attended these schools after he had attained manhood and was allowed to wear the toga of the Roman citizen. This took place when he was about seventeen years of age, and a special day was set apart by his family for the ceremonies connected with it. Early in the morning the youth laid the symbol of his childhood, his boy's tunic, before the Lares and Penates of his home and offered up a sacrifice. "Keep me," he said, "O Lares of my Fathers, for ye bred me to manhood when a tender child I played at your feet." Then his father took his bulla from his neck and hung it over the hearth, where it remained and was never worn again, unless the man who had worn it as a child was in some danger of his life from the envy of gods or men. A victorious general always wore it at his triumph. The youth was next clad in the toga and then, accompanied by his father, all his slaves and freedmen and a host of relatives and friends, he went to the Forum where he was greeted as a Roman citizen and his name inscribed on the roll of citizens kept in the Tabularium. Then followed the solemn sacrifice to Jupiter on the Capitol, and the youth entered on the duties, responsibilities and privileges of citizenship.

Roman youths belonging to noble and wealthy families nearly always completed their education by a period of travel and study abroad. They went to Greece, especially to Athens, to Rhodes, Alexandria and to cities in Asia Minor which were famous for their teachers.

The Romans had no special education for such professions as the law, political administration or the army, but the Roman gentleman was expected to take his share in these practical duties that concerned the state. In order to gain experience, sometimes after, sometimes instead of his travel and study abroad, the young man would attach himself to some distinguished lawyer, governor or general, and by observing and assisting him in his duties, he would gain practical experience that would be of the highest value to him later.

In all these ways, the Romans trained their sons and endeavoured to fit them for the strenuous life which lay before all Roman citizens who worthily fulfilled their obligations.

CHAPTER XVII

THE LIFE OF THE ANCIENT ROMAN

I. THE ROMAN GENTLEMAN

THE Roman Republic lasted for about five hundred years, and during this time Rome changed from being a small agricultural settlement to be the capital of an Empire. It was inevitable that during this long period great changes should take place in the habits and customs and the standards of living. But amidst all the change the Roman never lost his love of a country life. A Roman gentleman of the last century of the Republic took a keen and active interest in all the affairs of the city, but he was not a lover of city life as was the Athenian, and whenever he could, he escaped from the din and turmoil and restlessness of the city to the quiet of his country villa.

Life in the first century of the Republic was simple and stern, made so by the dangers which surrounded Rome on all sides, both from enemies and from nature. It was a country life, and men like Cincinnatus would go back to their farms and fields as soon as the immediate dangers to the state were over.

After the Punic Wars, however, when Rome was mistress not only of Italy, but of a large part of the Mediterranean, life in the city began to be of much greater importance than it had been before. The government of the Republic was carried on in Rome itself, and the fact that the headquarters of all the administrative and judicial councils and courts were in Rome, brought men from all parts of the Republic to the city. This of itself developed a city life and increased the population, and as the wealth of the Mediterranean began to pour into Rome, standards of living were raised and Roman life became a very different thing from what it had been in the old and primitive days.

Roman literature has told us most about life in the later days of the Republic and during the Empire, but in the life of Cato it has preserved for us a picture of how the earlier Roman lived and thought. Cato had a neighbour whose lands bordered on his and we are told how

he could not but admire how he laboured with his own hands, went on foot betimes in the morning to the courts to assist those who wanted his counsel: how, returning home again, when it was winter he would throw a loose frock over his shoulders, and in the summer time would work among his domestics, sit down with them, eat of the same bread, and drink of the same wine. . . . He cultivated the old habits of bodily labour, and liked best a light supper and a breakfast which never saw the fire, and he set his ambition rather on doing without luxuries than on possessing them. . . . He did all this not only when he was young, but also when old and grey-headed.

He himself says that he never wore a suit of clothes which cost more than a hundred drachmas; and that, when he was general and consul, he drank the same wine which his workmen did; and that the meat and fish which was bought in the meat market for his dinner did not cost above thirty asses.[1]

But Cato was probably the last of the great Romans who lived in this simple primitive way, for by the last century B.C. life in Rome had become the life of a great city. Rome had conquered both East and West and with that conquest and the wealth it brought came endless opportunities for self-indulgence. Oriental luxuries, rich food, rare wines and fruits were heaped in vulgar profusion on the tables of the rich. The great public baths, the Thermae, with their gorgeous halls with walls covered with marbles and floors inlaid with mosaics, with gymnasia and gardens, fountains and statues, became the lounging places of the idler and the gossip. There was waste and extravagance in all kinds of ways. It must be remembered, however, that much of our information about Roman society at this time comes from the history of the Caesars themselves, some of whom cannot possibly be taken as typical Romans of their time. Caligula and Nero were insane, and the fact that in spite of these wild rulers the Roman Empire maintained its greatness for centuries shows that somewhere there must have been other standards and other ways of living. The old Roman character had changed in many ways, but it was of too steadfast and too deeply-rooted

[1] Plutarch: *Life of Marcus Cato.*

a type to disappear altogether, and there is no doubt
that in many a quiet country place in Central Italy,
as well as in Rome itself, there were Roman families
still preserving the old upright, industrious manner
of life. Had it been otherwise, the Empire could
hardly have endured. Writers like Juvenal and
Martial would have us believe that there was nothing good in Roman society, yet the fact that they
complain shows that somewhere at the time there
must have existed a higher standard than shown by
those in Rome who, many of them, had so newly
acquired wealth and who, with no traditions of fine
living behind them, thought that vulgar ostentation
and profusion marked them out as men of importance
and position.

The Roman day was divided into twelve hours
beginning at sunrise and ending at sunset, and though
these hours would vary according to the time of
year, seven A.M. is usually reckoned as the first hour
of the morning. The early part of the day was considered the proper time for business and work, and
the later hours for rest and recreation.

The Roman rose early, generally before sunrise.
Workmen and shopkeepers, schoolboys and men of
letters were nearly always at work before the sun
was up, seeing to do their business by the light of a
smoky candle. The Roman gentleman, having risen,
expected all the members of his *familia* to salute him
and then he offered the daily prayers and made the
offerings to the Lares and Penates. Not much time
was spent over the morning breakfast. It consisted of bread dipped in wine, or eaten with honey,

olives or sometimes cheese. Workmen often ate this on their way to work and schoolboys, late for school, used to stop at the baker's to buy a kind of light cake which they ate as they ran along.

After his breakfast, when it was still barely light, the Roman gentleman attended to some of his business or wrote his letters. Then for about two hours he would receive his callers or *clients* as they were called. These were men who wished to be known as his supporters, or who wished his protection, or who were seeking some favour from him. They assembled in the vestibulium of the house, and when their patron was ready to receive them, they were admitted to the atrium, where they passed before him, bowing and uttering some courteous greeting. At the side of the master of the house stood a slave, called the *nomenclator*. It was the custom for the master of the house to address each of his clients by name, and to the more fortunate to give his hand. Did he forget a name, it was the duty of the nomenclator to whisper it quickly in his ear. This reception lasted for about two hours, and then, about the third hour of the day, the Roman gentleman set out for the Forum. His clients would form a kind of escort and accompany him, for the more followers he had, the greater was supposed to be his importance. "I press this strongly upon you," was the advice once given to a man who was canvassing for the consulship, "always be with a multitude."

During the morning a Roman might have to attend a trial or a meeting of the Senate; were he standing for some public office, this was the best time to do his canvassing; or there might be social functions to attend, for these all took place in the morning: the naming of a child, the assuming of the toga by the son of some friend, or a wedding. The Roman gentleman also attended to his own business during these morning hours, or he loitered about hearing what news had reached Rome from other parts of Italy or the provinces. Without the help of a newspaper, a Roman generally collected all the news of the day within a very short time of his appearing in the Forum.

All ordinary business was over by the sixth hour, though it sometimes went on until the ninth. At times of great crisis the Senate would sometimes prolong its meetings till late in the day, but law required that it should adjourn at sunset.

About the sixth hour the Roman gentleman returned home, where he had his midday meal, another light repast consisting chiefly of bread and fruit, nuts and wine, and then as a rule he took his siesta. Very important business was apt to go on without giving any time for this rest, but gradually it became so universal, especially during the period of the Empire, that during the noontide siesta everything stopped completely, leaving Forum and Senate, streets and colonnades so deserted, that the ghost stories of the time were as apt to be placed then as at midnight.

Between the siesta and the hour of dinner, which in ordinary times was usually about the ninth hour, the Roman took his exercise, in the Baths and in the Gymnasium. The younger men would go to the Tiber and the Campus Martius, and for the older men there were opportunities for all kinds of exercise in the halls adjoining the Thermae. The Roman Baths or Thermae played a great part in Roman life. They not only contained both hot and cold baths, but elaborate dressing-rooms and gymnasia, and in later days spacious courts for lounging, art galleries and libraries.

About the ninth hour the Roman dined. The business of the day was over, and he devoted the remaining hours to his family or to the entertainment of his friends. The dinner seems to have been the only form of purely social entertainment in Rome, so great care was taken in the preparation of everything connected with it. The dinner took place in the triclinium or dining-room. In the middle of the room was a square table with couches on three sides of it. Each couch held three people and it was rare for an ordinary dinner party to consist of more than nine people; if it did, another table was arranged, for it was considered very ill-bred to place more than three guests on one couch.

The guests arrived accompanied by their slaves, who removed their sandals, and they then took their places at the table, reclining on the couches and resting on the left elbow. The meal began with an invocation to the gods and then the dinner appeared. An ordinary dinner consisted of three courses, a light course at the beginning, then a dish of meat or fish, and dessert at the end. As the rare products of the Mediterranean world poured into Rome, the dinners became longer, more elaborate, costly and extravagant. In the matter of food the Roman never understood the moderation of the Greek. He generally preferred quantity to quality, and as the wealth of Rome increased, coarseness and vulgar profusion were found instead of delicacy and refinement.

After the main course of the dinner was removed, there was a moment of silence while the host made the offering to the Lares and Penates of the household, then as the dessert and wine were placed on the table, garlands of flowers and leaves were presented to the guests and fragrant perfumes were offered to them. Games and conversation followed the dinner, and then as the entertainment drew to a close, the guests called for their sandals which were brought by the slaves, and all departed home.

II. THE ROMAN LADY

All men rule over women, we Romans rule over all men, and our wives rule over us.

Cato the Censor.

The Romans held women in greater honour than any other nation of the ancient world. The words of Cato that "all men rule over women" were quite literally true, however, for in the eyes of the Roman law a woman had no freedom. Before her marriage she was entirely in the hands of her father, on her marriage she passed into a similar position towards her husband, and if she remained unmarried, she was under the control of her nearest male relative. Nevertheless, though legally she may have seemed to be little better than a slave, her position in the familia was a very honoured one. Ancient custom and tradition required that all women should be treated with reverence and honour, and a Roman matron was as much the mistress of her house as her husband was its master. In the old formula of marriage the Roman woman said simply: *Ubi tu Gaius, ego Gaia:* Where you are master, I am mistress. The Roman matron was addressed as Domina and she was expected to rule her household wisely and well, to be frugal and thrifty, industrious, simple and modest, grave and dignified.

During the early centuries of the Republic Rome had been ceaselessly at war, which meant that Roman men were constantly away from home for long periods at a time. This resulted in the Roman women becoming of necessity responsible for many of the duties usually performed by the men. They had to look after not only the house, but all the property and in some cases the farm; they controlled the slaves both indoors and out, and they superintended the education of the children, not only of the girls but of the younger boys as well. Unlike her Athenian sister the Roman woman grew up taking interest in the affairs of the state as well as of the household, she went in and out of the house, she walked at will in the streets, though not as a rule without an escort, and when she appeared everyone made way for her, and she might attend the public games and the theatre. She dined with her husband, she helped him receive his guests and he often consulted her on matters of business.

The early Roman lady led a very busy life. Roman girls did not as a rule go to school, but they were taught all that they were to know of book-learning at home by their mothers. A Roman maiden was generally married when she was about fifteen years of age, so the years given to her education were but short, and not much time was left to the early Roman maiden after she had learned all that concerned the management of the household. She learned to spin and weave and was expected to practise what she learnt in her home. Augustus himself, we are told, used to wear clothes spun for him by Livia and her maidens.

During the Punic Wars when Rome was under a great strain and needed a most careful control of all her resources, a law had been passed which

forbade any woman to have in her possession more than half an ounce of gold, to wear a dress of various colours or to ride in a two-horsed vehicle within a mile of the City or of any Roman town unless she was going to take part in some religious function.[1]

When the wars were over this law was much objected to and two of the tribunes proposed that it should be repealed, but two others

defended the law and declared that they would not allow it to be repealed; many of the nobility came forward to speak in favour of the repeal or against it; the Capitol

[1] Livy, XXXIV, 1.

was crowded with supporters and opponents of the proposal; the matrons could not be kept indoors either by the authority of the magistrates or the orders of their husbands or their own sense of propriety. They filled all the streets and blocked the approaches to the Forum; they implored the men who were on their way thither to allow the women to resume their former adornments now that the commonwealth was flourishing and private fortunes increasing every day. Their numbers were daily augmented by those who came up from the country towns. At last they ventured to approach the consuls and praetors and other magistrates with their demands.[1]

Such vigour on the part of the women greatly offended Cato who was consul at the time, for he thought that women were already interfering too much in public affairs, which he did not consider any of their business. "We suffer them now," he said, "to dabble in politics and mix themselves up with the business of the Forum and public debates and election contests."[2] This was bad enough, declared Cato, but it would be still worse to extend privileges to them by law, for he said,

if you allow them to pull away restraints and put themselves on an equality with their husbands, do you imagine that you will be able to tolerate them? From the moment that they become your fellows, they will become your masters.[3]

The women, however, were successful and the law was repealed.

[1] Livy, XXXIV.   [2] Ibid.   [3] Ibid.

Towards the end of the Republic Roman women began to be much better educated than they had been in earlier times. Cornelia, the second wife of Pompey, had, we are told,

other attractions besides those of youth and beauty; for she was highly educated, played well upon the lute, and understood geometry, and had been accustomed to listen with profit to lectures on philosophy; all this, too, without in any degree becoming unamiable or pretentious, as sometimes young women do when they pursue such studies.[1]

When a Roman maiden was old enough to be married, her parents generally arranged a suitable marriage for her. Special care was then taken to choose a day of good omen for the wedding and preparations were made. On the eve of her marriage, the Roman maiden took off her bulla and her child's tunic and consecrated them together with her childhood's toys to the Lares and Penates of the *familia*. She rose very early on her wedding morning, and her mother dressed her in the white tunic of the bride which was fastened with a woollen girdle. Her hair was then carefully arranged; tradition required that it should be parted by a spear-shaped comb into six locks which were kept in place by ribbons. On her head she wore a wreath of flowers and leaves which she had gathered herself, and over everything was draped the flame-coloured bridal veil. Then, dressed for her wedding, the bride awaited the coming of the bridegroom.

[1] Plutarch: *Life of Pompey.*

Whilst the mother had been dressing her daughter, the auspices had been taken, in order that nothing of bad omen might mar the ceremonies, and the guests had been arriving in the atrium of the house which had been decorated the day before with flowers and garlands. Here the bridegroom came, and when all was ready, the bride was brought to him and in the presence of her father and of all the guests she put her hand in his and plighted her troth to him. This ceremony was followed by the marriage feast, which lasted till late in the day. When the feast was over, the bride was led to the home of the bridegroom. An ancient custom required that she should be torn by force from her mother's arms, and then the wedding procession was formed.

Flute-players walked first and then came the bride, attended by three boys. She walked between two of them who led her by the hand, and the third walked in front bearing the wedding torch made of white thorn. Immediately behind her were carried her distaff and spinning-wheel, the symbols of domestic life, and then in a long procession followed all the wedding guests and friends. As they went along nuts were thrown to the slaves as a token of good luck.

When the bride reached the door of her new home, she anointed the door-posts with oil to symbolize plenty, and wound woollen bands about them to symbolize her duties as mistress of the household. She was then lifted over the threshold, probably to avoid any slip of her foot which would have been a bad omen, perhaps also in memory of the Sabine women who were carried by force into the homes of the first Romans.

Haunter of Mount Helicon,
　Who each tender maid
To her bridegroom bearest on,
Hear us now, Urania's son,
　Hymen lend thy aid!

Bend with marjoram thy brows;
　How its breath is sweet!
Don the veil, and come to us
Bringing joy, with saffron shoes
　On thy snow-white feet.

On this merry morning wake,
　Sound the wedding march
Clear and ringing: dance to make
Earth re-echo; seize and shake
　High the rosin-torch.

.　　.　　.　　.　　.　　.　　.

Fling the bolted portals wide!
She is coming now, the bride!
　How the torches toss
All the sparkles in their hair!

.　　.　　.　　.　　.　　.　　.

But she pauses blushing there,

.　　.　　.　　.　　.　　.　　.

Nay, she lists, and drops a tear,
　Knowing she must pass.

.　　.　　.　　.　　.　　.　　.

Come you forth, O bride, and hear
  If you will my lay.
Mark the golden torches, dear,
Tossing all their tresses clear,
  Bride do not delay.

.   .   .   .   .   o   o

Raise the torches, lads, on high;
  Lo, I see the veil
Coming now; and cheerily
All in time together, cry
  "Hymen, Hymen, hail!"

Shout aloud your jokes and glee;
  Bid the favourite throw
Nuts among the slaves, for he
Must have heard his destiny;
  He's forgotten now!

Throw the nuts, O favourite, now
  To the slaves; you're done.
You have played with nuts enow,
Now to Hymen you must bow.
  Throw the nuts, my son!

o   .   o   o   .   c

Good the omens are; be bold;
  O'er the threshold stone
Lift your little feet of gold;
Pass the polished portal's fold.
  (Hymen, help her on!)

> Maidens, shut the portals; we
> Now have played enough.
> Happy pair, live happily,
> Try your youth and energy
> In the lists of love.[1]

The bride was now led by her husband into the atrium, where they knelt together and lighted the first fire of their new hearth from the sacred fire of the wedding-torch. The torch was then thrown to the guests and great good luck was supposed to attend the happy person who caught it. The wedding festivities were concluded by a banquet given by the bride and bridegroom the following day, and then the young matron assumed the duties which she had learnt from her mother.

III. THE SLAVES AND WORKING PEOPLE OF ROME

Ancient history has left records about the life of the Roman gentleman and of the Roman lady, but it has told us very little about the life of the working-man and of wage-earners in general. We know a good deal about the slaves, because they ministered so directly to the well-being of the gentleman and formed a part of his household, but of the free-born working-man we know much less.

In earliest times Rome had been an agricultural community and the land belonging to her had been divided up into small holdings and worked by the farmers who owned their own farms. To many a

[1] Catullus.

Roman this early country life seemed one that was far more worth while than the restless, fevered life of the city, though one might question whether the busy Roman gentleman full of varied interests would have been really happy had he been obliged to live in the country all the year round.

Oh! all too happy tillers of the soil,
Could they but know their blessedness, for whom
Far from the clash of arms all-equal earth
Pours from the ground herself their easy fare!
What though no lofty palace portal proud
From all its chambers vomits forth a tide
Of morning courtiers, nor agape they gaze
On pillars with fair tortoise-shell inwrought,
Gold-purfled robes, and bronze from Ephyre;
Nor is the whiteness of their wool distained
With drugs Assyrian, nor clear olive's use
With cassia tainted; yet untroubled calm,
A life that knows no falsehood, rich enow
With various treasures, yet broad-acred ease,
Grottoes and living lakes, yet Tempes cool,
Lowing of kine, and sylvan slumbers soft,
They lack not; lawns and wild beasts' haunts are there,
A youth of labour patient, need-inured,
Worship, and reverend sires: with them from earth
Departing Justice her last footprints left.[1]

Towards the end of the Republic, however, this happy life in the country had very much changed, and the work of the farms was done almost entirely by slaves. At the head was the Steward, himself a

[1] Virgil: *Georgic*, II.

slave, who was responsible for all the buying and selling, for carrying out the wishes of his master and for administering discipline whenever necessary. Under him was the Stewardess who had charge of the house, kitchen and larder, the poultry-yard and the dovecot. Cato was always looked upon by the Romans as the model of what an old-fashioned farmer should be, and in a book he wrote on agriculture he describes the model steward. He should be the first to rise and the last to go to bed, strict with himself and with all those under him, and he should especially be able to keep the stewardess in order. He should be careful of his labourers and cattle, especially of the ox that draws the plough. He should always be at home and at work, he should worship the gods of the fields and be faithful and devoted to his master's interests.

The farm slaves had hard and heavy work. The Roman was a hard and stern man; he did not spare himself, so why, he would probably have argued, should he spare his slaves? They were to be cared for as long as they were useful to him, but then they were to be thrown on one side. Cato believed that "worn-out cattle, sick sheep, broken tools, old and sick slaves and all other useless things should be sold." He also gave instructions as to the food and clothing that should be given to the farm slave. In addition to his regular allowance, he might have a few of the "olives that drop of themselves," and a small quantity of sour wine. "As for clothes, give out a tunic and a cloak once in two years. When you give a tunic or cloak take back the old ones to make quilts.   Once in two years good shoes should be given."

The town slaves were generally better treated, they had lighter duties and as a rule lived under better conditions.   Their occupations were varied: some looked after the house, others worked in the kitchen, some superintended the toilette of the master and mistress; it was the duty of certain slaves to accompany the master whenever he went out and to clear the way for him if the streets were crowded, other slaves acted as pedagogues to the boys.

In every large household there were also well-educated slaves who had been trained as teachers, secretaries, copyists, musicians and even family doctors.   These were sometimes much loved and their relations with their masters were happy and often intimate.   They were the trusted friends of the *familia*.

In the imperial palace and in other great houses very large numbers of servants were employed. In order to ensure proper burial and to be remembered on the anniversary of their death these servants used to form associations to purchase burial-places.   It was the custom in Rome to cremate the bodies of those who died and to place the ashes in urns, and these associations of slaves and freedmen bought burial-places called *columbaria* in which they placed the urns in niches.   The inscriptions on these urns have provided a great deal of information concerning the households and the numbers of servants that were considered necessary.   Augustus and Livia lived far more simply than any other imperial family, yet Livia alone had six hundred servants and freedmen attached to her household. Such large numbers were necessary because the duties were so divided up. Amongst her servants Livia had a keeper of her purple robes, of her morning dresses, of her imperial robe, of her state robes, of her overcoats; she had folders of clothes and a hairdresser; a keeper of perfumery, eight goldsmiths and many other jewellers; a keeper of her imperial shoes and of her sandals; the regulator for the hot and cold water for her bath, and a keeper of her chair. There was also a governess for the favourite pet dog and a keeper of the family portraits.

In the eyes of the law, a slave was the absolute property of his master; he could not marry without his consent and his master could inflict any kind of punishment on him that he chose.

The country slave had very little opportunity of gaining his freedom. He could run away, but he was sure to be caught, and when he was returned to his master he was cruelly flogged and the letter F for *Fugitivus* (Runaway) was branded on his forehead.

For the town slave there was more hope that he might be set free. Sometimes his master would give him his freedom as a reward for long and faithful service, or he might buy it out of his savings, for it was possible for a town slave to earn and save a little money. He sometimes received gifts from his master or his master's friends, or if he were skilled in any occupation he could occasionally find opportunities to practise it for his own benefit. In such ways he could slowly and laboriously save enough, but at the best it was a long process, for the more valuable the slave, the greater was the price he must pay for his freedom. These freedmen were still looked upon as part of the *familia*. They still looked to their old master as to one whose interests they should serve whenever possible, and he, on his part, was expected to give them his protection.

Besides the slaves and the freedmen, there were in Rome the working people who were free-born Roman citizens. From very early times, tradition said it had first been done by Numa, the trades in Rome had bound themselves together into guilds, and in the time of Augustus there were more than eighty of these guilds in Rome itself. They included every possible occupation that received pay in return for work: bakers, shoemakers, potters, goldsmiths, porters, the vendors of oil, fish and grain, even doctors, teachers, architects, actors and jugglers. The lawyer occupied a different position in Rome. The well-born Roman gentleman despised the act of working for money and a lawyer received no pay for his services, though he seems to have had no scruple about receiving gifts from those whom he had served.

These guilds were not formed with any intention to improve the conditions of the workers, to regulate their pay or in any way to raise the standard of their work. Their object was to provide companionship and sympathy for the members, to arrange for social gatherings, and if necessary to see that the funeral of a member of the guild was properly conducted.

Those who followed all these varied occupations were looked down upon by the Roman gentleman, glad as he was to avail himself of their services when he needed them. They lived chiefly on the Aventine in large lodging-houses, three or four stories high. These houses contained a great many single rooms with only very small windows. Built of wood, they were frequently destroyed by fire, leaving a crowded population homeless.

It was only at the time of an election that these people became of any great importance in the eyes of the well-to-do Roman, for though they were poor and despised, yet they were free Roman citizens and as such had votes. Their votes were frequently bought, partly by the distribution of free corn, partly by the spectacles and shows in the circuses and amphitheatres provided by those who were seeking office.

But in reality we know very little about these workers in Rome, for ancient literature did not concern itself with them, Roman religion taught of no duties towards them, Roman patriotism did not require that they should be much regarded.

CHAPTER XVIII

THE WRITERS OF THE AUGUSTAN AGE

IT has been said by a modern historian, that "into the Roman Empire all the life of the ancient world was gathered; out of it all the life of the modern world arose."[1] Up to this time the richest thought of the world had been found in the great literature of ancient Greece, and this had formed an important part of the education of every cultivated Roman. But in the time of Augustus, Roman literature began to take its place beside that of Greece.

Not often has literature been so closely interwoven with history as it was in Rome during the closing years of the last century B.C. It was during these years that Latin prose became the matchless instrument it is by means of which human thought can be expressed. This was chiefly the work of Cicero, first as an orator, and then, when he had retired from public life, in his writings. We have his great speeches, a number of works on oratory and philosophy, and his letters, which are amongst the most valuable sources of our knowledge of the Roman world in his time. The Latin prose he

[1] Bryce: *Holy Roman Empire.*

created was not only great in itself, but has influenced the most cultivated and educated writing of the world since his day. Cicero represented the best mingling of Greek and Roman civilization of his time, and most of the leading men of the early part of the reign of Augustus had known and had been influenced by him.

The stirring events which had ended in the accession of Augustus had made Romans think more deeply than they had thought before. During the earlier part of the Republic war had succeeded war, one conquest had followed another, and in spite of periods when her very existence had seemed in peril, Rome had emerged victorious and had come to rule all the known world. The greatness of Rome captured the imagination of her poets and writers, but it was not only her greatness and power, but also her mission to the world which filled their minds.

In order to recall to the Romans the greatness of their past and their duty to the present, Livy (59 B.C.–17 A.D.) wrote his *History of Rome*. It was written on a hundred and forty-two rolls, but only thirty-five have come down to us, though we possess summaries of the missing books. As Livy looked about him, he saw that the wars and violence of the last century had done a fatal work in Rome, and that much of the old discipline and piety of the family life had disappeared. He believed that the greatness of Rome depended on the restoration of these qualities, and so in his history he dwelt on the heroic deeds of devotion to the State, on great

acts of valour, on the old Roman qualities of discipline and obedience, of self-sacrifice and duty.
He cannot always be relied on as an accurate historian, for he sometimes let the telling of a good story
interfere with strict accuracy, but the pageant of
Roman history unfolds itself in his pages in all its
richness and colour, and the stern, practical, pious,
disciplined Roman of the earlier Republic stood
out to the youth of a softer, more luxurious and self-
indulgent age as an inspiring and heroic example.

Latin prose became the perfect thing it is in the
late Republic, Latin poetry did not become so great
until the early years of the reign of Augustus. And
as it had been with Livy, so it was with the greatest
poets of this time: seeing that the old order of things,
the old ideals and standards were passing away,
they used their gifts as poets to call Rome back to a
sense of her duty and responsibility.

Horace (65–8 B.C.) was the son of a freedman,
and he had been given the best education Rome had
to offer. From school in Rome he had gone to
Athens, where he learnt to know and love the old
Greek poets. On his return to Rome he found civil
war raging, and for the moment he and his friends
were more interested in the politics of the time
than in the poetry and philosophy they had just been
studying in Greece. Horace was a friend of the
murderers of Caesar, and he fought on their side at
the battle of Philippi, but on the accession of Augustus he made peace with him, and later he became
one of his most faithful supporters. For out of all
these experiences Horace had learnt something.

He had come to believe that the Roman Empire needed the rule of one man, that she had fallen on evil days, not because of her enemies without, but because of the civil wars within.

In endless civil war imperial Rome
Plunges by her own strength to find her doom.
Not neighbouring nations, fiercely leagued in arms,
Not Porsena, with insolent alarms,
Not conquering Hannibal whose name of dread
On kindly mothers' lips deep curses fed,
Not one had compassed yet Rome's overthrow,
But by her children's hands she lieth low.

And as Horace believed that the strong rule of one man would save Rome, so did he also believe that Augustus was that man.

Horace was a man of the world, of the most intense human sympathies. He mingled with men in society and knew them well, and in his *Odes*, *Epistles* and *Satires* he wrote of men and of their lives and he has left us a valuable picture of the life and manners of Roman society in the days of the early Empire. But Horace has done more than that. Mingled with his pictures of the time are shrewd comments on the life and habits of those he met, and he told the world what, in his eyes, seemed wrong with it, and out of the treasures of a rich experience he gave wise and golden advice.

In the Augustan age Rome was entering on a new experience. She suddenly found herself very rich. The dignified, thrifty, frugal Roman had disappeared, and his place was taken by those who had grown rich suddenly, and who with no back-ground of tradition or of responsibility were self-indulgent, unrestrained and vulgar in their osten-tation. Horace, a man of the world and lover of all good things that life could give, as he was, hated above all things the vulgarity which mis-takes an outward show for happiness and greatness. True happiness, he always maintained, was to be found in simple things.

A clear fresh stream, a little field o'ergrown
   With shady trees, a crop that ne'er deceives,
Pass, though men know it not, their wealth that own
   All Afric's golden streams.[1]

Horace had a farm in the Sabine Hills which he liked to visit and where he was content with simple surroundings:

This used to be my wish: a bit of land,
A house and garden with a spring at hand,
And just a little wood. The gods have crowned
My humble vows; I prosper and abound:
Nor ask I more, kind Mercury, save that thou
Would'st give me still the goods thou giv'st me now.[2]

Horace believed that a hard life of discipline was good for a man in his youth:

To suffer hardness with good cheer,
   In sternest school of warfare bred,
Our youth should learn; let steed and spear
   Make him one day the Parthian's dread;
Cold skies, keen perils, brace his life.[3]

[1] Horace: *Odes*, III, 16.   [2] Horace: *Satires*, II, 6.
[3] Horace: *Odes*, III, 2.

Such a training in hardness of life and discipline,
Horace believed would lead a man to the highest
kind of patriotism, and he wrote that the name of
blest is given

> Of right to him who knoweth best
>   To use the kindly gifts of heaven,
> And bear adversity's hard hand;
>   Who dreads dishonour more than death;
> Yea, and for friends and fatherland
>   Stands forth to spend his dying breath. [1]

Horace was a great Roman poet, but Rome had
one yet greater: Virgil (70–19 B.C.). He led a quiet
and uneventful life. He was born in Mantua, but
went to Rome when he was about eighteen, and he
was able to devote the rest of his life to travel and
study. Virgil was very shy, reserved and sensitive,
and he preferred the quiet of the country to the noise
and bustle and society of the city. He had a house
in Rome, but he much preferred to be in Naples
by the sea or in the country. Like all educated
Romans he had studied Greek poetry, but when he
began to write himself, he did not merely imitate
the Greek writers. He had learnt from them that
poetry meant lifting the veil through which the
ordinary man sees the things of life and showing
their hidden meaning and beauty, and this Virgil
was able to do with that rare power that is only
granted to the very greatest of poets.

One of the early works of Virgil, that made the
Romans realize that a great poet was in their midst,

[1] Horace: *Odes*, IV, 9.

was called the *Georgics*. These were four poems in which Virgil described the life of the countryman as it might be. He wrote at a time when the agrarian troubles were causing discontent, and he showed what happiness might come from a life of industry and hard work. It was not an impossible world he imagined, he made no secret that there were hardships in it, but he showed that it is by overcoming difficulties that man becomes strong and able to endure, and that beyond the hardships lay the glory of achievement. In the *Georgics* Virgil showed a profound love for all living things, not only for man, but also for the birds and beasts, for flowers and trees, and for all the beauties of nature. Never before had poetry of such beauty been written in Latin. Virgil understood both the greatness of the language and also how to use it. He was never hurried in his work and he made it perfect. There are no useless words, no unnecessary lines. He knew the art "of saying much in little, and often in silence."

Before writing the *Georgics*, Virgil had written another poem in which he had foretold the coming of a great Deliverer, divinely-sent, who would free the world from its misery. As years went by Virgil believed more and more that Augustus was this divinely-sent Deliverer, and there took form in his mind the desire to set forth in poetry the mission of Rome which he believed was, under Augustus, to restore peace to the world. This poem was the Aeneid, and the writing of it occupied the rest of his life. It was not published till after his death, and as he lay dying, he asked that the manuscript might be brought to him in order that he might burn it. In the writing of the poem, so many great thoughts and questions had come to him one after the other, that he feared he had not put into his poetry all that he should have put or answered the questions that pressed upon him for an answer. Fortunately, the manuscript was not given to him, and the great poem was preserved.

The subject of the Aeneid is the mission of Rome in the world, and it shows how the gods had guided Rome through all her history to Empire, how a great people had been born and a great race founded. It is the story of how man has progressed through peril, toil and pain, through war and disorder, from barbarism to a state of peace and order. Virgil tried to show in the Aeneid how the sufferings and sacrifice of men are not wasted, but that in some way or other they are part of the purpose of the gods for the ultimate welfare of mankind. Aeneas is but a symbol: to the Romans he was Rome; later ages have seen in him the soul of Everyman setting out on a journey to some future glory. Whether Aeneas is Rome or the soul of Everyman, the success of his journey depends on the same thing, on that which the Romans called *pietas*, the fulfilment of duty to both God and man.

Virgil died nineteen years before Christ was born, but he was looked upon by the early Christians as one who was not far from the teachings of Christianity. Some even saw in his prophecy of a Deliverer who was to come a prophecy of the birth of Christ.

In the darkest years of early European history Virgil was never quite lost sight of, and when Dante wrote his great vision of the life after death, it was Virgil whom he chose to be his guide through Hell and Purgatory.

Few poems have opened so many windows into other realms as has the Aeneid, few poets have been the guide to so many others as has Virgil. More than a thousand years after his death, when the glory of English poetry was but beginning, Chaucer the Father of English poetry, paid homage to the great Roman Virgil:

> Glory and honour, Virgil Mantuan,
> Be to thy name! and I shall as I can
> Folow thy lantern as thou gost beforn.

CHAPTER XIX

ROME UNDER THE CAESARS

I. THE JULIAN LINE

(a) *Tiberius*

14–37 A.D.

AUGUSTUS died in the year 14 A.D. and there was no question but that the power he had exercised should be given to a successor. He had no sons, but he had a stepson, Tiberius, the son of his wife Livia, a very high-born Roman lady, by a former marriage. Tiberius was very young when his mother married Augustus and he was educated in every way as became a son of Caesar. Tiberius developed into a very able man, but Augustus was never fond of him and he slighted him and passed him by time after time, until Tiberius, who was by nature grave and serious, became bitter and suspicious. Augustus had two grandsons, the sons of his daughter Julia, and he had hoped that one of them might have been his successor, but they both died, and at last when there was no one else, Augustus announced that he would make Tiberius his heir. He went into the assembly of the people and tnere solemnly swore: "I adopt him for the public good."

After the funeral of Augustus the Senate met and asked Tiberius to take upon his shoulders the powers exercised by Augustus. At first he refused. "Only the intellect of the divine Augustus," he said, "is equal to such a burden," but his hesitation seems to have been more for the appearance of it than from any real unwillingness to hold the office, for he was soon persuaded to accept. At the time, the immediate successors of Augustus were still known only as *Princeps* or by the military title of *Imperator*, but they were Emperors, and later times have given them that title.

Tiberius was a tall, good-looking man, of great physical strength, but he was not a man who inspired enthusiasm. He is said to have walked stiffly, generally frowning and silent; and when he did speak, he spoke very slowly. He had not the tact of his stepfather who understood how to get on with all kinds of people; he was stern and unsympathetic, and he made himself very unpopular with the people, because he refused to spend vast sums of money on public amusements, one of the demands which the Roman people had always made on their popular leaders. The slights and disappointments which had been his lot as a young man had made him jealous and suspicious of anyone who seemed to be more popular than he was, and he was especially jealous of his nephew Germanicus. Ten years before, Tiberius had been sent to the German frontiers of the Empire and he had distinguished himself as an officer of great military ability, but since the death of Augustus he had not himself commanded any military campaigns.

Germanicus, a young man of great charm of manner, and a gallant and courageous soldier, was now on the Rhine, very near the place where Varus had been so badly defeated. The soldiers were devoted to Germanicus and they broke out into a mutiny, demanding that Germanicus should be Emperor. "The Roman world," they said, "is in our hands; our victories increase the state; from us emperors receive their titles." On hearing of the mutiny in the army, "Germanicus instantly went to the spot, and met the soldiers outside the camp, eyes fixed on the ground, and seemingly repentant. As soon as he entered the entrenchments, confused murmurs became audible. Germanicus then appealed to the men to remain loyal. Beginning with a reverent mention of Augustus, he passed on to the victories and triumphs of Tiberius, dwelling with especial praise on his glorious achievements with those legions in Germany. Next he extolled the unity of Italy, the loyalty of Gaul, the entire absence of turbulence or strife. He was heard in silence or with but a slight murmur."[1]

The influence of Germanicus had a good effect for the moment, but the men soon began to mutiny again. Germanicus had married Agrippina, known as Agrippina the Elder, the daughter of Julia and so the granddaughter of Augustus, and she and their young son were with him in the camp. When a

[1] Tacitus: *Annals*, I, 34.

rebellion broke out again, he decided that it was no longer safe for his wife and child to remain in the camp and he made arrangements for them to go away to a place of greater safety. The soldiers found this out and were deeply ashamed that their general should feel that his wife and child were not safe in their midst,

especially when they remembered her father, her grandfather Augustus, her own glory as a mother of children, her noble purity. And there was her little child, too, born in the camp, brought up amidst the tents of the legions, whom they used to call Caligula because he often wore the shoes so called, to win the men's goodwill. They entreated, stopped the way, that Agrippina might return and remain, some running to meet her, while most of them went back to Germanicus.[1]

The mutiny was ended, and the rule of Tiberius was accepted by the soldiers. Some time afterwards Germanicus was recalled from the German frontier and given a command in the East where he died, rumour whispering that Tiberius, ever jealous of his popularity, knew something about it. There was great grief in Rome when the news of the death of Germanicus arrived, for he was greatly loved, and men, remembering his gentle, courteous manner and the noble qualities of his character, mourned for him.

There were no further serious wars during the reign of Tiberius, so he was able to give all his time to the government of the Empire and he gave par-

[1] Tacitus: *Annals*, I, 41.

ticular attention to the affairs of the provinces, especially in matters concerning taxation. "He was careful not to distress the provinces by new burdens, and to see that in bearing the old they were safe from the rapacity of their governors."[1]

Tiberius governed the provinces well and the inhabitants respected and liked him. He maintained discipline in the army and kept the frontiers safe. He also carefully regulated the finances of the Empire and left a full Treasury. This economy, however, was very unpopular in Rome, for he spent no money on games and erected no great buildings.

Augustus had had the tact to leave the Senate and the assemblies of the people with the outward appearance of power, but Tiberius took away even that, and as he did nothing to gain the good will of the people he became more and more unpopular in Rome. As the years went by, he grew increasingly morose and suspicious and afraid of plots against his life. In order to guard against such dangers, he encouraged spies and informers, *delators* as they were called, to make known any attempts at treason, and a period of spying and accusations set in. In all this Tiberius was helped and encouraged by Sejanus, a scheming, unscrupulous man, anxious to get all the power that was possible into his own hands. He persuaded Tiberius to leave Rome and to live at Capri, a beautiful island not far from the Bay of Naples, which Augustus had bought and made into a country estate for himself. Sejanus remained in Rome, where as the Emperor's favourite

[1] Tacitus: *Annals*, IV, 6.

he was courted, flattered and obeyed, even while feared and hated. The days of his power were days of spying, informing, of false accusations and of cruel putting to death of Roman citizens who were in any way suspected of speaking against the Emperor.

There were ancient laws of treason in Rome which had come down from the earliest days of the Republic. These laws were intended to safeguard the state from acts that would bring upon it dishonour or the disloyalty of the citizens, but these earliest laws held only acts to be treasonable. In the terrible days of the Sullan proscriptions, words were considered just as treasonable as acts, but until the time of the Caesars, whether it was a deed or a word that was held treasonable, it was treasonable because it was against the state. But when the Roman people had numbered Julius Caesar among the gods, treason against the Emperor became a sin against the gods. The religious worship of the dead Caesar became confused with the loyalty given to the living Emperor, and gradually this loyalty itself became a kind of worship. This being so, any disrespectful word, even if spoken in jest, was held to be the same thing as speaking against the gods, and it was gradually coming about that divine honours were paid not only to the dead but also to the living Caesar.

With Tiberius in Capri, the ambitions of Sejanus knew no limit, and he even began to plot and plan how he might become Emperor himself. At length the suspicions of Tiberius were aroused. Sejanus was found guilty of treason, he was seized and was himself put to the death he had been inflicting on others.

Tiberius never returned to Rome. Never cheerful, gracious or kindly as a young man, as an old man he grew more and more gloomy and morose, and the last years of his life were marked by suspicions and deeds of cruelty. After a rule of twenty-three years he died in 37 A.D., an old man of seventy-five, unloved and unmourned.

(b) *Caligula*

37–41 A.D.

The only son of Tiberius had died suddenly and mysteriously while Sejanus was at the height of his power, and it was believed that he had been deliberately poisoned by the favourite of Tiberius in order to remove an heir. But Sejanus had failed in his ambitions, and Tiberius had appointed the young son of Germanicus his heir. This was Caius Caesar, or as he was always called Caligula, and on the death of Tiberius the Senate recognized him as Emperor. He was the last surviving son of Germanicus who had been so much beloved. By the scheming and cruelty of Sejanus, his mother Agrippina the Elder and her two older sons had been thrown into prison, where they had perished, and the people felt a great affection for the youth who had escaped. Tiberius had not been in Rome for years and so the presence of a young Emperor filled all Rome with rejoicing. Thank-offerings for his

accession were offered on all the altars, he promised
a period of good government, he distributed gifts,
and he recalled exiles from their wanderings.

Caligula had had no training to fit him for the
throne. Both Augustus and Tiberius had learned
in the discipline of the camp how to rule others.
They had both attended the Senate. Caligula had
experienced nothing of this kind. He was weak,
both in body and mind, and almost immediately
after the extravagant rejoicings at his accession his
health and mind gave way. The fair promise of
the beginning of his reign did not last, and the three
short years of his rule saw one insane act after another. He announced that he was a god and ordered
temples to be built in his honour; he sent far and
wide to collect all the statues of the gods that could
be found, and when they were brought to Rome, he
ordered that the heads should be removed and his
own put in their place; he had a marble stall and an
ivory manger built for his favourite horse and
announced his intention of making him consul, and
he is said to have built a bridge connecting his palace on the Palatine with the Capitol, so that he
might be "next door to his brother Jupiter."

Caligula was recklessly extravagant and in less
than a year he had spent all the money that Tiberius
had laid up in the State Treasury. Encouraged by
the Emperor the gladiatorial fights became fiercer
and more savage than ever, and Caligula used to
boast of the power he had over the life and death of
Romans, a power he used freely and madly. On
one occasion he is said to have uttered the wish "that

the Roman people had but a single neck," and he used often to say to his wife, "Off comes this beautiful head whenever I say the word."

After nearly four years of this insane rule, some of the officers of the guard made a conspiracy against him and one day as he was leaving his palace, he was slain.

(c) *Claudius*

41–54 A.D.

Caligula had named no heir and appointed no successor. Immediately after his death there was some discussion in the Senate as to whether it would not be a good thing for Rome that the early Republic should be restored, but the Senators were not given any real choice in the matter. Caligula had been so afraid of assassination, that he had surrounded himself with a strong imperial bodyguard of soldiers. It was some of these who had murdered him, and it was they who decided on his successor.

Claudius, the brother of Germanicus and uncle of Caligula, was in the palace at the time of the murder, and, terrified at what had happened,

he stole away to a balcony hard by and hid among the curtains which hung before the door. As he stood there, a common soldier who was prowling about at random, saw his feet, and intending to ask who he was, pulled him out and recognized him: and when Claudius fell at his feet in terror, he hailed him as Emperor.[1]

[1] Suetonius: *Claudius*.

He then conducted Claudius to the praetorian guards
and the next day, the Senate having come to no
conclusion, even after long discussion, Claudius was
accepted as Emperor.

Claudius began his rule in 41 A.D. when he was
fifty years old. He had spent most of his youth in
studying, but had never held any office under the
government, and no one thought of him as of one
capable of ruling or of gaining any kind of distinction.

His mother called him "a man not finished but merely
begun by Dame Nature," and when she wished to up-
braid anyone with dullness, she would say, "He is a
greater fool than my son Claudius." He was considered
of so little ability or importance that his sister, on hearing that he was about to be created Emperor, openly
and loudly prayed that the Roman people might be
spared so cruel and undeserved a fortune.[1]

It is possible that Claudius had made no effort to
change this opinion generally held of him, knowing
that his life was probably safer if he made no effort
to take part in public affairs.

Though not a man of strong personality, Claudius
left a mark for good on the Empire. He began,
what later Emperors completed, the giving to the
provinces political equality with Rome, and the
demanding from the provincial governors a fair share
in the responsibilities of government. After a long
struggle with the Senate, he made it possible for
some of the Gallic nobles to become senators. He
pointed out that it had been the custom in early

[1] Suetonius: *Claudius.*

Rome to unite the conquered on equal terms with the conqueror, and that the failure of the Greek states to do this had helped to bring about their downfall.

What [he said] was the ruin of Sparta and Athens but this, that mighty as they were in war, they spurned from them as aliens those whom they had conquered? Our founder Romulus, on the other hand, was so wise that he fought as enemies and then hailed as fellow-citizens several nations on the very same day. Strangers have reigned over us. That freedmen's sons should be intrusted with public offices is not, as many people think, a sudden innovation; it was a common practice in the old commonwealth.

On the whole, if you review all our wars, never has one been finished in a shorter time than that with the Gauls. Thenceforth they have preserved an unbroken and loyal peace. United with us as they now are by manners, education, and intermarriage, let them bring us their gold and their wealth rather than enjoy it in isolation. Everything, Senators, which we now hold to be of the highest antiquity was once new. Plebeian magistrates came after patrician; Latin magistrates after plebeian; magistrates of other Italian peoples after Latin. This practice, too, will establish itself, and what we are this day justifying by precedents will be itself a precedent.[1]

This speech of the Emperor was followed by a decree of the Senate, and certain tribes of the Gauls obtained the right of sending senators to Rome.

Claudius also added to the great buildings in Rome, by building two of the finest of the Roman

[1] Tacitus: *Annals*, XI, 24.

aqueducts, and he so improved the port of Ostia, that the corn ships could bring their freight right up the river to the city itself.

In 55 B.C. Julius Caesar had invaded Britain, but he had not completed the conquest of the island. The mad Caligula had planned an expedition there, but he got no further than the northern shores of Gaul, and all he brought back from the campaign were shells, which he ordered the soldiers to pick up off the shore to be shown in Rome as the plunder brought back from a distant land.

In 43 A.D. Claudius sent one of his generals with about fifty thousand men to Britain. They landed successfully and encamped not far from Londinium. The following year Claudius went himself and defeated the Britons in battle. The war continued, however, for another eight years and then at last the British chief Caractacus was captured and, with his wife and daughter, taken to Rome in order to walk in the triumph which celebrated the end of the war.

It was a great victory; the wife and daughter of Caractacus were captured; his brothers also surrendered. Caractacus had trusted himself to the loyalty of the Queen of the North, but he was put in chains and delivered up to the conquerors, nine years after the beginning of the war in Britain. His fame had spread thence, and travelled to the neighbouring islands and provinces, and was actually celebrated in Italy. All were eager to see the great man, who for so many years had defied the Roman power. Even at Rome the name of Caractacus was no obscure one; and the Emperor, while he exalted his own glory, enhanced the renown of the vanquished. The people were summoned as to a grand spectacle; the praetorian cohorts were drawn up under arms in the plain in front of their camp; then came a procession of the royal vassals, and the ornaments and neck-chains and the spoils which the king had won in wars with other tribes, were displayed. Next were to be seen his brothers, his wife and daughter; last of all, Caractacus himself. All the rest stooped in their fear to abject supplication; not so the king, who neither by humble look nor speech sought compassion.

When he was set before the Emperor's tribunal, he spoke as follows: "Had my moderation in prosperity been equal to my noble birth and fortune, I should have entered this city as your friend rather than as your captive; and you would not have disdained to receive, under a treaty of peace, a king descended from illustrious ancestors and ruling many nations. My present lot is as glorious to you as it is degrading to myself. I had men and horses, arms and wealth. What wonder if I parted with them reluctantly? If you Romans choose to lord it over the world, does it follow that the world is to accept slavery? Were I to have been at once delivered up as a prisoner, neither my fall nor your triumph would have become famous. My punishment would be followed by oblivion, whereas, if you save my life, I shall be an everlasting memorial of your clemency."

Upon this the Emperor granted pardon to Caractacus, to his wife, and to his brothers,[1]

but Britain was made a Roman province, and in honour of the conquest the little son of Claudius was given the name of Britannicus.

[1] Tacitus: *Annals*, XII, 36–37.

Claudius had married Messalina, known in Rome as a wicked, unscrupulous woman, and after her death, he married Agrippina the Younger. She was an ambitious and scheming woman and she married the Emperor chiefly in order that her young son, Nero, might be his heir. She gained great power for herself, sat on a throne near that of the Emperor, and her head even appeared on some of the coins. From the beginning she was cruel to Britannicus who was the rightful heir, and she succeeded at last in persuading Claudius formally to adopt his stepson Nero, and to name him as his successor. In 54 A.D. Claudius died, and without any protest, Nero was proclaimed Emperor.

(d) *Nero*

54–68 A.D.

Nero was seventeen years of age at the death of Claudius. Hailed Emperor on the steps of the palace, he was carried in a litter to the praetorian camp, and after a brief address to the soldiers was taken from there to the Senate House, which he did not leave until evening. Of all the honours that were heaped upon him, he refused only one, the title of Father of his Country, and that because of his youth.[1]

The young Emperor announced his intention of governing well and at first he seems to have made some effort to attend to his duties, but he soon tired of serious work. Nero had been educated by the Stoic philosopher Seneca, but he had not succeeded

[1] Suetonius: *Nero.*

in interesting the young prince in things which would have helped him to govern well and wisely, and all that Nero really cared for was music and singing and his own pleasure. Agrippina was quite willing that the young Emperor should pay no at-tention to ruling the Empire, for she wanted to keep the chief power in her own hands, but Nero, weak, vain, extravagant, and bad ruler as he was, had no intention of letting anyone take his place. This so angered Agrippina that she threatened to have Nero dethroned and Britannicus declared the right-ful heir. Nero at once settled that question by hav-ing a cup of poisoned wine prepared for Britannicus, who drank it and fell dead at the table of the Em-peror. This was only the beginning of those infa-mous deeds which have made Nero's name stand out in history as that of perhaps the wickedest and most worthless ruler who ever sat upon a throne. Soon after the murder of Britannicus, on the grounds that they were plotting against him, he had both his mother and his wife put to death.

As Nero added crime to crime, he lost whatever popularity he had had at the beginning of his reign. He neglected the affairs of the Empire and spent a great deal of time singing and playing on the harp and even appeared in Naples and other places on the public stage, an act which disgraced him in the eyes of the Romans, who believed that only slaves should take part in public performances of that kind.

In 64 A.D. a great fire broke out in Rome. It completely destroyed about half the city and devas-tated the rest. Tradition has handed down the tale that while the fire raged, Nero sat in his palace and played, a tale which gave rise to the saying that "Nero fiddled while Rome was burning." One story even hinted that Nero himself had set fire to the city in order that he might admire the sight of Rome in flames. However,

to relieve the people, driven out homeless as they were, he threw open to them the Campus Martius and the public buildings built in the time of Augustus, and even his own gardens, and raised temporary structures to shelter the destitute multitude. Supplies of food were brought up from Ostia and the neighbouring towns and corn was sold at a reduced price. These acts, though popular, produced no effect since a rumour had gone forth everywhere that, at the very time when the city was in flames, the Emperor appeared on a private stage and sang of the destruction of Troy, comparing present misfortunes with the calamities of antiquity.[1]

Many of the glories of ancient Rome perished in this fire. Among the oldest of the temples burnt were the Temple of the Moon, dedicated by Servius Tullius, and the temple which Romulus vowed to Jupiter, the Stayer of Flight. The palace of King Numa, the shrine of Vesta with the household gods of the Roman people were all burnt; so were many of the masterpieces of Greek art and treasures which Rome had brought from the East, and in spite of the beauty of the restored city, these could never be replaced.

[1] Tacitus: *Annals*, XV, 39.

Nero took the opportunity of the great fire to build for himself a new and magnificent palace, which is said to have covered the ground between the Palatine and the Esquiline Hill. It was so magnificent that he called it the Golden House.

Its vestibule was large enough to contain a colossal statue of the Emperor a hundred and twenty feet high; and it was so extensive that it had a triple colonnade a mile long. There was a pond, too, like a sea, surrounded with buildings to represent cities, beside tracts of country, varied by tilled fields, vineyards, pastures and woods, with great numbers of wild and domestic animals. In the rest of the house all parts were overlaid with gold and adorned with gems and mother-of-pearl. There were dining-rooms with fretted ceilings of ivory, whose panels could turn and shower down flowers and were fitted with pipes for sprinkling the guests with perfumes. When the edifice was finished and he dedicated it, he deigned to say nothing more in the way of approval than, "Now at last I have a dwelling fit for a man."[1]

Of Rome meanwhile, so much as was left unoccupied by the palace of Nero, was not built up, as it had been after its burning by the Gauls, without any regularity or in any fashion, but with rows of streets according to measurement, with broad thoroughfares, with a restriction on the height of houses, with open spaces, and the further addition of colonnades, as a protection to the frontage of the blocks of tenements. These colonnades Nero promised to erect at his own expense, and to hand the open spaces, when cleared of the débris, to the ground landlords. He also offered rewards proportioned

[1] Suetonius: *Nero.*

to each person's position and property, and prescribed a period within which they were to obtain them on the completion of so many houses or blocks of building. He fixed on the marshes of Ostia for the reception of the rubbish, and arranged that the ships which had brought up corn by the Tiber, should sail down the river with cargoes of the rubbish. The buildings themselves, to a certain height, were to be solidly constructed, without wooden beams, of stone from Gabii or Alba, that material being impervious to fire. And to provide that the water which individual licence had illegally appropriated, might flow in greater abundance in several places for the public use, officers were appointed, and everyone was to have in the open court the means of stopping a fire. Every building, too, was to be enclosed by its own proper wall, not by one common to others. These changes which were liked for their utility, also added beauty to the new city. Some, however, thought that its old arrangement had been more conducive to health, inasmuch as the narrow streets with the elevation of the roofs were not equally penetrated by the sun's heat, while now the open space, unsheltered by any shade, was scorched by a fiercer glow.[1]

In spite of all he did to restore Rome, Nero grew more and more unpopular, for he led a wild and wicked life. The story of his crimes has become proverbial. As nothing could get rid of the persistent rumours that the fire in Rome had been started by Nero, the Emperor laid the guilt at the door of the Christians and inflicted on them the most horrible tortures.

[1] Tacitus: *Annals*, XV, 43.

Mockery of every sort was added to their deaths. Covered with the skins of beasts, they were torn by dogs and perished, or were nailed to crosses, or were doomed to the flames and burnt, to serve as a nightly illumination when daylight had expired. Nero even offered his own gardens for these spectacles.[1]

The Christians were disliked and suspected not so much because they believed in a God not worshipped by the Romans, for on the whole Rome was tolerant to most forms of belief, but chiefly because they steadfastly refused to give divine honours to the Emperor, a refusal which was looked upon as treason to the state. But though the Romans considered the Christians worthy of punishment, yet when they saw the brutality with which Nero tortured them, they began to pity them, because they were not being sacrificed for the public good but simply to gratify the cruelty of one man.

At length the people could stand the crimes of Nero no longer, and a revolt broke out against him. Nero knew that in a serious rising very few would be found to support him, and when he heard of this revolt he was filled with terror. Then he heard that the Senate had declared him to be an enemy to the state and that he should be put to death. Upon that he fled from Rome and hid in the house of one of his freedmen. There he killed himself, saying as he did so: "What an artist the world is losing!"

Nero was the last Emperor who belonged to the

[1] Tacitus: *Annals*, XV, 44.

family of Augustus. He was succeeded by Galba, the general who had headed the revolt against him.

In the flower of his youth Galba had served with distinction in Germany. As pro-consul he governed Africa wisely, and in later years showed the same equity in Spain. When he was a commoner he seemed too big for his station, and had he never been Emperor, no one would have doubted his ability to reign.[1]

Civil war broke out almost as soon as he had been recognized by the Senate, and after a rule of seven months he was murdered.

Civil war over the succession continued for a year during which time two other generals in turn became Emperor and in turn were slain. At length in 69 A.D. Vespasian, a general of great ability belonging to the Flavian family, was made Emperor and peace was restored to Rome.

II. THE FLAVIAN LINE

(a) *Vespasian*

69–79 A.D.

During the days of the Republic and the early Empire one of the questions that was always pressing for an answer was that of the relationship between Rome and the Italians. It has already been seen that the Romans were so jealous of their privileges as Roman citizens that for a long time they

[1] Tacitus: *Histories,* I, 49.

were unwilling to extend the citizenship to the Italians whom they had conquered. By degrees, however, the Italians had gained equal rights with the Romans and certain privileges had even been granted to the inhabitants of some of the conquered provinces. From Augustus to Nero, the Emperors had all been Romans and they had all belonged to the family of Julius Caesar, but the death of Nero "revealed a secret to the Romans: an Emperor could be made elsewhere than at Rome."[1] Vespasian not only belonged to another family than that of Caesar, but he was an Italian, and with him began the period when the Roman Empire was to become united in a way hitherto not known.

In spite of the mad reigns of Caligula and Nero, much had been done in the last fifty years for the good of the Roman world, especially in the matter of provincial rule. But the extravagance of the last Caesars had emptied the Treasury and taxation had begun to be heavy again which was causing discontent, so that the new Emperor found a number of difficulties awaiting him. Vespasian was a man of character, of a firm will, and he had plenty of sound, practical commonsense. As soon as he became Emperor he set an example of simple living, and by reducing all wasteful expenditure he was able to replenish the Treasury emptied by Caligula and Nero. Where it was necessary to spend money, he spent it wisely. He continued the restoration of Rome which Nero had begun after the fire, but he did it well and without any of Nero's insane

[1] Tacitus: *Histories*, I, 4.

desire for display. The temple on the Capitol was restored, he built a new Forum, but the great building forever associated with his name was the Flavian Amphitheatre, known later as the Colosseum, built for the performance of the gladiators and the wild beast fights in which the Romans delighted. In order to build the Colosseum, Vespasian pulled down the Golden House of Nero and built the great amphitheatre on part of its site.

One great war was carried on in the reign of Vespasian. For some time there had been discontent in Palestine. Before becoming Emperor, Vespasian had himself commanded the army there, but when in 70 A.D. the Jews broke again into revolt, Titus, the son of Vespasian, was sent to quell the disturbance. After a siege of some months, during which the Jews in the city suffered both from famine and pestilence, Jerusalem was taken and utterly destroyed. The golden vessels of the Temple which had escaped destruction and some of the prisoners were taken to Rome, where they were displayed in the great triumph given to Titus on his return. [1]

For ten years Vespasian ruled, never sparing himself where work was concerned, and he left behind him a record of restored order and content and of good government. Towards the end of his life he was advised to take more rest and to work less hard, but "an Emperor," he said, "should die upon his feet," and he attended to the affairs of state until the end. He died in 79 A.D. and was succeeded by his son Titus.

[1] See *The Book of the Ancient World.*

(b) *Titus*

79–81 A.D.

Before becoming Emperor, Titus had gained for himself the reputation of being a good general, but of being not only severe but also sometimes cruel in his treatment of those whom he conquered. He had held various offices of state, but he was feared rather than loved. When he became Emperor, however, all this changed and he sought to win the love rather than the fear of his people. He succeeded in doing this so well, that he was spoken of as the "Delight and Darling of Mankind."

As a ruler Titus showed himself kindly and peace-loving, and it is said of him that when a day passed in which he could not recall any kindly action done that day for someone else, he would say: "My friends, I have lost a day."

Three dreadful calamities happened in the reign of Titus: another great fire in Rome, a plague which ravaged Italy, and an eruption of Mount Vesuvius which buried beneath its ashes the cities of Pompeii and Herculaneum. A letter written at the time describes the awful sight of the eruption:

For many days previous there had been slight shocks of earthquake, which were not particularly alarming, because they are common enough in Campania. But on that night the shocks were so intense that everything round us seemed not only to be disturbed, but to be tottering to its fall. My mother rushed into my bed-chamber, just as I was myself getting up in order to arouse her if she was still sleeping. We sat down in the courtyard of the house, which was of smallish size and lay between the sea and the buildings. I don't know whether my behaviour should be called courageous or rash—for I was only in my eighteenth year—but I called for a volume of Titus Livius, and read it, as though I were perfectly at my ease, and went on making my usual extracts. Then a friend of my uncle's, who had but a little time before come to join him from Spain, on seeing my mother and myself sitting there and me reading, upbraided her for patience and me for my indifference, but I paid no heed, and pored over my book.

It was now the first hour of the day, but the light was still faint and weak. The buildings all round us were beginning to totter, and, though we were in the open, the courtyard was so narrow that we were greatly afraid, and indeed sure of being overwhelmed by their fall. So that decided us to leave the town. We were followed by a distracted crowd, which, when in a panic, always prefers someone else's judgment to its own as the most prudent course to adopt, and when we set out these people came crowding in masses upon us, and pressed and urged us forward. We came to a halt when we had passed beyond the buildings, and underwent there many wonderful experiences and terrors. For although the ground was perfectly level, the vehicles which we had ordered to be brought with us began to sway to and fro, and though they were wedged with stones, we could not keep them still in their places. Moreover, we saw the sea drawn back upon itself, and, as it were, repelled by the quaking of the earth. The shore certainly was greatly widened, and many marine creatures were stranded on the dry sands. On the other side, the black, fearsome cloud of fiery vapour burst into long, twisting, zigzag flames and gaped asunder, the flames resembling lightning flashes, only they were of greater size. . . .

Soon afterwards the cloud descended upon the earth, and covered the whole bay. Then my mother prayed, entreated, and commanded me to fly as best I could, saying that I was young and could escape, while she was old and infirm, and would not fear to die, if only she knew that she had not been the cause of my death. I replied that I would not save myself, unless I could save her too, and so, after taking tight hold of her hand, I forced her to quicken her steps. She reluctantly obeyed, accusing herself for retarding my flight. Then the ashes began to fall, but not thickly. I looked back, and a dense blackness was rolling up behind us, which spread itself over the ground and followed like a torrent. "Let us turn aside," I said, "while we can still see, lest we be thrown down in the road and trampled on in the darkness by the thronging crowd." We were considering what to do, when the blackness of night overtook us, not that of a moonless or cloudy night, but the blackness of pent-up places which never see the light. You could hear the wailing of women, the screams of little children, and the shouts of men; some were trying to find their parents, others their children, others their wives, by calling for them and recognizing them by their voices alone. Some were commiserating their own lot, others that of their relatives, while some again prayed for death in sheer terror of dying. Many were lifting up their hands to the gods, but more were declaring that now there were no more gods, and that this night would last for ever, and be the end of all the world. Nor were there wanting those who added to the perils by inventing new and false terrors, for some said that part of Misenum was in ruins and the rest in flames, and though the tale was untrue, it found ready believers.

A gleam of light now appeared, which seemed to us not so much daylight as a token of the approaching fire.

The latter remained at a distance, but the darkness came on again, and the ashes once more fell thickly and heavily. We had to keep rising and shaking the latter off us, or we should have been buried by them and crushed by their weight. . . . At length the blackness became less dense, and dissipated as it were into smoke and cloud; then came the real light of day, and the sun shone out, but as blood-red as it is wont to be at its setting. Our still trembling eyes saw that everything had been transformed, and covered with a deep layer of ashes, like snow. Making our way back to Misenum, we refreshed our bodies as best we could, and passed an anxious, troubled night, hovering between hope and fear. . . . But though we had passed through perils, and expected still more to come, we had no idea even then of leaving the town until we got news of my uncle.[1]

Pliny and his mother escaped, but the people of Pompeii experienced a different fate. They were keeping a holiday when the eruption took place, and nearly everyone in the city had gone to the amphitheatre to watch a great entertainment, when the darkening sky alarmed them. They started up to return to their homes, when they felt the earth trembling beneath their feet and showers of hot ashes began to fall upon them. A large number made efforts to get to their houses and these lost their lives, buried beneath the burning rain of ashes, but a still larger number escaping from the amphitheatre fled to the shore and so were saved. For about eighteen hundred years Pompeii lay silent and buried,

[1] Pliny the Younger, VI, 20. His uncle was Pliny the Elder, a scholar. He lost his life in this disaster.

but the city has now been excavated, and it is possible to walk along the streets, to go into the houses on the walls of which the paintings that once made them gay can still be seen, to stand in the Forum, once humming with the busy life of a Roman provincial town, and to sit in the theatre which was once thronged with pleasure-seekers.

Titus was greatly distressed at the calamity which had befallen his people, and he began to make arrangements for their relief. But he did not live to finish them for, quite suddenly, as he was on his way to his country villa in the Sabine Hills, he caught a fever and died, greatly lamented by all his subjects.

(c) *Domitian*

81–96 A.D.

Titus was succeeded by his younger brother Domitian. The name of this Emperor has come down in history as that of a harsh and cruel man. Like Vespasian, he beautified Rome with great and splendid buildings; he gave magnificent entertainments to the people of Rome; and, knowing how important it was that the army should be faithful to him, he increased the pay of the soldiers. All this required money, and to obtain it, he decided, not to increase taxation, which would have made him unpopular with the people, but to force the rich to give it to him, a method which made him many enemies.

Domitian had no son and he lived in constant fear that, having no successor, a conspiracy would be formed by some powerful leader and that he would

be put to death.   In order to guard against this, the
old system of delators was introduced again and
many innocent men lost their lives.   Domitian was
fearful of losing any of the respect due to him.   He
enforced the observance of many religious duties,
especially that of worship of the Emperor; this
brought the Christians under his notice, and the
persecutions began again with renewed severity.

These things made Domitian hated and feared in
Rome, but his rule in the provinces was good.   He
sent capable men as governors and the frontiers were
well defended.   Agricola,[1] a very able general, was
sent to Britain, where he extended the boundary of
the province as far north as Scotland, known then as
Caledonia.

The fears of Domitian as to a conspiracy were not
groundless.   He was disliked and feared, and at
last a plot was formed against him, in which even
his own wife joined, and he was assassinated.   The
soldiers mourned for him and would have numbered
him among the gods, but the Senate rejoiced at his
death, and orders were given that all images of him
should be destroyed, and that wherever his name
was found in the annals of the state or on monuments it should be erased, in order that his memory
might be wiped out for ever.

A century had passed since the accession of
Augustus, and in spite of the misrule of some of
his successors, two great tasks had been accomplished
in the Roman world.   The government of the
provinces had been much improved, they were no

[1] See Tacitus: *Life of Agricola.*

390 BOOK OF THE ANCIENT ROMANS

longer at the mercy of an ambitious or unscrupulous
governor, they had been given more privileges, and
there was a growing feeling that they were parts of
one great Empire with the same interests and the
same citizenship.

The danger from unprotected frontiers that had
threatened Rome for so long had been greatly less-
ened. The great African desert in the South and the
Atlantic Ocean on the West made these frontiers
secure, but the North and North-East had always
been sources of danger. Vespasian and his sons
made the northern frontiers as secure as it was perhaps possible to make them. Walls of defence were
built and strong fortifications erected, so that there
was little danger to be expected from the North.
Rome was united and strong; the only real danger
still left was in the East.

CHAPTER XX

Rome in the Age of Trajan and Under the Antonines

I. NERVA

96–98 A.D.

As soon as the Senate heard of the assassination of Domitian, they met and appointed his successor. Their choice fell upon Nerva, one of the Senators, a man already sixty-five years of age, kindly and benevolent, but not one who would leave any great mark on the Roman state.

During his short reign he made various efforts for the relief of the poor, and he interested himself in the education of their children. But perhaps his most important act was the choice he made of a successor. He adopted as his son and heir Trajan, a young Spaniard, who was at the time the general in command of the army in Germany. The Senate made no objection to his choice and when, very soon after, Nerva died, Trajan followed him as Emperor.

II. TRAJAN

98–117 A.D.

The accession of Trajan marks another important step in the development of the Roman Empire. The first Caesars had all been Romans, Vespasian and his sons were Italian, but Trajan was neither Roman nor Italian, but a provincial, yet he was accepted without protest. Rome was fulfilling her task of uniting the Roman world and of making all who dwelt there feel that they were citizens of the same great Empire.

Trajan was a greater Emperor than any who had ruled since Julius Caesar and Augustus. He was a soldier-statesman, and the first thing he did was to turn his attention to the one danger spot on the Roman frontier, the East. He marched to the Danube, where the Dacians were making trouble, and after two long and severe wars he conquered them and Dacia was organized as a Roman province. On his return to Rome, Trajan celebrated a great triumph, and to commemorate his victory he set up a tall column in the middle of the Forum he was building. Winding round the column from top to bottom was the story of his campaign told in magnificent sculpture.

But the eastern frontier was still unsettled and in 113 A.D. Trajan set out to subdue the Parthians. He was successful at first and he conquered Armenia, Assyria, Mesopotamia and Media. He would have liked to have marched on still farther, but the new provinces were still restless, the news from Rome was

laws of their own, the local authority was given great
freedom to legislate for the special needs of the
place, but the underlying principles were the same
for the whole Empire, and a Roman citizen was
sure of the same justice and protection wherever
in the Empire he found himself.

The Roman Empire had reached its greatest
extent under Trajan, but it was Hadrian who completed the task of making the Empire one in fact as
well as in name. He was able to do this because
there was no part of the Roman world he had not
personally visited, and he knew from what he had
himself seen what were the conditions in the most
outlying parts of the Empire. It was said of him
that he wished "to see himself all that was to be
seen, to know all that was to be known, to do all
that was to be done," and as far as was possible he
gained his wish, for he spent a great part of his reign
travelling from Britain in the North to the distant
lands of the South, and from the West he went to
the East. In most of the provinces he visited, he
left some abiding mark of his presence. In Athens
he built a great Temple to the Olympian Zeus, part
of which is still standing, and in the North of Eng-
land one can today walk along the Roman wall
built by Hadrian to keep out the barbarian from
the North.

Both Trajan and Hadrian were builders, and they
left Rome still richer in great buildings than they
found it. Hadrian rebuilt the Pantheon, begun by
Augustus, a circular temple surmounted by a magnificent dome; towards the end of his life he lived in

the beautiful villa he had built for himself in the country outside Rome, and when he died he was buried in the tomb he had erected on the further side of the Tiber.

IV. ANTONINUS PIUS

138-161 A.D.

As he lay dying, Hadrian appointed Antoninus, a Gaul, as his successor. Antoninus was surnamed Pius by his people because of his gentle, peace-loving character. The twenty-three years of his reign were marked by no very important outside events, but they were years of peace and of great content within the Empire. The life of Antoninus Pius was characterized by the old Roman sense of duty and a deep sense of religion. He had a great regard for law and for the just observance of it, and he was the first to insist on that principle on which all modern trials are now conducted, that every man should be regarded as innocent until he has been proved guilty.

Antoninus Pius adopted his nephew Marcus Aurelius as his son and successor, and after his death Marcus Aurelius wrote of all that he had learnt from the character of his adopted father:

In all things be the disciple of Antoninus. Remember his resolute championship of reason, his unvarying equability, his holiness, his serenity of look, his affability, his dislike of ostentation, his keenness for certitude about the facts; how he would never drop a subject till he saw into it thoroughly and understood clearly; how he bore unjust reproaches without a word; how he was never in a hurry; how he gave no ear to slander; how accurately he scrutinized character and action; never carping, or craven, or suspicious, or pedantic; how frugal were his requirements, in house and bed and dress and food and service; how industrious he was and how long-suffering. Remember his constancy and evenness in friendship, his forbearance to outspoken opposition, his cheerful acceptance of correction; and how god-fearing he was, though without superstition. Remember all this, that so your last hour may find you with a conscience as clear as his.[1]

V. MARCUS AURELIUS

161–180 A.D.

Within the Empire all had been at peace during the happy but uneventful years of the reign of Antoninus Pius, but beyond the frontiers there was restlessness. Only a strong hand and stern military discipline had protected the Roman frontiers and whenever that was withdrawn, there was danger. When Marcus Aurelius became Emperor, he had to go immediately to the East and wage war against the Parthians. He conquered them, and made the frontier safe, but Rome paid a heavy price for this war. The returning troops brought back with them the plague, and just at a time when Rome needed all her men, the plague struck them down and they died in thousands.

Then another war broke out on the German fron-

[1] Marcus Aurelius, VI.

tier, and again Marcus Aurelius had to take the field. Again he was successful, but the war had been so costly, that no money was left in the public Treasury. The resources of Rome had been severely drained both by the plague and the wars, and the Emperor was unwilling to tax the provinces, so in order to obtain the necessary money he sold all his valuable bowls of gold, crystal and porcelain, his rare vases, the gold-embroidered robes of the Empress Faustina, and even the crown jewels.

Although Marcus Aurelius defeated the barbarian tribes on the northern frontier, he could not keep them from breaking through some of the defences into Roman territory. In order to maintain peace, he at last assigned certain border lands to some of these tribes, a policy which kept the peace for the moment but which was fraught with dangerous consequences for the future.

The reign of Marcus Aurelius was almost entirely taken up with wars, and yet he was no warrior at heart. He was the philosopher-king, one of the few rulers in the world who have been like the ideal ruler described by Plato. He lived a simple and austere life, and he looked upon the office of King as a sacred trust to which he must dedicate his whole life, his every thought and deed and word. All that he did was guided by what he believed to be his duty. The man who would have been most happy could he have spent his life in quiet study and thought, was forced to spend most of it on horseback at the head of his army in the midst of din and excitement. He accepted what came to him as his duty, and wherever he was, he was thinking, planning and working for the good of the Empire and the welfare of all who dwelt within it. He made the sacrifice without a murmur, and as far as he was able, he left the Empire safe.

But the greatest gift Marcus Aurelius gave to the world was his character, and we learn to know it best in a slender volume he left containing his *Thoughts* or *Meditations*, written at odd moments, whenever he had a few moments to spare, whether in the city or in the camp.[1]

Marcus Aurelius died in 180 A.D., the last of the great Emperors of Rome. He was greatly loved, but on the day of his death no one, we are told, thought of mourning for him, for all were sure that he had come to them from the gods and had now returned to heaven.

[1] See p. 403.

CHAPTER XXI

RELIGION IN THE ROMAN EMPIRE

I. DECAY OF THE OLD ROMAN RELIGION

THE old Roman religion was very formal and had consisted to a great extent in a careful carrying out of certain forms and ceremonies. It had but little to do with the spirit of man, but it had undoubtedly influenced the Roman character in giving to it a respect for authority, self-restraint, discipline and duty, virtues which to the Roman were inseparable from patriotism. The practical, industrious, sober-minded Roman of the early Republic had believed firmly in his gods and in their power, if he kept his word to them, of aiding him in all his undertakings. But during the last two centuries of the Republic, influences were at work which began to undermine the position and authority of the old gods.

The opening of the East to Romans brought with it many new ideas. Greek mythology and Egyptian cults in particular introduced elements of superstition and excitement in religious worship that had hitherto been almost unknown in Rome. The long century of revolution had not only upset ordinary ways of living, but also ordinary ways of thinking, there was restlessness and a craving for something new. Greek philosophy had also had a share in weakening the power of the old gods. It encouraged questioning, and the old-fashioned Romans who disapproved of it maintained that it developed doubt, scepticism and irreligion. No honest and sincere questioning ever does any harm, but the great days of Greek philosophy were over, and since the death of Aristotle at the end of the fourth century B.C. philosophy had been taught by smaller minds. There are two kinds of questioning: the questioning of the big mind which is honestly seeking to understand something which is vast and great and far beyond the questioner, and there is the questioning of the little mind which is not based on sound knowledge of that which has already been comprehended, but which only seeks to cast doubt on that which for various reasons the questioner would find it either more convenient or more comfortable not to believe. Both these kinds of questioning were at work in Rome, though the Roman never delighted in the abstract search for truth as did the Greek.

Again, that which is built on a sure foundation need fear no questioning of any kind. Now the old Roman religion had not provided ideals after which the individual could strive, it had not provided any certainty that wrong-doing would be forgiven, and above all it had provided no belief that brought any real assurance with it of a future life, and when it was seriously questioned as to these things, it failed. Augustus tried to bring about a reform in religion and a return to the "religion of Numa," but it was an outward return only, for real belief in the power of the old gods to heal and to save was dead.

The old religion had failed them, and so Romans began to turn to other philosophies and other cults in order to try and find that which they sought.

II. STOICS AND EPICUREANS

It was not only in Rome that the old order of things was passing and that thinking men believed no more in the old gods, the same thing had already happened in Greece, and it was there that a new philosophy was first found to take the place of the old. Towards the end of the fourth century B.C. Zeno, a stranger from the East, came to Athens which he made his home for the rest of his life. It was in one of the Stoa, the Painted Porch, that he taught this new philosophy, and it has been known since as that of the Stoics, taking its name, not from that of its founder, but from the place where he taught.

The Stoic philosophy spread very soon to Rome and it was one which was specially suited to the hard Roman temperament. It endeavoured to answer the questions which were pressing for an answer: How was a man to live, and what was he to believe? To the first, the Stoic answered that the aim of man should be to live a life devoted to virtue, that he should cultivate an unbroken serenity of mind, that he was to hold in contempt both worldly goods and misfortune, that all men were equal and formed one brotherhood, and that life should be spent in the service of man.

To the second question the Stoic had a less definite answer. He was to believe that nothing was good in the world but goodness, that the world was ordered by a divine plan and was working towards some great end, but he stopped short there. He did not fill in the blank or strive much to gain any real perception of what that end was.

Stoicism lifted up ideals and standards at a time when they were sorely needed, and during the early Roman Empire it found many followers. Two of the greatest Stoic philosophers, whose teachings and writings have greatly influenced the moral thought of thinking men, were Epictetus, who lived in the first century A.D., and the Emperor Marcus Aurelius.

Epictetus was originally a slave. He was lame and later had been given his freedom. He then began to give lectures, first in Rome, and then at Nicopolis in Epirus, where he had many followers. He lived to be an old man, and he was so greatly revered that at his death a large sum of money was offered for the little earthenware lamp he had used, in the hope that by its light it would guide others to the same wisdom that Epictetus had attained.

Marcus Aurelius has been called the "Stoic Saint." He lived the life he preached. Placed in a position of great trust and power, he did his duty unflinchingly to the end. To the Stoic life was a game, but he was taught to be indifferent as to whether he won or lost, whether he gained possessions or lost them, the thing that mattered was, how had he played the game?

Remember that you are an actor in a play, and the Playwright chooses the manner of it: if he wants it short, it is short; if long, it is long. If he wants you to act a poor man you must act the part with all your powers, and so if your part be a cripple or a magistrate or a plain man. For your business is to act the character that is given you and act it well; the choice of the cast is Another's.[1]

Marcus Aurelius acted the character that was given him and he acted it well. As he lay dying, his last thoughts were for the safety of the Empire: "Why weep for me? Think of the army and its safety; I do but go on before."

But in the end Stoicism failed to satisfy the spiritual side of man, and it failed largely because of the reasons it gave for the life a Stoic should live. It was a philosophy for the individual, not for society, for all that man was to do, was to be done for the sake of his own soul. He was to serve his fellowmen, but he was not to concern himself with them, for that would have troubled the serenity of his mind. He was never to feel pity as an emotion. He might sympathize and help, but his object was not to get rid of pain and disaster, of wrong and evil, but to see that they were borne nobly. When he helped, it was not to matter to him whether he succeeded or failed, so long as he had done his best and borne himself well. How a man suffered and how he carried himself in the hour of death were what mattered to the Stoic, not the loss and the suffering itself. The Stoic was not to say, "The

[1] Epictetus.

thing is a misfortune," but "To bear it bravely is good fortune."[1]

Stoic teaching was not always consistent. It professed to teach a man humility, but in much of its teaching it so exalted man that it raised him to be on a level with God Himself. It taught him indifference to worldly fortune, yet it encouraged a man to take his own life when it satisfied him no longer. It made many of its followers hard, narrow and unsympathizing, nevertheless in an age that was spiritually dark and groping after better things, it set up standards that were worth striving for, it emphasized the importance of conduct, and it did much to free men from bondage to material things.

Another philosophy which sought to answer some of the questionings of man's mind and spirit was that of Epicurus. The Stoic had said that virtue was the highest good, the Epicurean said that it was to be found in happiness. Epicurus taught that to attain happiness a man must live wisely, temperately and uprightly, and he, like the Stoic, believed in turning aside from any emotion that would disturb the serenity of the mind. Epicurus himself lived a very simple life, one that was self-denying and even ascetic, but his teaching was dangerous. It gave opportunity to the self-indulgent to become more so, it encouraged the making of one's self and one's own pleasure the beginning and end of things. Epicureanism lacked the self-discipline and restraint of the Stoic. It, too, was tried and found wanting.

[1] Marcus Aurelius, IV.

III. THE MYSTERY RELIGIONS

Rome had always shown herself tolerant to the introduction of foreign gods or forms of worship and her persecution of the Christians was mainly on political, not religious grounds. When the East came under Roman dominion, with all else that came from those lands, there came also their gods and forms of worship, and three of them in particular attracted many followers. Neither the Stoic nor the Epicurean teaching satisfied all the longings and cravings of man's spirit. The old Roman gods, even when most firmly believed in, had been far away; man sought now a closer communion between himself and the divine, he was still seeking for some assurance of forgiveness and reconciliation with God, and for some more definite hope of immortality.

Three foreign worships seemed for a time to give what was wanted. These were the worship of Cybele, the great Mother-Goddess of Asia Minor, of the Egyptian Isis, and of Mithra, the Persian God of Light. The worship of Cybele and of Isis was chiefly practised by women. The ritual was full of symbolism and emotion and for a time seemed, to those who followed it, to give a promise of satisfying the longings and desires of the spirit. But both these cults encouraged superstition and proved to be weakening and emotional and neither lasted.

The religion of Mithra took hold more firmly than that of either Cybele or Isis. From ancient times in the East the cave had been the place where he was worshipped, and all the shrines of Mithra that have been found were built underground. Mithra was a legendary spirit of light and truth. He was supposed to have been miraculously born, and though no written records of his story remain, the sculptures in the shrines dedicated to him tell his story. He seems to have been thought of as the mediator between the good and evil powers in nature, to have championed the weak, and to have conquered over death. It was a religion full of combat and of struggle, and he was called "Unconquered Mithra." Mithraism was very symbolic and largely a nature-worship. It gave hope of immortality, hence much of its popularity, but it, too, failed as a lasting religion, for it was founded on belief in a god who had never existed, who was only a symbol of nature. Something greater was needed to satisfy the searching of man's spirit.

There are no real beginnings or endings of periods in history. Empires have risen and fallen, great men have lived and died, civilizations have flourished and declined, and it would seem as if the changes that came were the result of some dramatic event that took place suddenly. As a matter of fact the changes have come owing to influences unnoticed or disregarded that have been at work sometimes for long periods of time, and the dramatic event, which to a later age seems to have been a sudden beginning or ending, has, as a rule, been only the outward sign that the change is there and that men are conscious of living in a new era.

It was partly thus with the beginnings of Christianity. For ages that which it had to teach had

been sought after, and various religions and philosophies had been tried, and though some of them
contained much that was of eternal value, they had
in the end been found wanting. When Christ was
born, the way had been prepared, and the world
was found ready for Him.

IV. THE CHRISTIAN CHURCH IN THE ROMAN EMPIRE

(a) *The First Centuries of Christianity*

For a long time the spirit of man had been searching for something that neither the old Roman religion of the gods, nor the philosophy of the Stoics and
Epicureans, nor the Mystery Religions had been
able to give him. He was still longing for some
closer communion between himself and God, for
some assurance of forgiveness and of reconciliation
with God, and for some more definite hope of immortality, not only for himself, but for his fellow-
men. These longings were satisfied by the teaching
of Christianity.

Christ was born in the reign of Augustus and He
was crucified when Tiberius was Emperor, and the
story of His birth and life, of His death and resur-
rection is found in the four Gospels. His teachings
were spread in the Roman world by His followers
and especially by St. Paul, a Jew born in Tarsus, but
a free born Roman citizen, a man of learning and of
great eloquence, who spent his life travelling through
the cities of Asia Minor and Greece, preaching and
teaching. Accused by the Jews as teaching strange
things contrary to the Scriptures, and by the Ro-

mans of creating disturbance, he appealed to Caesar and was taken to Rome as a prisoner, where he was put to death during the reign of Nero. In nearly every place to which St. Paul went, he founded a community of Christians to whom he afterwards wrote letters, known as the Epistles of St. Paul, and which together with the Gospels and the Acts of the Apostles, an account of the journey of St. Paul and of the work of others of the immediate followers of Christ, form the principal part of the New Testament.

The teachings of Christ and of how they satisfied the yearnings of men can be read in the Gospels. At first the groups of Christians were small, and were composed of men and women of lowly estate, of slaves, of many who had been outcast and oppressed. By degrees, however, this new faith began to attract others. The extraordinary thing about it was that those who became Christians showed it by a complete transformation of their lives. Nothing quite like it had ever been seen in the world before. We, who have lived all our lives under a civilization that has been Christian for nearly two thousand years, can hardly realize what those early days of Christianity were like. The characters of those who believed were transformed by the love which through the Spirit of Jesus they showed to their fellow-men.

At first the Christians were left alone by the government. So long as they remained good citizens, Rome did not care in what God Romans believed, but as their numbers increased and as men and women of more importance in Rome became Chris-

tians, certain things were noticed about them which
the Roman government considered disquieting. In
a court of law, no Christian would take the usual
oath, because he refused to swear by the pagan
gods; all Christians refused the customary worship
given to the Emperor; the Christians talked of another King and His Kingdom, and they held secret
meetings which were never approved of by Rome,
as they might be the beginning of a plot or conspiracy. All these things cast suspicions on the loyalty of Christians as good Roman citizens. And
there were other things as well. At banquets the
Christians present refused to make the usual offering
to the Lares and Penates of the household, and they
hated the spectacles in the amphitheatre, so that
they kept more and more to themselves, taking but
little part in the social life around them. These
things were also looked upon as suspicious, as showing an unfriendly spirit to one's fellows.

And so it came about that the Christian was
looked upon as a dangerous character, but it was
not until the reign of Nero that active persecutions
began. There were periods when they were very
violent, then there would be times of quiet, and then,
often on some slight pretext, they would break out
again with great ferocity. It was said of this time
by a later Christian writer that

if the Tiber floods the city or the Nile refuses to rise, or
the sky withholds its rain, or disasters occur in the
shape of earthquake or famine or pestilence, the cry is
raised at once: "The Christians to the lions !"

Under Nero, Domitian and in the third century under Diocletian the persecutions were especially fierce and cruel, but they also took place even under such Emperors as Trajan and Marcus Aurelius. The steadfastness with which the Christians bore not only death, but torture and sufferings of the most horrible kind amazed those who watched them. Seneca, a Stoic and so one taught to practise unflinching endurance of any hardship, was astounded not only at what they bore, but at how they bore it. He wrote to a sick friend:

What are your sufferings compared with the flame and the rack? And yet, in the midst of suffering of that sort, I have seen men not only not groan, that is little; not only not complain, that is little; not only not reply, that too, is little; but I have seen them smile, and smile with a good heart.

In spite of the persecutions the Christians grew in numbers. Under Trajan no man was allowed to be persecuted until it had been proved that he was a Christian, and the test generally applied was that of making the customary offering before the statue of the Emperor. In answer to a letter written by Pliny when he was governor of a province concerning the methods to be employed in finding out the Christians, Trajan answered:

It is not possible to lay down any fixed rule by which to act in all cases of this nature. The Christians are not to be sought out; but if brought before you, and the crime is proved, they must be punished; with this restriction, however, that where the person denies that he is a Christian, and gives a practical proof of the fact, as, for example, by showing his reverence for our gods, then he is to be forgiven on account of his recantation, notwithstanding any suspicion there may be against him with regard to his past life. Anonymous informations are not to be received in prosecutions of any sort: they are the worst of precedents, and not consonant to the spirit of our time.[1]

The spirit that filled the Christians was so steadfast that they refused to deny their God. When Polycarp, the aged Bishop of Smyrna in the middle of the second century, was asked if he would not deny Christ rather than submit to torture, he answered: "Six and eighty years have I served Him and He has done me nothing but good; and how could I curse Him, my Lord and Saviour?"

The first Christians had been simple and uneducated men and women, but as those who were better educated became Christians, questionings of a different kind had to be answered. Among those who followed the new teaching were often men who had been trained in the schools of Greek philosophy, men who gave to their religion all their mind as well as all their heart. To meet their difficulties Christian scholars began to write about the Christian faith. These scholars are known as the Fathers of the Early Church.

(b) *The Early Church*

As soon as any large number of people live together in any community or association, some kind

[1] Trajan to Pliny the Younger.

of organization is necessary, and it was soon found that the Christians scattered in all directions, living in many different parts of the Empire, required some kind of government that would bind them together. The word *Church* means *belonging to the Lord*, and all Christians everywhere were a part of it. The only ordered government known to the men of the first century was that of the Roman Empire, and to a large extent its forms were borrowed for the early Church. The Apostles who had been the immediate followers of Christ Himself had naturally been the first leaders in the Christian communities, and their successors were men who had been solemnly set apart for the same office. They were given the title of *Bishop*, a word meaning *overseer*, and their work was to have the oversight of all the Christian communities in certain districts which were called dioceses or sees. Under them were the priests, men also specially set apart for the work of the Church, and to help these again there were deacons, an order first instituted to help the priests in the practical affairs of the Church, so that the latter might have more time for the spiritual side of their work.

In the fourth century, the most important sees were those of Rome, Constantinople, Alexandria and Antioch, and except in Rome, the Bishops of these sees were called Patriarchs. Tradition has always held that St. Peter was the first Bishop of Rome, and that he and St. Paul were put to death there during the persecutions under Nero. From the beginning this gave the Bishop of Rome great importance in the eyes of the Church.

In the reign of Constantine a controversy arose in the Church, concerning what was believed about the Person of Jesus Christ. The Emperor probably understood very little about it, but he was far-seeing enough to realize that the Christian Church was to be one of the great powers in the world, and that for the work it had to do, it was important that it should not be divided, so when an appeal was made to him to settle the question, he called a Council of the whole Church together at Nicaea in Asia Minor. This Council met in 325 A.D. It was the first great council of the whole Church and was attended by Bishops and other clergy from all over the Roman world. The controversy was settled, and as a result of the Council the Nicene Creed was drawn up, a statement in noble language of what the Church held to be essential in Christian belief.

During the fourth and fifth centuries, as the Empire began to fall before the barbarian invaders, the Church grew more powerful, especially in Rome, for as the civil government became more and more incapable of keeping order, the Church gradually began to take its place. The Roman rulers were weak and incompetent, but the Bishops of Rome of this period were statesmen as well as churchmen. When the Emperor and his court went to Constantinople, the Bishop was the most important man left in Rome, and he gradually assumed a position of great power and responsibility. In 445 A.D. a decree was passed which declared that the Bishop of Rome had supremacy over the whole Church, and for more than a thousand years this supremacy was never seriously questioned on the continent of Western Europe.

The Church had inherited two things from the Roman Empire. She had taken and adapted to her own needs the Roman form of government, and she had also made her own the old Roman ideal of unity. The Roman ideal had been that of one political empire, with its centre in Rome, the city that had been divinely founded and that was to last for ever. The ideal of the early Church was that the whole world should be united in a great spiritual kingdom of which Rome was to be the earthly centre, but of which Christ was to be the King and which was to last for ever. Transformed and adapted to the needs of later times, that which Roman civilization had put into the world was destined to endure.

CHAPTER XXII

The Civilization of the Roman Empire

THE threefold mission of Rome in the world was to conquer, to rule and to civilize, and the records of her history show in what manner she carried out her task. For the fulfilment of it Rome needed certain instruments, and these have profoundly influenced the modern world which grew out of the life of the ancient world, as it was moulded by Roman influence. To conquer the world, Rome needed an army; to rule it, she needed law; to civilize it, she needed great buildings by means of which the strength and might of her power should be known, a language, by means of which the thought and wisdom of the ancient world could be handed on to the newer nations which were growing up protected by her law, and good roads and communications to serve as channels along which her civilization should pass. These things are among the great gifts that Rome has given to the world.

I. ROME THE CONQUEROR OF THE WORLD

The Roman Army

In the early days of Rome, every able-bodied citizen had been expected to serve in the army to defend his home and the state, and this citizen army was commanded by the King. Every citizen had to provide his own armour and weapons, and as some ranks required more costly equipment than others, Servius Tullius, who made a number of reforms in the Roman army, divided the citizens of the state into five classes according to the kind of equipment each could best provide. But it was still a citizen army. It was not until the time of Marius that the army became a profession and that men enlisted in it for a definite term of years. In the main the Roman army kept the character given it by the reforms of Marius, not only during the period of the later Republic but also during the Empire.

There were two main divisions of the Roman army: the Legions and the Auxiliaries. There were thirty legions which were known by numbers. Each legion consisted of about six thousand foot-soldiers and a hundred and twenty horsemen. The legion was subdivided into ten regiments known as cohorts and these again into groups of a hundred men, called centuries, each of which was commanded by a centurion. In republican days the army had been commanded by the Consul, under the Empire the Emperor became the commander-in-chief of the whole army.

A Roman soldier generally enlisted for a term of twenty years. He had to be a free Roman citizen, and on entering the army he took an oath of allegiance. He swore never to desert the standard, to be absolutely obedient to orders given him and to be willing to give up his life for the safety of the Emperor and the Empire. These men were given a thorough military training: they were taught not only to handle weapons of all kinds and to fight, but to march, to face hardships, to grow steady, disciplined, stubborn and determined. When not engaged in fighting, they were used to build roads, bridges or walls in the provinces where they were stationed.

Attached to the legions were the Auxiliaries. These were provincials and not necessarily Roman citizens. They were troops raised in the various provinces, though they were not as a rule allowed to serve there. The Briton and the Gaul would be found serving on the Euphrates, the African, Syrian or Spaniard on the Rhine and Danube frontiers or in Gaul. These men enlisted for twenty-five years and when discharged they became Roman citizens.

In addition to the Legions and Auxiliaries, there were the Imperial Guards. These consisted of twelve regiments of a thousand men each which were stationed in Italy. They were a specially picked body of men, some of whom were always in attendance on the Emperor's person. They had higher pay than any other soldiers, and were only required to serve for sixteen years.

One important characteristic of the Roman army was its camp. The site was carefully chosen, and was always within easy reach of food supplies, wood and water. The space determined on was marked out and a ditch dug all round it. Inside the ditch a rampart was built of the earth thrown out of the ditch and of stakes. The camp was nearly always rectangular and was entered by four gates, one on each side. Two hundred yards were left clear on all sides between the rampart and the rows of tents, where the troops could exercise and which served as an additional defence. The tents were set up in streets laid out in perfectly straight lines and crossing each other at right angles. Every part of the army had its own place and knew exactly where to set up the tents. The general's quarters were in the centre, with a platform from which he could address the troops, and an open space for a soldiers' forum near it. These camps were not only speedily laid out, but when the trumpet gave the signal, they could be broken up at a moment's notice. Such a camp could only have been achieved by men accustomed to hard discipline and prompt obedience. It was such men that made up the armies of Rome.

The Roman legions were stationed on the frontiers of the Empire, for it was there that danger was chiefly to be feared. Egypt, Africa and Spain had one legion each, there were three in Britain, eight on the Euphrates, and sixteen on the Rhine and Danube. These armies were kept chiefly for purposes of defence, and for nearly five hundred years after the reign of Augustus they kept the frontiers safe and the Empire at peace.

II. ROME THE RULER OF THE WORLD

ROMAN LAW AND UNITY

The Roman citizen was essentially law-abiding. The discipline of his early training had taught him the duty of obedience, as perhaps no other nation has ever been taught it. And as he had been taught first to respect and obey his father, so did he grow to respect and obey the state.

In 509 B.C. when the Roman Republic was founded, Rome had been but a small city-state; by 264 B.C. she had become mistress of Italy; by 133 B.C. she was the mistress of the Mediterranean; and at the death of Augustus in 14 A.D. she ruled the whole civilized world. The laws that had been adequate for the small city-state proved wholly insufficient for the ever-growing world-state, but by the period of the Empire, Rome had shown her genius for law and had learned how to govern her wide dominions. That which she learned has been one of her great gifts to the world. The subject of Roman law is too vast to be dealt with here, all that can be done is to point out some of the directions in which it travelled.

The city laws were made less rigid and more applicable to a large state. The conquered provinces were left free to make their own local laws, but all citizens of the Empire, wherever they lived, could be sure of the same justice and the same protection. The whole Empire was included in what was known as the *Pax Romana*. In the eyes of the law, those who dwelt within the Empire were not members of different nations, there was no difference made between races, but all were Romans. It was under the great Emperors that certain principles of justice and humanity were firmly planted at the root of the law, principles which are still at the foundation of all civilized law today.

The Roman law was collected and written down at various times in Codes, the most important of which was made by Justinian, an Emperor of the sixth century, and which served as the foundation of the later law of the countries of Western Europe. In the preceding century Claudian, an Egyptian by birth, but a Roman citizen, gave voice to what Rome had accomplished in the world she had conquered:

> Rome! Rome! alone has found the spell to charm
> The tribes that fell beneath her conquering arm,
> And given one name to the whole human race,
> And clasped and sheltered them in fond embrace;
> Mother, not mistress, called her foe her son,
> And by soft ties made distant countries one.
> This to her peaceful sceptre all men owe—
> That through the nations, wheresoe'er we go,
> Strangers, we find a fatherland; our home
> We change at will; may watch the far-off foam
> Break upon Thule's shore and call it play,
> Or through dim, dreadful forests force our way,
> That we may tread Orontes', Ebro's shore—
> That we are all one nation, evermore!

III. ROME THE CIVILIZER OF THE WORLD

(a) *Roman Architecture*

Rome was more than a conqueror, for more than five hundred years she was a great civilizing power. The spirit of a nation expresses itself in its building as well as in its political history, and in her architecture Rome has shown how practical and con-

structive was her spirit. The greatest Greek architecture was seen in the temples, the greatest Roman
architecture in her great public buildings. Just as
the Roman citizen was trained to put the state before every personal interest, so did the buildings
put the state first. Rome was the first city of the
ancient world in which the public buildings of the
state are greater than the temples. The Roman
mind was not adventurous or speculative, it concerned itself chiefly with the practical things of life
and was filled with the sense of the might of this
world, and held that as Rome was the ruling power,
so should all things be done to symbolize her might
and majesty by great buildings of practical use to
the state. To this end there were built, not only
in Rome itself, but in all the provinces of the Empire, great public buildings for the service of the
state and for every need of the people: basilicas and
fora, bridges and aqueducts, triumphal arches, public baths and places of amusement, circuses, theatres
and amphitheatres.

The contribution made by Rome to architecture
was the development of the arch. It is thought
that the Babylonians were the first to make use
of the arch in building, but they had not developed
it very far. The Greeks had hardly used it, and
it was the Romans who made it a very important
part of construction. They were the first people to
build bridges on a large scale, and from the arch of
the bridge came the greater development of the
arch of the aqueduct, that great engineering triumph
of the Romans.

As the inhabitants of the provinces, going about their daily business, looked up at the massive, magnificent buildings which had been built in all their cities, they must have been filled with a sense of the might of the Empire of which these buildings were in some sense the symbol, and of pride that they were counted amongst its citizens.

(b) *Language and Literature*

Something has already been said of how the Latin language was made into the perfect instrument it is for the expression of human thought, and of the greatest writers of the Augustan Age.

Language is the means by which thought is expressed, and the spirit of a nation is expressed by its language and literature as well as by its deeds. One of the chief characteristics of Latin is its power of expressing thought in a few words, a characteristic of the Roman himself. The civilization we have inherited was Greek in its origin, but it came to us first through the Romans. The Romans were not creators, as were the Greeks. Great poetry, great drama, great history had all been written several centuries before the age of Augustus, and the practical mind of the Roman never at any time concerned itself with the speculations and questionings which so much interested the Greek philosopher. But Rome did not copy Greek literature. What her writers wrote was their own, inspired, doubtless, by Greece, but in form and substance Roman. The two great Roman poets of the Augustan Age were essentially Roman in all their thought, and they represent those qualities which were most characteristically Roman. Virgil shows that greatness of spirit, nobility of mind and devoted patriotism that characterize the Roman spirit at its best; and Horace the wide human feelings and interests, sympathy with and understanding of man in all that concerns his human life.

For nearly five hundred years Rome kept the frontiers of her Empire safe, and by so doing gave the civilization of the ancient world time to take such root that it would never die. For a thousand years after the break-up of the Roman Empire it was the Latin language which helped to preserve that ancient heritage. All through the Middle Ages Latin was the language of the educated world, and when, out of what had once been the Roman Empire, new nations arose, the peoples of those nations developed languages directly descended from Latin. If Rome had not once ruled in Italy, Gaul and Spain, Italian, French and Spanish would never have come into being. In whatever direction we turn today, we find ourselves on a path made possible to us by Rome.

(c) *Roman Roads and Commerce*

All nations have a centre, the capital of the nation, which is the seat of government and the centre of commerce. Such a city draws so much of the life of the nation into itself and wields so great an influence over the rest of the nation, that it is sometimes forgotten that there are other important and influential cities doing their share, and often a large one, in the building of the nation. This was especially true of Rome and the provincial cities of the Empire. When Rome conquered, she immediately settled and organized the new territory that belonged to her, and one of the first things she did was to plan and develop cities. Of course in the East the conquering Roman found cities and an ancient civilization. These yielded to the superior power of Rome, but they never became romanized and they preserved their own characteristics. Such cities as Alexandria, Antioch, Damascus, Tarsus, Ephesus and Smyrna flourished exceedingly under the Roman rule, but in character they always remained Greek rather than Roman.

In the West and North of the Empire it was different. Before the Roman conquest, the inhabitants had lived in villages, knowing nothing of municipal life. In these places Rome founded cities, in order that the conquered province might have a centre which was Roman and from which Roman civilization might spread over the province. These cities were walled and entered by gates. The streets were laid out at right angles to each other, and in the centre of the city was the Forum with a basilica near by and temples, porticoes and triumphal arches; theatres, amphitheatres and baths were built, until a rich provincial city became almost a little Rome. Life in these cities was a Roman life. The governor and his suite introduced Roman habits and customs and amusements: the circus, theatre and gladiatorial shows.

There is not a country conquered by Rome that

cannot still show signs of the mighty power that once ruled it. In Europe the Roman city has frequently become the site of a modern city, for the Romans knew what made a good site. In lands where centuries of silence have succeeded the Roman rule, the spade of the archaeologist is laying bare the foundations of ancient Roman cities. Out of the silence of the African desert there are arising temples, arches, amphitheatres, basilicas and fora haunted by the spirit of the Roman power which once covered the North of Africa with busy populous cities.

These cities were connected by the great Roman roads, the first of which had been built during the Republic in the fourth century B.C. and which had been added to in every direction during the succeeding centuries.

The oldest roads leading out of Rome were the Appian Way, the Flaminian Way and the Aemilian Way. The Appian Way was built by Appius Claudius the blind Censor, and was the main road from Rome to the South. The Flaminian Way was the main road North to Rimini, where it connected with the Aemilian Way and went to Turin, Milan, Verona and then across the Alps to the North. Another road, the Aurelian Way, went North from Rome along the west coast to Genoa, then across the Alps to the South of Gaul and thence across the Rhone and the Pyrenees into Spain. The main centre for roads in Gaul was at Lyons, and from that city one road went East to Besançon and Belfort to the Rhine and the German frontiers, and another

North through Rheims and Amiens to Boulogne, the port for Britain. In Britain great roads went from London to York, Chester and Bath.

Roads were also built in the East. From Damascus in Syria roads went out through Baalbek, famous for its great temple, to Antioch and Asia Minor, and South to Egypt. All these roads connected the most distant provinces with each other and with Rome and knitted the whole Empire closely together.

The Roman roads were the best, the safest and generally the shortest from place to place. The practical, determined Roman was never daunted by obstacles. If he came to a river, he bridged it; was there a narrow valley to be crossed, he spanned it with a viaduct; was there a hill, if possible, he carried the road over it. That the Roman roads were well-built, practical and followed the best routes can be seen today. They are still some of the best in Europe, and modern railways in most cases follow the same route.

Over these roads passed all the travel of the Empire. One language and one coinage carried the traveller everywhere, from the distant East through Italy and across the Alps to Gaul and Britain, or along the shores of the Mediterranean and over the Pyrenees to Spain. Everyone who had leisure and who could afford it, could travel in safety and with comparative speed to visit places full of interest because of their historical associations or because of some natural beauty. All kinds of reasons took people travelling then as now. There were tourists, merchants, government officials, students and soldiers.

Travellers on the roads used different means of transportation. The poor man went on foot, either carrying his pack or placing it on a mule if he could afford one. The well-to-do generally drove in travelling carriages, some of them exceedingly comfortable, and followed by their luggage in waggons looked after by slaves. Government officials travelled on horseback, soldiers marched on foot, ladies were always in covered travelling carriages or for short distances outside the city were carried in litters.

In the larger towns and cities there were inns where the traveller could rest for the night, and then, as now, they were recognized by signs. One inn at Lyons had a picture of Apollo and Mercury on the sign-board with this inscription beneath:

Here Mercury promises gain, Apollo health, Septumanus (the innkeeper) meals and rooms. Anyone coming in will be the better for it; stranger, look to where you stay.

The products of all the civilized world were to be had in Rome, and merchants with their wares travelled freely both by land and sea. From the East came all kinds of luxuries: from Syria, purple dye and rare glass; from Arabia, spices, perfumes and gems; from India, pepper and pearls; from the Greek lands, beautiful woven fabrics, wine and marble; from Egypt, fine linen; from North Africa, grain and ivory. From Gaul came pottery; from the Danube lands, iron and gold, and amber which had reached those regions by the trade-routes from the Baltic; from Spain, copper, tin, lead and gold; and lead came also from Britain. All that the civilized world produced could be had in Rome, and it travelled over Roman roads and highways. It is probable that until the beginning of the nineteenth century travel in Europe was never so safe, swift and easy as it was during the first two centuries A.D.

What could be better [said one who lived in the first century A.D.] or more profitable than the present state of affairs? Now any man can go whither he pleases with absolute confidence, the harbours all over the Empire are full of business, even the mountains are as safe for those who journey over them as the cities are to those who dwell in them.

This was the result of the *Pax Romana.*

PART IV

THE DECLINE AND FALL OF ROME

CHAPTER XXIII

THE DECLINE OF ROME

I. THE SOLDIER EMPERORS

180–284 A.D.

THE year 180 A.D. marks the last turning point
in the history of Rome. For two hundred years
the civilized world had enjoyed a peace and prosperity that it had never known for so long a period
before. There had been wars, but these were chiefly
on the eastern frontiers. Some of the Emperors
had been wild and extravagant and others harsh
and cruel, but these things had only touched the
surface of the life of the Empire. In the main,
peace at home and good government of the provinces
had brought prosperity everywhere. Nevertheless
there were things silently at work in the Empire
that were gradually weakening it and which were
in time to ruin it.

The great wealth of Rome had brought with it

luxury and especially the luxury of the East. The
courts of the later Emperors became more like those
of oriental monarchs in their pomp and display, and
vast sums of money were spent on outward shows
and magnificence. But the money of the Empire
was becoming more and more needed to keep up
the armies which defended the frontiers. During
the great days of the Empire the frontiers had been
kept safe, but the barbarian tribes who lived beyond the Roman boundaries were growing stronger
and more threatening to the peace of the Empire.
In spite of the wealth of Rome, the money needed
for defence was difficult to raise and the taxes became increasingly heavy and oppressive. The provinces were decreasing in population, for pestilences,
famine and war had wrought havoc among the inhabitants. This decrease in population made it
difficult to till the land and much of it was beginning
to run to waste. Yet outwardly there still seemed
prosperity, and in Rome itself the love of pleasure
and extravagance gave a false air of security. There
was discontent among the poorer people, but instead of asking for reforms in taxation which might
have bettered conditions, they only demanded more
free corn and more spectacles and games in the
amphitheatre. If they had bread and circuses they
were content.

Another source of danger to the Empire lay in
the frequent civil wars over the election of the
Emperors, and the frequency with which these were
deposed and put to death by their political opponents or by the army, for the bodyguard of the Em-

peror, the Praetorian Guard, had grown so powerful that no one could be Emperor without its good
will. For a hundred years after the death of Marcus Aurelius, Rome was ruled by soldier Emperors,
elected by the army. Between 180 and 284 A.D.
there were twenty-nine Emperors, of whom only
four died natural deaths. All the others were murdered either by a rebellious army or by a rival.

But perhaps the greatest danger of all to Rome
in these centuries was the change in the Roman
character. The old Roman ideal of discipline and
duty, of self-control and self-restraint, of seriousness of purpose and dignity of demeanour had begun to disappear when Rome became mistress of
the world, and by the second century A.D. there was
practically none of it left. The pestilences, famines
and wars which had caused the decrease in population had carried off some of the best of the old
Roman stock, and there was not enough of it left
to do the work of Rome as it had been done in the
days of her greatness.

Marcus Aurelius had been succeeded by his son
Commodus, a weak and incapable ruler who let
the Praetorian Guard get control of the state. After
twelve years of bad government, Commodus was
murdered and an Emperor, Pertinax, put in his
place. He tried to restore some order and discipline
amongst his guards, but he, too, was murdered and
then followed one of the most disgraceful scenes in
all Roman history: the office of Emperor was sold
at auction to the highest bidder. The Praetorian
Guard seemed to have lost all sense of decency or

honour and to have believed that there was nothing that could not be purchased by money. An auction was actually held, and the Roman Empire was sold to a man who had been Consul, Julianus, and for about two months he reigned as Emperor. But there were still some Roman soldiers left with a sense of honour and decency. The legions on the Danube, under the command of Septimius Severus, an African, marched to Rome and avenged the murder of Pertinax. Julianus was deposed and Septimius Severus made Emperor in his place.

For thirteen years Septimius Severus maintained order in Rome. It was a military rule, for he was Emperor at the will of the army, but the soldiers followed and obeyed him and for the time his strong hand prevented any breakdown of the frontiers. He took from the Senate what little power it seemed to have, but he encouraged the great lawyers of the time, and Roman law was well administered in the provinces.

Septimius Severus was succeeded by his son Caracalla, who completed the work of enfranchising the provinces, for he made all freemen in the Empire Roman citizens. He added to the great buildings of Rome by having magnificent baths erected. Caracalla, however, was cruel and made himself disliked, and he, too, was murdered. Then followed a time of great danger to the Empire. For fifty years there was constant civil war over the succession to the throne. This weakened Rome within, and in consequence withdrew large numbers of soldiers from the frontiers, and as a result, Rome was assailed on all sides by the barbarians who broke over the frontiers into Spain, across the Rhine and the Danube, and into Asia Minor.

In 270 A.D. Aurelian became Emperor and in five years his energy and vigour had in some measure restored order. He gave Dacia to the Visigoths, the first land lost to the Roman Empire, and he made the Danube once more the boundary. Then he turned to Syria where the rulers of Palmyra, a flourishing city midway between Damascus and the Euphrates, had set up an independent kingdom. For seven years Palmyra had been ruled by Zenobia, a capable and energetic Queen, but she was defeated by Aurelian who destroyed Palmyra and took Zenobia as a captive to Rome, where she was made to walk in his triumph, though afterwards she was well treated and allowed to live in a palace near Rome. Aurelian then turned to the North and made those frontiers once more secure. But not all the barbarians were driven back. Numbers of them were beginning to remain in the Empire. Attracted by the order kept by the Roman government, they began to settle near the frontiers, and though for a time they were peaceful, their presence within the Empire was before long to prove a source of danger.

II. DIOCLETIAN AND THE DIVISION OF THE EMPIRE

284–305 A.D.

After the death of Aurelian, the next Emperor to leave a mark on the Empire was Diocletian who reigned from 284 to 305 A.D. His immediate predecessor had been murdered and Diocletian, Commander of the Bodyguard of the Palace, was chosen Emperor. He followed the custom established by the later Emperors of modelling his court in large measure on that of the King of Persia. He wore gold-embroidered garments and a diadem and required those who entered his presence to prostrate themselves on the ground before him. He also revived the worship of the Emperor which led to a renewed persecution of the Christians, one which was carried out with greater ferocity than almost any other had been.

A century before, the Senate had been deprived of any remnants of authority it still had, but Diocletian abolished it altogether and ruled alone. But Diocletian was a statesman and knew that one man could not rule such an Empire without assistance, and he set himself to re-organize the administration of the government. His object was to centralize it in the Emperor. To this end he continued the policy, begun by Augustus and continued by later Emperors, of dividing the large provinces into a number of smaller ones, in order to reduce the power of the provincial governors. In the time of Diocletian there were more than a hundred provinces. He divided these into four large groups, each called a Prefecture, those of Gaul, Italy, Illyricum and the Orient, and each was ruled by a Prefect who was directly responsible to the Emperor. The Prefectures were then subdivided into dioceses each ruled by a vicar, and these again into small provinces ruled by a governor. In this way the government of the whole Empire was centralized in the hands of the Emperor to whom all the subordinate rulers were responsible.

For purposes of still better government Diocletian then divided the Empire into two parts, the East and the West, and associated Maximian with himself as Emperor. Diocletian was to rule the East, and Maximian the West. Both were called Augustus, but Diocletian, the Emperor of the East, was the real head of the government. A little later two men were appointed to assist the Emperors. They were given the title of Caesar, and it was their duty to command the armies on the frontiers. On the death of either of the Emperors, the Caesar was to succeed to the throne. In this way it was hoped to avert the constant civil war over the succession.

For a time this arrangement worked successfully and the Empire enjoyed peace and good order. But in 305 A.D. Diocletian abdicated and forced Maximian to do the same. The two Caesars became Emperors and new Caesars were appointed. Constantius, one of the Emperors, was in Britain where he died at York the year after his accession, but instead of allowing the legally appointed Caesar to succeed him, his army made Constantine the son of Constantius Emperor. The army in Rome set up another Emperor and for several years there was civil war, for Constantine marched at the head of an army to Rome and fought against his rival. He defeated him and became Emperor of the West. A few years later, he warred against the Emperor of the East whom he also defeated and put to death, and Constantine was then acknowledged as Emperor of both the East and the West.

III. CONSTANTINE THE GREAT

306–337 A.D.

Constantine had been proclaimed Emperor on the death of his father in 306 A.D. but it was not until 324 A.D. that he became sole ruler of Rome. He was as absolute a ruler as Diocletian had been, and the government was now so centralized that all officials of the Empire, whether civil or military, were directly responsible to him alone. But the two facts for which the reign of Constantine the Great is chiefly remembered are the recognition by the state of Christianity, and the choice of Byzantium as the eastern capital of the Empire.

The mother of Constantine, Helena, was a Christian, and it is said that she went on a pilgrimage to the Holy Land, whence she brought back with her a piece of the wood of the cross on which Christ had been crucified. Constantine himself was not at first a Christian, but he had always treated the Christians under his rule with tolerance. The story is told that as he approached Rome in order to fight his rival, he saw in the sky a great flaming cross with the words *In hoc signo vinces* inscribed beneath it. Constantine believed that this was a sign to him from the God of the Christians that He would be on his side in the coming battle, and he commanded that the sign of the cross should be placed on the shields of the soldiers. Constantine regarded the victory that followed as directly given to him because of his obedience to the vision, and soon after he became Emperor of the West he published the Edict of Milan (311 A.D.), which granted tolerance to all Christians and which placed Christianity on the same footing as all other religions of the Empire.

Only one Emperor after Constantine opposed Christianity. This was his nephew Julian, a capable ruler, but he did his best to restore the worship of the old gods, and for this reason he is known as Julian the Apostate.

Constantine was the Emperor of the Roman Empire, but at heart he was not a Roman of Rome. He had been born in one province and brought up in another still more distant, and no ties bound him to the city. It was not surprising, therefore, that he decided to found an eastern capital for the Empire. He was also far-seeing enough to realize that the days that Rome would rule the West were numbered, and that if the Empire were to endure there must be a strong centre in the East. He chose the ancient Greek city of Byzantium, which he strengthened with walls and beautified with great buildings. In 330 A.D. the city was solemnly dedicated to its founder and its name changed from Byzantium to Constantinople. The new capital occupied one of the finest situations in the Empire, looking on one side to Europe, on the other to Asia.

The history of civilization has been different because of the founding of certain cities, and in this history Constantinople has played no small part. In barely a century from the founding of the new capital, the western part of the Empire was to be invaded by the tribes that had for so long menaced the frontiers. Rome was to fall, and it was to appear as if the mighty civilization she had built up was to be ruined and disappear. But the Eastern Empire was to last for yet a thousand years, and though politically the power of the Empire was gone, it was in Constantinople and the East that the ancient civilization was partly preserved. When in 1453 Constantinople fell before the invading Turk, Western Europe, the new world which had grown out of the fragments of the Roman Empire, was ready to receive the ancient heritage that came to it from the East.

CHAPTER XXIV

The Fall of Rome

I. THE BARBARIAN INVADERS

AFTER the death of Constantine, the power of Rome steadily declined. For nearly five hundred years Rome had been able to keep her frontiers safe, and the barbarian tribes who lived beyond them had been unable seriously to threaten the Roman boundaries. But with a weaker and less capable government, with provinces so heavily burdened with taxation that their old prosperity was vanishing, there was less resistance to any invasion from beyond the frontiers. Up to the end of the second century, the East had been the danger spot for the Roman Empire; from about the third century onwards the danger came from the North and North-East.

These barbarians, as the Romans called them, were Germanic tribes who had lived originally in the North, but who, in search of food, had migrated to other parts of Europe. One tribe in particular, the Goths, had left Northern Europe and had settled on the northern shore of the Black Sea. The Roman historian Tacitus has left an account of these German tribes. He says:

They take pleasure in the size of their herds: these are their sole form of wealth, and they are very proud of them. Whether it is in mercy or in anger that the gods have denied them silver and gold, I do not know: nor could I definitely assert that Germany produces no vein of gold or silver: for no one has explored. But they are not affected in the same way that we are by its possession and use.

The Germans fight with spears which have a short narrow head, but are so sharp and handy that they use the same weapon, as circumstances demand, for close and open fighting. The cavalry are content with shield and spear; the infantry also shower javelins: each man carries several, and they can throw them a very long way. They fight naked or in a very light plaid. They have no elaborate apparel, and merely paint their shields with distinctive colours of the brightest hue.

Their number is fixed: a hundred come from each village, and they are known to their own people as "the hundred." Thus what was at first a mere number has come to be an honourable name. The line is drawn up in wedge-battalions. To retire from your post, provided you charge again is thought to show prudence not fear. They carry away their dead, even after a doubtful battle. To lose your shield is the most dishonour of all: one thus disgraced may not be present at a sacrifice or enter a council. After a defeat many survivors have been known to hang themselves to end their infamy.

When the fighting begins, it is shameful for a chief to be outdone in bravery, and equally shameful for the followers not to match the bravery of their chief: to survive one's chief and to return from battle is a foul disgrace which lasts as long as life.

When they are not fighting, they spend little time in hunting, much more in doing nothing. They devote themselves to sleeping and eating. Even the bravest and most warlike are quite idle, for they give over the care of house and fields to the women and the old men, and to all the weaklings of the household. They themselves merely lounge for from a strange contradiction of character they love idleness yet hate peace. It is usual for the tribe, man by man, to contribute a voluntary gift of cattle or corn for the chiefs. They accept this as an honour, and it meets their needs.

It is well known that none of the German tribes live in cities. They cannot endure undetached houses. Their houses are separate and scattered, pitched at the call of river, plain or wood. They build villages but not as we do with the buildings all adjoining and connected. Each man has an open space round his homestead, either as a protection against risk of fire, or because they do not know how to build otherwise.

The husband brings a dowry to the wife, not the wife to the husband. The parents come to the wedding and inspect the presents. They are not designed to please a woman's taste, nor can a young bride wear them in her hair: they are oxen, a bridled horse or a shield with spear and sword. This is the dowry which wins a wife, and she in her turn brings her husband some gift of arms. A woman must not think herself exempt from thoughts of bravery or the chances of war. By the ceremony which begins her married life she is warned that she comes to be her husband's partner in toil and in danger, to suffer and to dare with him alike in peace and war. This is plainly shown by the yoked oxen, the bridled horse, and the gift of arms. Thus she must live, and thus she must die. She is receiving a trust which she must keep worthily and hand on to her children, a trust which her sons' wives must receive in turn and pass on to their children.[1]

These were the people who now began seriously to cross the Roman frontiers. For a century or more many of them had been coming peaceably. They had settled on the border lands just within the Roman frontiers where they could enjoy the order kept by the Roman government, they had made homes there and by the third century German influence was very marked. As time went on, Germans were even found serving in the Roman armies and in some cases acting as officers. The latter were often men of great ability, they had served in Roman armies and had learnt Roman habits of military discipline and obedience.

It has already been seen that Aurelian had given Dacia to the Visigoths. These had lived as friendly allies of Rome and had been influenced by the habits and customs of their Roman neighbours. When they, in their turn, were threatened by a savage enemy coming from the East, they appealed to Rome for help. This enemy was a tribe of Asiatic people known as Huns. They were so fierce and savage that it was thought they were hardly human, and the very name of Hun terrified all who heard it. These Huns invaded Dacia and defeated the King of the Visigoths, who immediately sent an imploring message to the Roman Emperor asking that the survivors with the women and children

[1] Tacitus: *Germania*.

should be allowed to cross the Danube and come into the Roman Empire, where they hoped for protection. Valens, the Emperor at the time, consented, and Roman officers were sent to see that proper protection was given to them. But the Romans plundered, robbed and ill-treated the unfortunate Goths, so that those who might have become firm friends and allies of the Romans became their deadly enemies and in 378 A.D., rebelling against the cruel and unjust treatment they had received, the Goths rose up in arms and in a battle fought at Adrianople, not only defeated the Roman army, but also slew the Roman Emperor.

Valens was succeeded by Theodosius, who wisely made peace with the Goths. He was known as "Lover of peace and of the Goths," and as long as he lived, they gave Rome no trouble. Theodosius was the last Emperor to rule over both the East and the West. From the time of his death in 395 A.D. the East and the West, though nominally still one Empire, each went its own way, along a different path which led to a different future.

Theodosius had kept peace with the Goths, but his successor was weak and hardly interested himself at all in the affairs of the Empire. It was then that the Goths grew very powerful and under a strong leader, Alaric, they ravaged the lands of the East and then entered Italy. Alaric wanted land for himself and his followers, but he does not seem to have been a wilful destroyer for the sake of destroying, and he generally spared life, did he but receive the submission of his enemies. He advanced to the walls of Rome and besieged the city. When the inhabitants sent out a messenger asking him on what terms he would raise the siege, he agreed to depart if all their gold, silver and movable property were sent out to him. "What will be left to us?" they asked. "Your lives," was the short answer. Some treasure was sent out to him, but it was not enough and the siege continued. At length in 410 A.D. Alaric entered Rome and allowed his followers to burn and pillage at will. A great deal of damage was done, though probably not as much as was supposed, and it is said that Alaric gave orders that the Churches should be spared.

Although the days of her greatness had passed, the name of Rome was still one which stood to the world for all that was great and unconquerable, and when the news of the sack of Rome by Alaric spread to distant places, everyone was stupefied with horror and dismay. The news reached St. Jerome who, far off in his cell at Bethlehem, was living the life of a hermit, and he could hardly believe what he heard. In a letter written shortly afterwards, he said: "The City which had taken all the world was itself taken. . . . The Roman world is falling." As people began to recover from the shock, they began to ask why such a disaster could have fallen upon Rome. There were still large numbers of pagans in the Empire and they blamed Christianity for the catastrophe, for the Christian religion, they said, had caused the neglect of the old Roman gods who in their anger had allowed the city to fall. But St. Augustine, the

Bishop of Hippo, who was himself the son of a pagan father, but of a Christian mother, Monica, wrote a book called *The City of God*, in which he answered the pagan accusations, and in which he declared that Rome was of the world and therefore could not last, but that the Kingdom or City, as he called it, of God was to triumph over the whole world, and that this spiritual empire would endure.

After taking Rome, Alaric left the city and soon made himself the master of Italy, and then he died. His name has become well-known in history, not so much because he was himself a great man, but because he, a tall, fair-haired barbarian from without the Empire, had broken the spell that had hung about the name of Rome. His followers buried him in a river, turning it aside from its course in order that they might dig his grave in its bed. In it they placed the body of Alaric together with rich treasure, and then turned back the waters into their accustomed channel. And that none might ever know where his body had been laid, they put to death the men who had made the grave.

Rome had been sacked, but she had not yet ceased to be the seat of government. The Goths withdrew from Italy and overran Spain, where they set up a Visigothic kingdom which lasted until early in the sixth century. Other tribes wandered about the Western Empire, and those who were most restless and destructive were the Vandals. At one time they lived near the Danube, then through the South of Gaul they forced their way into Spain. The Goths drove them out of Spain and they crossed to Africa, pillaging, ravaging, burning, destroying wherever they went. "Where are we going next?" a Vandal once asked his chief. "Wherever there is a people with whom God is angry," was the answer. The Vandals seized the harbours of North Africa and built themselves ships, in which they sailed like pirates over the Mediterranean, until, in the middle of the sixth century, they were subdued by the Eastern Emperor.

But now the Huns again became troublesome, and under a powerful leader, Attila, they came plundering into Europe and reached Gaul. It is said, that it was the boast of Attila that grass never grew again where the hoof of his horse had trod. He was known as the Scourge of God, and he inspired such terror, that the Romans and Goths were willing to make friends in order to drive him away. In 451 A.D. their combined armies inflicted such a tremendous defeat on Attila at Châlons, that all fear of Hun dominion in Europe was dispelled. Attila left Gaul, but the next year he entered Italy and actually reached the neighbourhood of Rome. The Bishop of Rome, Leo I, called the Great, went out of the city and fearlessly confronted the savage Hun. "Thus far shalt thou come, and no farther," he said to him and demanded that he should immediately leave the land. Legend says that as he spoke, a vision of St. Peter and St. Paul with their hands outstretched in blessing over the city appeared in the sky, and that, awed and terrified, Attila withdrew. He died soon after, and the Huns troubled Europe no more.

Of all the invading tribes none survived, except as a memory and a name, but the Franks who invaded Gaul and the Angles and Saxons who invaded Britain. They invaded, but unlike the other Germanic tribes, they stayed in the lands they conquered, and their story does not belong in this place.

II. THE FALL OF ROME

By the middle of the fifth century these barbarian invaders were occupying most parts of the Western Roman Empire, and the Emperor at Rome ruled over little more than Italy. In name, he ruled over the barbarians, but these were really independent and gave him but little support. They lived in the Empire side by side with the Romans, from whom they learnt a great deal and to whom they also taught much.

The Germans learned to speak Latin, some of them adopted Christianity, they paid taxes and they served in the army. They were often brutal and violent, but they were a young, vigorous and healthy race, and they valued above all things their personal independence. The Roman held the state greater than himself, the German valued more highly the importance of the individual.

As the years of the fifth century went by, anxiety and apprehension seized upon the people of Rome. At the end of the first century B.C. the augurs had declared that each of the twelve vultures said to have been seen by Romulus represented a century in the life of the city and that at the end of twelve centuries Rome would fall. Was this true, they asked each other, and was the end approaching? or was Rome, as they had always believed, eternal?

In 476 A.D. the end came. Odoacer, the chief general of the army, himself a German, demanded of the young Emperor, Romulus Augustulus, that land in Italy should be given to the Germans who were serving in the army. The Emperor refused, and quietly he was set aside. For fourteen years Odoacer ruled in the name of the Eastern Emperor, but never again was there an Emperor in Rome, and never again was Rome the seat of the government of the Roman Empire.

CHAPTER XXV

THE PRESERVATION OF THE ANCIENT HERITAGE

ROME had fallen, the Empire was broken up and overrun by invaders who, if not as uncivilized as they have sometimes been painted and though they were learning much from the Romans, were certainly not civilized as the Greeks and Romans understood civilization. Undoubtedly during these centuries of invasion much that was material was lost, and especially was this true of many manuscripts of the ancient writings. Written on fragile papyrus rolls by the copyists in Athens, Alexandria and Rome, they were not replaced when they fell into bad condition, and in consequence many of them perished. In the first centuries A.D. parchment had to a large extent taken the place of papyrus, and more parchment manuscripts have been preserved than those written on papyrus. This loss fell most heavily on the older Greek manuscripts, yet all was not lost there.

Much ancient art was lost. When Christianity became the recognized religion of the Empire, pagan temples were closed and allowed to fall into bad condition, and statues lay about uncared for. Many have been recovered by modern excavations carried out on ancient sites, but often they are damaged beyond repair. Nevertheless, our modern civilization is based on the foundations laid by Greeks and Romans. How has it been preserved?

In Europe, new nations were being formed, Christianity spread into these new countries, and with Christianity went the monks. It is to the founder of two monasteries in particular that we owe the preservation of many of the ancient classics. After the fall of Rome, there arose in Italy a flourishing kingdom of the East Goths, with Ravenna as its capital. For over thirty years this kingdom was ruled by Theodoric the Great, a wise and statesmanlike ruler. Attached to his court was Cassiodorus, a scholar who was especially interested in classical literature. Throughout a long life of political activity, Cassiodorus had been able to collect a large number of Greek and Latin manuscripts, rescued, many of them, from the ruined libraries of cultivated Romans. Towards the end of his life, and he lived to be over ninety years of age, he founded two monasteries, probably of the Benedictine order. Every monastery had its scriptorium, where the monks copied the Scriptures and service-books and illuminated them with skill that has rarely been surpassed. Cassiodorus gave his magnificent collection of Greek and Latin manuscripts to the two monasteries he founded, and in addition to the Scriptures and service-books, the monks copied those writings of the great classic writers which Cassiodorus had collected and wished preserved.

But reading and writing, painting and sculpture alone do not make a man or a nation civilized. Civilization has many meanings and may be interpreted in many different ways. One way, and not the least important by which civilized nations may be known is by their relations with other men, both with those of their own nation and with those of other nations. Wherever men live together there must be some kind of law and government. The Roman Empire had been well governed. After its break-up, its form of ordered government was carried on in the organization of the Church, Roman ideas of justice profoundly influenced the law of the growing states in Europe, and the heritage of law and order given by Rome to her vast dominions was never entirely lost to the world.

Another important factor in preserving the Roman civilization was the Latin language. Latin had been the language common to all parts of the Western Empire, and when in the thirteenth century the first universities were founded, Latin was still the language most widely used in Europe. The services of the Church had always been conducted in Latin, every educated man, were he priest, administrator or lawyer, knew Latin, and it was in Latin that all study in the early universities was carried on. Those who studied the Latin language read Roman literature, in which were found the old Roman stories of what Romans of old had done, stories of patriotism, courage, discipline and obedience, and later ages have been greatly influenced by the Roman character.

In all these ways the ancient tradition was handed on with almost no break, but there was much that was still unknown to the younger nations of Europe.

For a thousand years after the fall of Rome, Constantinople was the capital of the Eastern Empire, where Greek scholars and artists kept alive the old learning and habits of thought. In 1453 the Turks conquered Constantinople and the Eastern Empire came to an end. All who could do so fled, taking with them what they could of their belongings. Scholars took their precious manuscripts, and to the cities of Europe to which they fled, they opened what seemed like a new world of story, myth and legend, of ways of thinking, of new paths to tread, which were found in the wealth of the ancient world.

Europe as we know it today is built on the foundations laid by the civilization of Rome, which was in its turn influenced both by the new ideas brought to it by the Germanic tribes and by the Christian Church. Slowly, but surely, it has grown out of the past.

When a Greek left his home to found a colony in another place, he took with him some of the sacred fire from the city hearth of the home he was leaving, in order that his old traditions might not be broken and that he might hand on to his children that which he had received. Rome lit her torch at the sacred fire of Greece and by its light she made her own that which Greece had given to the world. She gave to it the strength and stability that had been wanting in the character of the Greek. She carried it into distant lands far beyond the horizon of the Aegean Sea, and when the time had come and her race was run, she handed the torch still alight to younger hands who took it and tended it and in turn handed it on to succeeding generations. And the torch is still alight.

SUGGESTIONS ABOUT BOOKS FOR FURTHER READING

THIS book has been intended for those who were reading about Rome for the first time. The following list is for those older readers of the book who would like to know more of this great civilization. It only contains suggestions as to how to begin, and is in no way meant to be a full bibliography.

I.—*Books about Rome*

MOMMSEN	*History of Rome.* (The great history of the Republic.)
H. STUART JONES	*The Roman Empire.*
GIBBON	*The Decline and Fall of the Roman Empire.*
CYRIL BAILEY (Edited by)	*The Legacy of Rome.*
CYRIL BAILEY (Edited by)	*The Mind of Rome.*
CYRIL BAILEY	*Roman Religion.*
T. R. GLOVER.	*The Conflict of Religions under the Roman Empire.*
W. WARDE FOWLER.	*The City-State of the Greeks and Romans.*
W. WARDE FOWLER	*Social Life at Rome in the Age of Cicero.*
SAMUEL DILL	*Roman Society from Nero to Marcus Aurelius.*
J. W. MACKAIL	*Latin Literature.*
M. P. CHARLESWORTH	*Trade Routes and Commerce of the Roman Empire.*
MRS. STRONG	*Roman Sculpture.*
WALTER PATER	*Marius the Epicurean.*

II.—*Latin Writers*

Reference to Latin writers will have been found all through this book and in the list of acknowledgments at the beginning. The following list of the more important writers and their works referred to in this book has been put together here for the purpose of easier reference.

LIVY	Translated by W. M. Roberts.
TACITUS	*Annals*, translated by Church and Brodribb.
	Histories, translated by W. Hamilton Fyfe.
	Germania, translated by W. Hamilton Fyfe.
	Agricola, translated by W. Hamilton Fyfe.
EPICTETUS	Translated by P. E. Matheson.
MARCUS AURELIUS	Translated by G. H. Rendall.
PLINY THE YOUNGER	*Letters*, translated by J. B. Firth.
VIRGIL	*The Poems of Virgil*, translated by J. Rhoades.
	The Aeneid, translated by Fairfax Taylor.
HORACE	*Odes*, translated by W. S. Marris.
	Odes, Satires and Epistles, translated by Conington.

"The Claim of Antiquity," an excellent pamphlet published by the Oxford University Press, gives a much fuller and more complete list of books and translations for those who would like further suggestions.

INDEX

A

457

Photo Alinari.

FORUM ROMANUM.

Looking towards the Capitol.

A ROMAN GENTLEMAN OF THE REPUBLIC AND HIS WIFE.

A VESTAL.

Museo delle Terme, Rome.

JULIUS CAESAR.
British Museum.

AUGUSTUS CAESAR.
Vatican Museum, Rome.

AUGUSTUS WEARING A TOGA.
Museo delle Terme. Rome.

FORUM ROMANUM.

Looking towards the Arch of Titus.

Photo Alinari.

THE PERISTYLE OF A ROMAN HOUSE.

Pompeii.

Photo Alinari.

A ROMAN HOUSE.

Pompeii.

INTERIOR OF A ROOM.

Pompeii.

THE COLOSSEUM.

Rome.

ROMAN GIRL, OF THE EMPIRE.

Museo delle Terme, Rome.

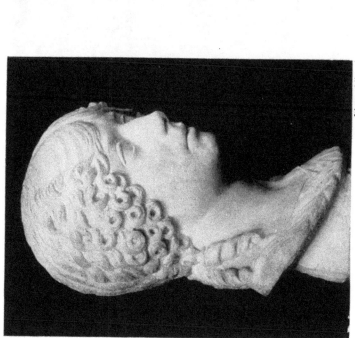

ROMAN GIRL, PROBABLY OF THE REPUBLIC.

Museo delle Terme, Rome.

TRAJAN.
Vatican Museum, Rome.

MARCUS AURELIUS.

Piazza of the Capitol, Rome.

THE PANTHEON, ROME.

Begun by Augustus—Reconstructed by Hadrian.

N.D. Photo.

ROMAN AQUEDUCT.
Pont du Gard, Nîmes.

ROMAN AMPHITHEATRE.
Arles.